Helping Students T̲ of Their Own Learning

MW00800889

What does learner-centered education look like, and how can we best put it into practice? This helpful book by experienced educators Don Mesibov and Dan Drmacich answers those questions and provides a wide variety of strategies, activities, and examples to help you with implementation. Chapters address topics such as positioning students at the center of the lesson and teachers as coaches, making tasks relevant and engaging, incorporating the affective domain and social-emotional learning, assessing learning, and more. Appropriate for new and experienced teachers of all grades and subjects, this book will leave you feeling ready to help students take control of their own learning so they can reach higher levels of success.

Don Mesibov has worked at a school for emotionally disturbed children, been a middle school English teacher, taught courses on constructivism at local colleges for 22 years, and worked for a teacher's union. Additionally, he is director of the Institute for Learning Centered Education, an organization he founded in 1995.

Dan Drmacich was principal of the nationally renowned School Without Walls in Rochester, New York, a public school, and a member of the New York State Performance Standards Consortium, which requires performance-based assessments and a yearlong project to demonstrate competency for graduation rather than standardized tests. Dan is currently cofounder and coordinator of the Rochester Coalition for Public Education, an organization focused on research-based, progressive school reform and social justice.

Helping Students Take Control of Their Own Learning

279 Learner-Centered, Social-Emotional Strategies for Teachers

Don Mesibov and Dan Drmacich

Routledge
Taylor & Francis Group

NEW YORK AND LONDON

Cover image and interior illustrations by Afzal Khan

First published 2022
by Routledge
605 Third Avenue, New York, NY 10158

and by Routledge
4 Park Square, Milton Park, Abingdon, Oxon, OX14 4RN

Routledge is an imprint of the Taylor & Francis Group, an informa business

Library of Congress Cataloging-in-Publication Data
Names: Mesibov, Don, author. | Drmacich, Dan, author.
Title: Helping students take control of their own learning : 279
learner-centered social-emotional strategies for teachers / Don Mesibov
and Dan Drmacich.
Description: New York, NY : Routledge, 2022. | Series: Routledge eye on
education | Identifiers: LCCN 2022000872 (print) | LCCN 2022000873 (ebook) |
ISBN
9781032257211 (hardback) | ISBN 9781032246635 (paperback) | ISBN
9781003284697 (ebook)
Subjects: LCSH: Student-centered learning. | Affective education. |
Activity programs in education.
Classification: LCC LB1027.23 .M46 2022 (print) | LCC LB1027.23 (ebook) |
DDC 371.39/4--dc23/eng/20220209
LC record available at https://lccn.loc.gov/2022000872
LC ebook record available at https://lccn.loc.gov/2022000873

ISBN: 978-1-032-25721-1 (hbk)
ISBN: 978-1-032-24663-5 (pbk)
ISBN: 978-1-003-28469-7 (ebk)

DOI: 10.4324/9781003284697

Typeset in Palatino
by SPi Technologies India Pvt Ltd (Straive)

Dedicated to the many wonderful professional educators who strive so hard on a daily basis to provide meaningful, engaging learning opportunities for today's youth. They are overworked, under-paid, and so often, under-appreciated. It is those educators from whom we have learned so much, and without whose on-going efforts this book could not have been written.

Contents

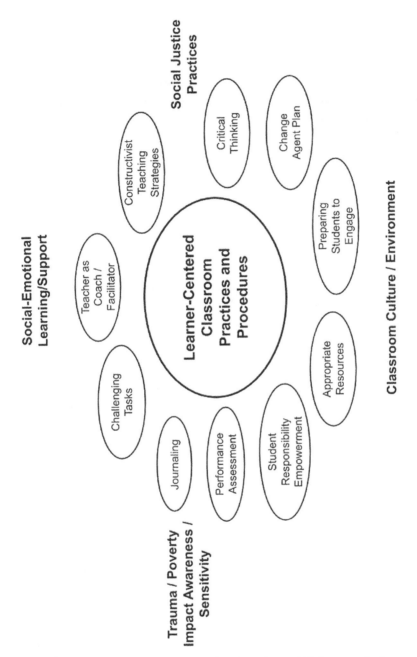

Graphic by Pat Flynn. With permission

Acknowledgments

With deep appreciation, for their contributions of time and material, to Carol Amberg, Jacqueline Grennon Brooks, Pat Flynn, Madi Fortier, Nicole Freeman, Susan Herman, Christina Luce, Terry Mazany, Deborah Meier, Raina Mesibov, John Myers, Henry Padron, Raamitha Pillay, Angela Premo, Tim Rudan, Paul Vermette, and Diane Watkins.

Illustrations by Afzal Khan

Editing by Carol Lamb, Michelle Hunter, Jim Shuman, and Steve Viau

A Message from the Authors

If you are not into constructivist theory of how people learn (which we'll define more later in this book), then you will probably assign this book to the lengthy list of books on student-centered learning, none of which you have actually read.

However, if you are among the growing number of educators who are focusing on the learner rather than the teacher, then you understand that the more you learn about how to be a constructivist-based teacher, the more you want to know. Starting the journey into student-centered teaching is like entering a huge forest: the more you travel, the more it seems there remains to be traveled. When someone says, "Now I know what I need to know about student-centered teaching," then it becomes clear they really don't understand that it is more than simply letting students work in groups.

- ◆ If you are taking the journey along with us on the road to becoming even better at centering units of study on the students, then this book is for you. In other words, the more advanced you are with student-centered teaching, the more we think you will find value in the pages that lie ahead.
- ◆ If you are relatively new to student-centered learning, then this book can also be for you, especially if your gut tells you that we can't expect students to learn if we tell them what we want them to know and test them only for their ability to memorize and regurgitate.
- ◆ If you are a future teacher or a university instructor, this book can be for you because it offers practical application strategies, and the research to support them.
- ◆ If you are a professor of education courses, or a person interested in the best way to educate people whatever your motivation, this book can also be for you.
- ◆ Finally, if you are a parent who wants to understand what is happening in education and how to support your child, this book can be for you. In fact, many of our more than 250 suggested classroom strategies can also be used by parents with their children at home.

Helping Students Take Control of Their Own Learning can be read cover-to-cover and then kept as a resource book for times when a particular section is appropriate. We tried to make it encyclopedic in nature. Or a teacher, parent, or professor may want to select a certain section for a particular reason. There is even a section with examples of how this book can be used in a university education course.

We hope that our combined 100+ years of experience have enabled us to provide ideas to support you on your endless journey into constructivist-based teaching. If we can be of personal assistance, you can reach us through the Institute for Learning Centered Education website: www.learningcentered.org. If we're lucky to still be alive, you will hear back from us.

Don Mesibov   **Dan Drmacich**

Introduction

As educators, school administrators, and parents, we all want similar things for our children: to develop into thoughtful, healthy, independent individuals; to become responsible, contributing people in a democratic society; and to gain the necessary skills to find personal happiness and well-being.

What if our schools could help *all* children achieve these outcomes in a way that is cost-effective and backed by research? Consider the following scenario:

> Imagine that you've just walked into the main entrance of a school, where you are greeted by a smiling student. As you walk through the hallways, you ask your guide how she feels about the school. She bubbles over with excitement as she describes a science project she is working on with two classmates.
>
> Your guide leads you to a classroom where students are tackling a personalized learning project. Each student, your guide explains, has been working for the past week on a topic they chose, either alone or in collaboration with other students. Each project must address specific learning objectives, regardless of the topic.
>
> As you cast your eyes around the room, you notice that some students are working in pairs, others in groups of three or four. Three students are working alone—two at computers and the third with a book, pen, and paper.
>
> Then you realize you have not seen the teacher. Your eyes search the room until you spot her. She's pulling up a chair to engage with three students who are in the middle of a passionate discussion.
>
> It strikes you that all of the students are approaching their tasks in different ways, yet each one looks motivated and engaged. Many even seem happy.

The previously described classroom is *learner-centered*—meaning students are actively engaged in their own learning, through methods that are individualized to suit their personal learning styles. Research compellingly demonstrates that learner-centered practices are the best way to maximize student learning. Unfortunately, our imaginary scenario likely does not mirror many people's lived experiences with public education.

Public Education Today

Despite four decades of reform efforts, schools and school systems remain remarkably unchanged, and performance has not appreciably improved. Under the crippling pressures of standardized testing, many teachers are forced to focus their time on teaching for memorization rather than developing critical thinking. Large-scale reform is not happening fast enough, and solutions are often perceived as costly. The result: higher rates of absenteeism and dropouts, and more and more students at risk of failing to develop the skills they need to lead successful, happy, and fulfilling lives.

Is This the Reality of Public Education?

Graphic by © Peter Kuper. Used with permission

Some readers may consider this a disturbing illustration. Take a minute to think critically about whether you believe it accurately represents the general reality of our public education system. We encourage you to share the illustration with colleagues, friends, family members, and others to get their reactions. Your personal analysis and conversations with others may give you some new perspectives—or perhaps they will confirm what you already believe about public education.

Why Does It Matter?

Young people today face more complex challenges than any previous generation: a worldwide pandemic that forced many into months of remote learning, systemic racism and racist behaviors that continue to tear our country apart, the January 6 attack on our democracy, growing concerns over the environment, mental health, the racial wealth, and achievement gaps—the list goes on. Now more than ever, every child living in the United States needs and deserves a relevant, quality education that will prepare them for the challenges of today and tomorrow.

Learner-Centered Education: A Way Forward for All Students

The authors have been involved in education improvement efforts since the 1983 Carnegie report and the 1988 *Nation At Risk*. We believe that more could be done to improve educational opportunities for *all* children if schools would make the design of learner-centered classrooms, with an emphasis on social-emotional learning, their highest long-term priority.

Learner-centered practices allow teachers to address the needs of students with a diverse range of interests and abilities in the same classroom at the same time. They address the whole student and can be used to teach content in any subject at any level, from prekindergarten to university.

Focusing on learner-centered strategies motivates students to take responsibility for their own learning and allows teachers to challenge students to think critically about topics such as social justice, the qualities of good citizenship, ethical practices, and the traits of a life-long learner (Lam, Cheng, & Ma, 2009). We are sure you would agree that our nation, and the world, need critical-thinking citizens who have moral compasses that reflect in their day-to-day behaviors (Boekaerts, 2002).

Unfortunately, the successful education reform approaches toward raising student achievement and preparing students, ethically and morally, for a future beyond schooling, are coming about too slowly. Why should students in today's schools miss out on changes we know work?

Rochester's School Without Walls (1971), and Ithaca's Lehman Alternative School (1974), both in New York State, and a few schools in California, as well as in some schools across the country, are demonstrating how active engagement of students in the learning process can motivate student learning while affording teachers and parents opportunities for authentically assessing student progress. Typical of these schools is this statement from the

Lehman school's website: "Students demonstrate essential skills and knowledge through portfolios and performances rather than credits and reflect on their learning through written evaluations rather than grades."

Or this from the website of the School Without Walls: "We are a learner centered school. Our students participate in interdisciplinary classes with project based curricula. We use the community as a base and resource for our work. Our students … are involved in school governance. Graduation requirements include completion of portfolios and Senior projects instead of standardized testing requirements."

Learner-centered practices enable teachers to simultaneously meet the needs of higher-performing students, children being raised in concentrated poverty, students with physical or learning disabilities, and students with diverse learning styles that are not necessarily a match for the average teaching style—in other words: *all* students.

What Do Learner-Centered Practices Cost?

With pandemic-related costs added to perennial issues around school budgeting, any education solutions will not be viable if they are accompanied by increased costs. This book prescribes the best medicine for what ails our schools, and, best of all, it is not another 'throw money at the problem' solution. In fact, most of what we prescribe costs not a penny—just a change in the way we think.

Learner-centered practices can be put into effect immediately. All that is required is a shift in mindsets and a commitment by school administrators to prioritize the training and implementation of these practices. Ask the forward-looking classroom teachers about the proposals in this book, and they will most likely tell you, "It's just plain good old common sense!"

What This Book Offers

This book gives readers an overview of what learner-centered education is and how to put it into practice. To do this in as concrete a way as possible, we have included 279 **activities and sample lessons** that can be easily utilized in classrooms. While activities are usually specific to one discipline and/or grade level, most can be used for any discipline or level (from prekindergarten to graduate school) with slight adjustments by a creative teacher. We trust the reader will focus on the quality of the activity rather than the specific level or discipline.

Who It Is For

Teachers—The role you play in students' lives and development is second only to that of parents and caregivers. We wrote this book to give you a practical, hands-on guide for bringing learner-centered practices into your own classrooms.

Education professors and students—We have included a brief outline for an education course using this book as text, as well as an invitation for professors to contact us for additional support.

Administrators—As school leaders, you are essential to supporting your teachers' abilities to develop learner-centered classrooms. While you can benefit from everything in this book, Section Six ("What Makes for a Good Administrator?") was written specifically with you in mind.

Parents—This book is not just for educators in schools. As your child's first and most important teacher, you can use learner-centered strategies to support their growth and development at home. Any of this book's 293 activities can be easily adapted for home use.

Who Are the Authors?

Dan Drmacich and Don Mesibov are two guys with last names difficult to pronounce and more than 100 years of experience in the trenches of education. We do not claim to be intellectuals, have no doctorate degrees, and have written only a few books. *However*, what we do have are track records of success helping teachers adjust their classroom strategies, challenging administrators to think about their approaches to leadership, and supporting school reform initiatives.

For 23 years, Dan was principal of the nationally renowned School Without Walls in Rochester, New York, a public school, and a member of the New York State Performance Standards Consortium, which requires performance-based assessments and a yearlong project to demonstrate competency for graduation rather than standardized tests. Dan is currently cofounder and coordinator of the Rochester Coalition for Public Education, an organization focused on research-based, progressive school reform and social justice. He continuously struggles to demonstrate performance-based competency to meet his own standards on the golf course.

In the past five decades, Don has worked at a school for emotionally disturbed children, been a middle school English teacher, taught courses on constructivism at local colleges for 22 years, and worked for a teacher's union.

Additionally, he is director of the Institute for Learning Centered Education, an organization he founded in 1995. The Institute has conducted 28 week-long summer conferences modeling learner-centered strategies and has organized more than 1,000 workshops on learner-centered practices. Beginning in 2015, the Institute has supported more than 40 schools engaged in its Student Poverty/Trauma Initiative.

Section One
Why Do Schools Need to Change?

Learner-Centered Education (LCE) and Social-Emotional Learning (SEL): You Can't Have One without the Other
The Iron Is Hot
Research Supports the Need for Change
Best Practices Are for All Students
Many Students Are Bored and Unmotivated

One day, in the middle of a lecture,
I looked up, saw the yawns and
bored looks of my students, and
I interrupted my lecture and asked,

"Are you as bored as I am?"

Carol Amberg, High School English Teacher
and Department Chair, retired

1

Learner-Centered Education (LCE) and Social-Emotional Learning (SEL)

You Can't Have One without the Other

Scenario One: *Dwayne enters class excited. Yesterday, the class identified an issue that is relevant to their school and personal lives: the lack of local employment opportunities for youth. Dwayne is looking forward to investigating this issue with his peers and developing solutions to a problem that has negatively impacted so many of his friends, family, and neighbors.*

Scenario Two: *Dwayne enters class with the attitude of many students: "This is going to be a waste of my time." Before the teacher even speaks a word, he is sliding a book or video game out of his desk, hoping it is hidden from the teacher's view.*

It is apparent that more needs to be done to motivate students to want to come to school and learn. Otherwise, absenteeism, dropout rates, and discipline problems will continue to increase. Fortunately, the irony is that lack of student motivation has become such a problem that many educators are becoming more receptive to the ideas that are explored in this book than would have been the case years ago when students were more likely to comply with parent and teacher directives.

This is not to suggest that education was better years ago. The traditional teaching that most of us experienced as students was never the best way for students to learn—we were just able to delude ourselves into thinking it worked. It was a time when most students came to school because their parents held them accountable, and once in school, a threat to send a student

DOI: 10.4324/9781003284697-2

to the office was often enough to control behavior. If that did not work, the threat of a lower grade or a call to a parent often sufficed.

Here are some highlights of what many teachers and students are telling us:

- ◆ Teachers face increasing difficulty as they struggle to motivate students to take their studies seriously.
- ◆ School curricula are often overloaded with subject content students are expected to memorize and regurgitate, even though many students are not interested in learning content that they find irrelevant. It is no more possible to teach content to a student whose mind is tuned out than it is to enter a locked room without a key.
- ◆ There is too much focus on teaching students for memorization as opposed to teaching for understanding, ability to apply, and the skill to create.

Our premises are simple:

- ◆ Classrooms that are learner-centered, as opposed to more traditional, teacher-centered classes, afford all students the best opportunities to achieve their maximum potential as they prepare to be contributing members of society.
- ◆ While many experts compartmentalize learner-centered education (LCE) and social-emotional learning (SEL) as if they are two distinctly separate approaches to teaching, we believe that any definition of learner-centered classrooms has to include a classroom where SEL strategies are an integral part of the learning process. In other words, if there is not a focus on SEL, then it cannot be considered a learner-centered classroom. SEL practices are the door that opens the mind to the content we want students to understand and be able to apply. Aren't each of us more likely to consider what is shared by someone we respect and whom we believe to truly *care* about us?

What Are SEL and LCE?

SEL is an educational approach that focuses on the teacher-student relationship. The principal idea behind SEL is that the stronger the connection between teacher and student, the better the teacher's chances of getting the student to engage. SEL requires teachers to consider the following:

- Understanding and managing emotions
- Setting and achieving goals
- Empathizing with other points of view
- Taking responsibility for developing and maintaining positive relationships
- Making responsible decisions

In *LCE*, students are actively engaged in the learning process, while the teacher plays a facilitative or supportive role. Learner-centered instruction focuses on skills and practices that enable students to engage with experiences and information for becoming lifelong learners, critical thinkers, and independent problem-solvers. For teachers, this means a shift away from treating students as if their heads are receptacles into which knowledge can be poured. Instead, teachers challenge students to become more responsible for their own learning by having them make choices about what and how they will learn.

Image by Afzal Khan. With permission

True or False: If It Is Group Work, It Is Learner-Centered

False. While having students work in pairs or small groups very often reflects LCE because the need to collaborate encourages critical thinking, students can also work individually on tasks that require them to think critically. In fact, sometimes a teacher can accommodate different learning styles by offering students the option of working individually or with others on similar assignments at the same time. The test of whether a task is learner-centered is whether it requires critical thinking. It depends on the type of thinking in which students are involved.

 Strategy 1: Critical Thinking Activity

An obvious and simplistic example would be if students were asked, in pairs, to agree on what Little Red Riding Hood wore on her walk through the woods. This question is not likely to require students to put on their thinking caps. Similarly, students can easily be challenged to think critically with a well-designed individual assignment, such as writing a short story or drawing a picture of what else Little Red Riding Hood could have done when encountering the Big Bad Wolf. While students should frequently be challenged to collaborate on tasks, it is incorrect to believe that there are not times when students should work individually on tasks, or that a class cannot simultaneously have some students working individually while others are paired or in small groups.

In a learning-centered classroom integrated with SEL approaches, what matters most is for teachers to strive toward building rapport with each student, identifying each one's learning style, and offering as many personalized learning approaches as possible.

What Are the Authors' Experiences with SEL and LCE?

We began our careers as classroom teachers, and we continue to work with classroom teachers conducting professional development and consulting with the people who know best what needs to change and what needs to remain the same in our schools. In the following stories, we share some of the earliest and most formative experiences in our individual journeys to understand how education could be different.

DAN: One day after school, in 1973, a ninth grader whom I had taught the previous two years, but was now in a traditional high school, visited to show me the results of a quiz that her social studies teacher had given her class. The quiz consisted of three questions that would generally require only rote memorization for a response. The first two questions she answered correctly. The third asked, "What are two symbols that represent the United States?" My student responded creatively with two drawings: one of the Holiday Inn and the other of McDonald's. The teacher's question did not ask that responses be limited to words. Instead of recognizing the student's creativity by submitting drawings—which asking for symbols implies—the teacher gave her a big red checkmark and provided no comments or questions for the student to contemplate.

What an opportunity this could have been to enliven the class with a discussion by having my former student share her artistic response and asking the class to explore the many different ways people can express themselves. The teacher also missed an opportunity to convey her support for the use of artistic expression and creativity. I often wondered how most teachers would have handled this same situation, but I knew creative problem-solving and critical thinking were, unfortunately, falling by the wayside to standardized test-driven instruction.

DON: My first class with students continues to shape my attitude toward teaching: It was September and I stood before 23 eighth graders, who were about the same age as the youngsters I had worked with the previous eight weeks at an overnight summer camp where I was usually able to establish a rapport with my campers.

But that first class, those eighth graders were looking at me with an expression that said, "I dare you to teach me anything." These were basically the same children I had worked with at camp. It felt like I would have had a better chance of teaching someone if I had walked off the ball diamond as the shortstop, put my arm around the second baseman, and said, "Let's sit down so I can help you with your pronouns." And on top of the resistance to being taught, the curriculum was so crowded that it did not allow time to get to know my students and establish a relationship with them, which is a critical part of successful teaching.

When teachers use learner-centered practices integrated with SEL strategies, it allows students to know they are respected and cared about. The best teachers understand that this approach is key to their ability to open students' minds to new learning and possibilities.

When we speak of schools not being as successful with all students as they might be, let us be clear there is little blame to be placed on teachers, administrators, and the many other school employees, parents, and community members whose efforts to educate students are often admirable and praiseworthy. If the suggestions in this book are adopted, it will result in arming the many wonderful educators, parents, and others with the resources, training, and support they are currently lacking as they strive to do what is best for children.

The only question that should be addressed when deciding how to conduct our schools and classrooms is the obvious one: What is best for *all* students?

COMMONSENSE CONCLUSION

LCE and SEL go together like the proverbial horse and carriage: You cannot have one without the other.

2

The Iron Is Hot

At the dinner table, Malcolm's parents were discussing whether to attend a meeting to discuss how parents can opt out of statewide standardized tests. While Mom and Dad did most of the talking, and arguing, Malcolm interrupted once to complain, "The questions on those tests are stupid. I studied real hard for the last one and got marked off because I couldn't remember the name of some obscure war hero."

Just before dessert was served, Malcolm spoke up again: "Mom, school really is a waste of time. It's boring. Do I really have to go to college?" His parents were alarmed, and based on their own experiences in school, they sympathized with Malcolm. Yet, they felt it necessary to reassure him things would get better and more interesting as he progressed through high school.

Why is *now* the most important time in history to focus on learner-centered practices? Because the most significant improvements in educating all of today's youth can be brought about by increasing the pace of transforming classrooms from traditional into learner-centered. Right now, the iron is hot. This is due to

- Rising rates of absenteeism and dropouts,
- Increased difficulty in motivating students, and

DOI: 10.4324/9781003284697-3

◆ A decrease in support for schools from some (not all) parents and an increasing number of parents who have to work outside the home and are not in a position to monitor their children's progress in school.

Learner-centered classrooms are not, by themselves, the solution to what ails our schools, but they will significantly enhance the ability of professional educators to motivate students and contribute to improved student learning. A learner-centered classroom not only improves students' learning of subject-area content, but it also requires a focus on social-emotional learning (SEL) practices. A learner-centered classroom prepares students for entry into the world after graduation. It motivates students to want to learn, teaches them critical thinking and other executive functioning skills, and addresses good citizenship, social justice, and other relevant issues that are often ignored in mandated curricula.

Brain research documents the importance of student engagement as part of an effective learning process. A growing number of educators are accepting the fact that teaching strategies must become more learner-centered, meaning the question is shifting from whether classrooms should be learner-centered to *when* and *how* it should and can happen (Schwartz, Tsang, and Blair, 2016).

Many teachers who resisted moving from teacher-directed to learner-centered lessons are now recognizing the importance of change—some because they believe it is more effective and others because they see it happening and do not want to be left behind. More than 30 years' worth of published research, publicized success stories, and progressive professional development programs are finally having a positive impact. As frequent workshop designers, we have noticed a significant change in the concerns of participants. Until recent years, most participants wanted (or needed) to be convinced to try learner-centered classroom lessons. More recently, however, a growing number of teachers do not have to be convinced; they just want to learn how to do it (Polly, 2011).

Similarly, whereas until recently, educators often dismissed SEL and other aspects of the affective domain[1] as "that touchy-feely stuff we tried years ago and found doesn't work," there is now growing acceptance of the need to link subject-area content with strategies for SEL. In 2019, author Amy Takabori of the University of Arizona blogged that "educators across the country already knew that such classroom practices that foster **social-emotional learning (SEL)** have become increasingly common in K–12 schools (emphasis in the original)."

The iron is hot!

COMMONSENSE CONCLUSION

The time is right to provide all teachers with the professional development and resources needed to conduct learner-centered classrooms integrated with effective use of social-emotional strategies.

Note

1 The affective domain involves our feelings, emotions, and attitudes. It includes the way we deal with values, appreciation, enthusiasm, and motivations (Bloom, 1956). SEL, with its inherent focus on relationships, addresses aspects of the affective domain.

3

Research Supports the Need for Change

Carol Amberg, who recently retired as an outstanding secondary English teacher and department chair, began her career as a self-described "traditional teacher." One day, in the middle of a lecture, she looked up, saw the yawns and bored looks, and inter-rupted her lecture to the class, saying, "Are you as bored as I am?"

Once she established credibility and showed that she wanted candor, the students acknowledged that they, too, were not finding her class a place that was among their top choices to be. So, Carol said, "Look, what you have to learn is non-negotiable. But I do not have to teach it any particular way. Let's discuss how you would prefer to learn what I am required to teach." This started Ms. Amberg on a never-ending journey toward mastering the skills required of a teacher seeking to design a learner-centered classroom.

DOI: 10.4324/9781003284697-4

Image by Afzal Khan. With permission

This chapter provides a brief overview of the educational thinkers and theories that gave us learner-centered practices. While the content here is particularly intended for teachers and teachers-in-training, parents and care-givers may find it valuable as well.

Two Schools of Thought

Researcher Patrick Flynn, from the Institute for Learning Centered Educa-tion, told us that in the early 1900s, there were two dominant philosophies of education vying for acceptance: Thorndike's and Dewey's. Edward L. Thorndike, an American psychologist, educator, lexicographer, and pioneer in educational research, focused on behaviorist theory, which asserts that thinking and feeling have little to do with learning because each cannot be measured (Thorndike, 2011).

Thorndike's theory contrasted with the philosophy advocated by John Dewey, whose view of education emphasized the need to learn by doing. Dewey believed that human beings learn through "hands-on" and inter-active approaches. Constructivist theory, as advocated by Dewey, suggests that humans construct knowledge and meaning from their experiences (Dewey, 1938).

Dewey provides some insight into the "nuts and bolts" of this construc-tivist process: "Thinking is not like a sausage machine which reduces all materials indifferently to one marketable commodity but is a power of following up and linking together the specific suggestions that specific things arouse." The phrase "following up and linking" suggests an active process initiated by the learner.

In brief, Thorndike's theory leads to traditional, teacher-centered "behaviorism and operant conditioning" and "direct instruction" practices, whereas Dewey's theory aligns with "hands-on/minds-on," constructivist, learner-centered instructional practices.

In a traditional classroom that adheres to Thorndike's philosophy, the teacher does most of the speaking, and students, seated quietly in rows, listen, take notes, and are expected to regurgitate their notes upon command by the teacher or as required on a test.

The Thorndike method can result in students who get high test grades because of good memories yet frequently fail to understand the deeper meanings of the correct responses on the test (Silberman, 1967). The following is an example of the fallacy of learning solely through memorization reinforced by testing for memorization:

> One of the authors rates poorly on any measure of spatial intelligence; hence, he struggled in high school with geometry. Yet, he scored a 91 on the statewide standardized test. How? He has a good memory and strong linguistic and mathematical-logical intelligences. He reviewed tests from previous years and memorized the kinds of questions that would be on the test. Yet, on the day of the exam, if you had asked him to demonstrate an understanding or application of any of his correct responses, he could not have done it.

For meaningful learning to occur, students must actively engage with the content and be able to apply it to real-world situations. For many students, taking notes distracts them from thinking about what is being taught. There are, of course, exceptions that may justify requiring students to take notes:

◆ If the ability to take notes is a lesson objective (after all, note-taking is an important real-world skill)
◆ If the information being taught is not easily accessible in written form
◆ If the student is a "tactile dominant learner" who learns more effectively by taking notes

Exceptions notwithstanding, teachers could distribute notes to students and actively engage them with the information that would otherwise be the subject of the note-taking ("Put Down That Notebook! New Studies Find Taking Notes Is Bad for Your Memory," 2018).

Flynn concluded that, in Dewey and Thorndike's time, it was Thorndike's views that won out. By the 1990s, however, the pendulum was swinging toward Dewey. Happily, it is picking up speed in the United States and around the globe. Professor Michael Smith spent many summers teaching in Thailand and now, having retired, spends a majority of the year there. Dr. Smith reported over a decade ago that the Thai government was encouraging schools to focus on constructivist theory. Additionally, secondary math teacher Nicole Freeman says, "I was fortunate this year to visit an elementary school in Uganda. They are turning away from Thorndike and trying to use learner-centered strategies."

Brain research informs us that students must be actively engaged with the information we want them to learn and apply to the real world. Learner-centered classroom instruction is supported by years of research and has been promulgated in periodicals such as *Education Leadership* and *Kappan* (Willingham, 2009).

Constructivist Theory

Learner-centered teaching strategies are based on the constructivist theory of how people learn. Constructivism has epistemological and philosophical roots going as far back as Socrates and then all the way from Immanuel Kant to John Dewey, Jean Piaget, Jerome Bruner, Lev Vygotsky, Jacqueline Grennon Brooks, and Martin G. Brooks. It is "an educational theory that emphasizes the importance of being hands-on and activity-based" to create new understandings and knowledge to act upon (Brooks & Brooks, 1983).

According to researcher Flynn, the main tenets of constructivist theory include the following:

- Learning occurs when people construct their own knowledge by connecting new information with prior knowledge
- Learners must be offered cognitively challenging tasks
- Learning grows out of social interaction
- Learning that is essentially experiential is learning that lasts
- Learning lasts when learners are actively engaged with the information
- The foundation of long-lasting learning is critical thinking

A chart designed by Flynn to demonstrate the correlation between the tenets of constructivism and learner-centered classroom practices is available at www.learningcentered.org or by email to institutelce@gmail.com. Teachers can use the chart as a checklist to determine if their lessons are consistent with constructivist theory.

Three Myths about Constructivism

Myth One: In a constructivist environment, students always decide what they will learn.

This myth suggests that teachers who adhere to constructivist principles allow students to make all decisions without having to meet teacher, school, or state standards. However, constructivist practices can work in a standards-based classroom. As we'll explain in Chapter 4, teachers have a range of options for how students will address required learning objectives. It is possible to meet state standards while giving students agency in their learning.

Myth Two: Constructivism means students are given an assignment and the teacher then leaves them completely alone to complete their task until/unless the students ask for assistance.

This myth is ridiculous on the surface. Constructivist-based lessons require significant amounts of student-teacher interaction. In a well-designed constructivist lesson, the teacher assigns (or negotiates) a task that will enable students to address specific, teacher-determined learning objectives or teacher-student negotiated objectives. The teacher then scaffolds the lesson to the degree necessary to support the student. By adjusting the scaffolding to the requirements of each student, a teacher can individualize instruction.

Myth Three: There is no place for lecture in a constructivist environment.

Is there room for a lecture, or any other strategy often viewed as "traditional," in a constructivist classroom? Yes, definitely! Having students pair-share after a mini-lecture, followed by whole-class sharing, is an effective example of a constructivist "lecture." Intervening during student-led activity with a mini-lecture is another example.

Whether a lecture constitutes a constructivist-based approach depends on the context in which it is delivered. A key question that teachers must address in creating a constructivist-based lecture is, "Is there a reason my students should want the information I want to impart?" For additional information, see Flynn, Mesibov, Vermette, and Smith, *Captivating Classes with Constructivism*, Chapter 12 (2004b).

Why Has It Taken So Long for Learner-Centered Practices to Gain Traction?

In the past, if students fell behind on their work or caused a discipline problem, a trip to the principal's office was the first option for many teachers. If that did not work, the teacher merely had to hint at calling a parent or lowering a grade. Comedians of the mid-twentieth century would joke that if they told their parents the teacher had hit them on the knuckles with a ruler, the parent would hit them again, saying, "If the teacher hit you, there must have been a good reason." But times have changed. In an ironic reversal, today it is often the parents of a high-performing student who receive that call from the teacher if there is a problem, not the parents of a child who is causing discipline problems. And those trips to the office might now be made by parents whose child complained about a teacher—unless those parents skip the office visit and go straight to court to file a lawsuit.

There is one positive side to the increase in students who either do not care about learning or are simply disruptive in class: It has sped up teachers' realization that unless the focus is on intrinsically motivating students to learn, little meaningful learning will occur. When students were well-behaved, sitting quietly in rows, listening to the teacher, and taking notes, the profession had little reason to care about motivating students to engage in learner-centered practices that would require teachers to learn a whole new way to teach. However, to quote Bob Dylan, "The times they are a changin'." And, hopefully, this book will encourage the pace of educational change.

The traditional way of teaching was never the best way for students to learn the skills necessary to become responsible, critical-thinking individuals, but until student motivation and behaviors became intolerable, there was little motivation to move toward Dewey's far more effective philosophy of learning experientially through doing.

COMMONSENSE CONCLUSION

For a variety of reasons, the field of education is gradually, yet steadily, accepting the research that indicates students learn best in a learner-centered environment. While many educators still resist this trend, a growing number are either welcoming it or at least accepting that it is happening and recognizing that they need to become part of the process.

4

Best Practices Are for All Students

The classroom appears to be in chaos; there is no discernable pattern. Three students with high class averages are huddled in a corner, challenged by a problem that would exceed the capabilities of most other students in the class. Another four are working individually at computers using software designed to help them practice tasks reinforcing what they had recently learned using math manipulatives.

Mr. Barrington is in a corner of the room assisting four students with learning disabilities, all of whom have a high intellectual capability when given accommodations for their disabilities. He alternates between working with these four students and another group to whom he has assigned an easy-to-understand task because of their limited ability to keep up with their classmates. Approximately every 15 minutes, Mr. Barrington makes a quick trip around the room to see if any of the students working individually or in small groups have questions or need assistance. A large sheet of paper on the wall allows students to post questions that do not require immediate attention.

Why Does It Matter If Our Classrooms Are Teacher-Centered or Learner-Centered?

Learner-centered teaching strategies are best practices for *all* students, whereas a teacher-centered approach focuses only on the *average* student. In the latter scenario, struggling students get left behind and higher-performing ones are inadequately challenged. And if a lecture-style teacher spends much

DOI: 10.4324/9781003284697-5

of his time talking, too little time is left to assess what students are learning. It is difficult to talk, listen, and observe at the same time.

Personalizing (or individualizing) instruction is an important goal of learner-centered teaching. To do it well, we must separate in our minds the objectives of the lesson (the "what") from the means (the "how"). In other words, there are two aspects to any lesson: *what* we want the students to learn and *how* we want them to learn it. Carol Amberg recognized this distinction when she invited her students to share in deciding how to learn what she was required to teach. This flexible approach helps teachers understand what students do and do not know and allows teachers to adjust their expectations accordingly.

Certain learning objectives required by local, state, or federal standards—*what* each student must learn—are non-negotiable, meaning teachers have little control over them. Teachers do have flexibility, however, when it comes to *how* they will address these required learning objectives with their students. This does not preclude the addition of student-generated learning outcomes in addition to the mandated ones.

The learner-centered classroom allows students to learn—and exceed—required standards, while a teacher-centered classroom often limits students to the teacher's decisions on what students must learn and how they learn it. Additionally, a learner-centered teacher encourages students to add their own goals to those set by the teacher for a particular learning experience. When students can pursue their own learning goals, they are more highly motivated than when they are restricted to goals set by the teacher.

DON: High school teachers John Waterhouse and Tom Youssi designed the "Venture Program," a four-year curriculum in which students learn through four ten-week interdisciplinary units each year. Mr. Waterhouse brought a student, Ginny, to my undergraduate education class to discuss their process for having student-led, parent-teacher conferences in which the student would demonstrate to the parent and teacher her mastery of some of the 38 district standards required for graduation. The standard she addressed was her understanding and effective use of technology. But having been given the choice of topics through which she could demonstrate her technological skills, she had chosen to prepare a report on how ponies are born and then raised.

The student sent surveys to a dozen veterinarians and created a video that not only demonstrated her effective use of technology but also how much she had learned about her own interest in the topic she chose. As this student spoke with poise and eloquence to my 20 students who were gathered around a circular table, Mr. Waterhouse passed me a note: "Do you know what a learning disability is?"

Following his student's articulate presentation, he explained that when the semester had begun a few months earlier, she would have been too nervous to have spoken before my class or any group. Being able to choose her own topic motivated her to accomplish her own objectives in public speaking, as well as the district-mandated technology standard.

In a learner-centered classroom, many students can work alone or independently for significant periods of time, allowing the teacher to work with individual students, or small groups, who may need teacher attention. Consequently, a learner-centered classroom focused on individualizing and personalizing instruction allows the teacher to

- ◆ Keep those students with the greatest needs from falling through the cracks;
- ◆ Adapt strategies to those students who simply have different learning styles;
- ◆ Address the unique needs of students who are being raised in concentrated poverty, are experiencing severe trauma (regardless of their economic situation), or are learning English as a second language; and
- ◆ Simultaneously challenge the higher-performing students.

In other words, learner-centered education helps create equity in the classroom because it allows teachers to meet each student where they are.

 Strategy 2: Tailoring a Lesson for Each Individual Student

Here is an example of how one teacher might individualize a lesson for a class of 25 students:

STEP ONE

Students are given a written statement of a lesson objective: "You will learn to provide a rationale for your opinions in an essay you will write."

STEP TWO

The teacher asks students to select a topic for their essay. This can be open-ended, or there can be a list of topics from which each student will choose.

STEP THREE

The teacher puts students in pairs or small groups (no larger than four) and then asks each group to agree on a facilitator, who will listen to the teacher's directions and keep the group on task, and a recorder, who will write down decisions of the group. The teacher allows ten minutes for each group to agree on an explanation of what it means to provide a rationale for an opinion.

STEP FOUR

The recorder from each group shares the group's definition of rationale and the teacher facilitates a class discussion.

STEP FIVE

The teacher asks students to begin writing their essays individually and to do their best to provide a sentence or paragraph with a rationale for each opinion they express, reminding the class to call her over if they have a question, are uncertain how to proceed, or think they have completed the task. The students are allowed to request assistance from members of their group, but each is responsible for their own essay.

The teacher immediately begins to work with the individual student or small group she anticipates may have the most difficulty with the task. She continues to rotate around the room, working with groups and individuals struggling with the task and checking the essays of those who think they have completed their work.

There are two keys to the success of this individualized approach:

1   By allowing students to choose the topic for their essays, it increases the likelihood they will be motivated to work individually for a while, thus allowing the teacher to work individually with each student.

2   The teacher has a different, but related, task to offer students who complete their task satisfactorily while others need more time. However, it is important that students view the additional task as fun, or at least interesting. One veteran teacher often asks groups that finish early to design a test on the topic being studied, which he then pledges to take and allow the group to grade. Sometimes he goes a step further and requests that the test model what the students would consider to be a good exam. He is then able to review their test through the lens of whether it would require him to think critically.

COMMONSENSE CONCLUSION

Learner-centered strategies benefit *all* students and help create equity by meeting learners where they are.

5

Many Students Are Bored and Unmotivated

Mr. Green in classroom 109 is speaking before the entire class. As he looks around the class, while still concentrating on what he intends to say, he can see some students are not paying attention. He also knows that he cannot be certain that students with good eye contact and body language are thinking about what he is saying—especially if the activity is a lecture or one with little student interaction.

Mr. Brown in classroom 110 has challenged his students with a well-designed, learner-centered activity. He observes that every student is actively engaged. He can see and hear what they are thinking because he can overhear discussions as he works the room, unencumbered by the need to focus on what he intends to say. He can focus all his attention on observing his students and not be distracted by thinking of what he wants to say.

Ms. Freeman, a high school math teacher, observes, "When my students are engaged in off-task conversations, I explain that their brain is engaged in their conversation, not my task. The next step is to change my task to force them to engage with my topic."

In his autobiography, Tony Bennett says he used to start concerts with a lively number to grab the attention of his audience. Then, on advice from Count Basie, he switched to starting concerts "with a medium-tempo number to give the audience a chance to settle in" before moving into an up-tempo number later. This decision shows Bennett's thoughtful consideration of the best way to grab and maintain the audience's attention. He also, through smiles, friendly gestures toward the audience, and frequent complimentary

DOI: 10.4324/9781003284697-6

observations about the locality, demonstrates at each performance how much he cares about the people for whom he is performing.

Think about this: People pay $200 to $400 to see a Tony Bennett concert, and yet *he* feels the need to shower *them* with praise throughout his 90 minutes on stage. Why? Because Bennett understands that the audience is the reason he is there, that he needs them to "buy-in" to what he is doing.

Conversely, many students, if they were allowed and had the means, would pay $200 to $400 *not* to be in class. This is because too many teachers believe they can simply walk into class and start teaching without doing anything to grab the students' attention. Though we may be able to compel students to be physically present in a classroom, we cannot compel them to have their minds present as well.

In later chapters, we suggest strategies for motivating unmotivated students. For now, let us simply cite the increasing problem of students who are unmotivated and willing to express their discontent through anything from refusing to do assigned work, to disrupting classroom lessons, to even dropping out of school.

COMMONSENSE CONCLUSION

An unmotivated student often has a closed mind to what is being taught. What is the purpose of teaching if there is little chance that what is being taught will be learned and applied to the real world by a student?

Section Two

How Do the Teachers' and Students' Roles Change?

It All Starts with the Teacher

Prioritize What Impacts Student Learning

Student Needs, Interests, and Learning: Styles Should Be at the Center of a Lesson

Motivation Is Derived from What Students: Find Interesting, Relevant, or Just Plain Fun

Teachers Are Classroom Coaches

Critical Thinking Is the Main Focus for Student Learning

Advisories, Journaling, and Conferencing Are Essential

Music and Art Facilitate Learning in All Disciplines

Students Need a Vision

Introverted (or Quiet) Children Require Special Strategies

Educators Can Make Use of Lectures and Be Effective

Student-centered learning encourages and
allows for individualizing and personalizing
instruction; the needs of all learners—high performing,
identified, introverted, artistically or
musically intelligent, or slower learning—
can be addressed in a single classroom by
a single teacher

6

It All Starts with the Teacher

The school principal, Ms. Wonderly, gazed upon the classroom and saw students sitting quietly in rows as Mr. Glade spoke with little expression or movement except for his mouth. A few students appeared to be paying complete attention. Several were talking to the student behind or across from them. One was designing paper planes, waiting for Mr. Glade to look away, and then throwing them at predetermined targets throughout the room. Two kept their heads on their desks with no pretense of paying any attention to what Mr. Glade was saying.

It took a good deal of restraint for Ms. Wonderly to resist the temptation to stick her head in the door and ask, "Why is there no learning taking place in this class?"

Understanding Student-Centered Schools

Call it learner-centered, student-centered, or constructivist-based, what counts is the school's commitment to encouraging teachers to empower students to take responsibility for their own learning. There must be a priority to improve students' academic growth, citizenship, and ethical/moral behaviors.

What Is Missing from These Recommendations for School Reform?

- ◆ Revise the curriculum
- ◆ Improve and expand training for school administrators

DOI: 10.4324/9781003284697-8

- ◆ Reduce student loan requirements
- ◆ Reduce or increase the number of state and federal mandates
- ◆ Significantly increase, and equalize, school funding
- ◆ Raise teacher pay
- ◆ Increase or decrease the number of charter schools

HINT: All of these are important to consider, but something more important is missing from this list. Any idea what it is? If you had to name one factor that is more important to a child's education than any other, what would it be?

Got it yet? Missing from this list of critical factors in a child's formal education is *what happens in the classroom.*

Nothing can influence student success more than the impact of the classroom teacher. That is why it is of the utmost importance to ensure teachers thoroughly understand the concept of learner-centered pedagogical practices ("Eliciting Engagement in the High School Classroom: A Mixed-Methods Examination of Teaching Practices," Cooper, 2014).

In a perfect world, all children would be in classrooms with the latest technology, expensive resources, an ideal schedule, a forward-looking administration, and a passionate, effective teacher. But we do not live in a perfect world yet. If it came down to a forced choice in which only one of the aforementioned could be in a classroom, wouldn't we all choose that passionate, effective teacher?

School reform must focus on support for the classroom teacher because this is the person with the most significant impact on student learning.

Traditional vs. Learner-Centered Teachers

Traditional teacher: Abraham Lincoln is considered to be one of our greatest presidents because he opposed slavery and led the country during the Civil War. Take careful notes and be prepared for this to be on the unit test.

 Strategy 3: Ranking-by-Priority Activity

Learner-centered teacher: Rank all the presidents we have studied so far from most effective to least effective and write an essay that explains your ranking for each. You may work with a partner or work alone. Either way, please keep a daily journal that records how your research is attempting to address this assignment's criteria. The criteria will be posted by the class's student website committee, where you will also find a list of readings, videos, and other resources that may help you in your research. Feel free to use other sources.

COMMONSENSE CONCLUSION

A child's most valuable school-based resource is a learner-centered teacher, especially given that *all* students need to be appropriately engaged.

7

Prioritize What Impacts
Student Learning

After he denied some of his teachers' requests to attend a workshop on learner-centered practices, Principal Miles Archer prepared himself for pushback. "After all," he thought to himself, "the ones I turned down are the same teachers who attended a two-day workshop on the same topic a year ago, and our budget isn't elastic."

At home, Mr. Archer complained to his spouse, "These teachers just want to get out of the classroom for a few days, and they just don't understand that substitutes cost money." When Ms. Archer, a high school teacher in another district, tried to explain how difficult it is for a teacher to feel comfortable with learner-centered practices, he lamented, "I didn't have learner-centered teachers when I was in school, and I turned out OK, didn't I?" Ms. Archer, herself a believer in active learning, just looked toward the ceiling and didn't say a word.

If we can agree that the single most important factor for a student's in-school development is the teacher, doesn't it follow that the most significant step a school administrator can take is to ensure sufficient learner-centered professional development opportunities and resources to support classroom teachers and specialists?

Most administrators and teachers did their own learning in traditional classrooms, were trained to teach by professors who modeled traditional teaching practices, and got jobs at schools where a majority of instructors taught using traditional methods. The skills required to manage a learner-centered classroom differ significantly from those required in traditional classrooms, where students are expected to sit quietly and speak only when

DOI: 10.4324/9781003284697-9

called upon. It takes an understanding of learner-centered research and practice to become proficient in actively engaging students in developing the skills needed to become active, critical-thinking citizens.

Administrators have an important role to play in helping staff recognize the importance of learner-centered education and understand where the design of a learner-centered school or district ranks among their school's priorities. For an example of a process for helping teachers design a learner-centered activity, lesson, or unit, visit www.learningcentered.org or email institutelce@gmail.com.

Moving learner-centered, social-emotional classrooms to the top of a school's or district's list of priorities need not be accompanied by new costs. Funding is already provided for professional development, conferences, and classroom supplies in every district, although in varying degrees. Prioritizing learner-centered practices simply requires shifting these resources in alignment with a determination that every classroom shall be as learner-centered as possible, as quickly as possible. It also requires recognizing the difficulty that most teachers encounter when they begin the journey from traditional to learner-centered teaching. This professional goal is not one that can be accomplished overnight. Teaching in a learner-centered classroom requires a significantly different skillset, one that is not part of the average teacher's bag of tools.

Constructivist practice requires teachers to put in substantial time creating learning experiences that engage students. It is the teacher's "scaffolding" assistance throughout these experiences that enables students to learn to think critically, not just memorize or regurgitate existing formulas and information. When first engaging students in cooperative work, or any other learner-centered activity, teachers often feel they are losing control. But with sufficient practice and support, they can master the art of learner-centered teaching and witness the positive difference it will make for their students.

COMMONSENSE CONCLUSION

Administrators need to focus on what's most essential—supporting teachers in developing the skills to facilitate learner-centered instruction in their classrooms and communicating to staff that they understand this will be a lengthy, though worthwhile, journey.

8

Student Needs, Interests, and Learning Styles should be at the Center of a Lesson

Joel Cairo grew up idolizing Jackie Robinson. So when his teacher, Effie Perone, assigned the class Silas Marner, *a book in which he had no interest, he asked if he could choose another book. When Ms. Perone explained she wanted him to write about plot, character, setting, and conflict in* Silas Marner, *Joel asked, "Why can't I write about those things in* The Jackie Robinson Story?"*

Ms. Perone refused to even offer a compromise. When Joel couldn't find a movie about Silas Marner, he located a summary of the story on the internet and completed the assignment in less than an hour.

In a student-centered learning space, students are often involved in choosing what they will learn, how they will learn, and how they will assess their own learning. The teacher mainly controls the environment and makes final decisions where necessary and appropriate. However, the teacher empowers students by turning over a significant amount of control of the learning process. A learner-centered classroom is tightly structured and allows for what may initially appear, to unaware observers, to be chaos.

Consistent with constructivist theory, a learner-centered classroom should

- ◆ Cognitively challenge students,
- ◆ Experientially engage students (physically, mentally, and emotionally), and
- ◆ Use inquiry-based techniques that challenge students with teacher and student questions.

DOI: 10.4324/9781003284697-10

The following is another example of the difference between a typical teacher-directed and learner-centered classroom activity:

Teacher-centered: "Review the first ten amendments to the Constitution and prepare for a test."

Strategy 4: Ranking-in-Order Activity

Learner-centered: "Rank the ten amendments from most important to least important. Then, pair with another student and compare your lists. You must either reach consensus on one combined list or be prepared to share where you disagree and offer your reasoning. Then pair with another pair and try to reach consensus on one list. If you cannot, you must once again be prepared to defend your positions. Having a rationale is more important than whether I, as the teacher, agree with you."

One teacher explained the shift in his thinking as he transitioned from traditional methods of teaching to learner-centered:

> I used to approach a lesson with the mindset of, "I know what I want them to learn. How do I get the information from my head into theirs?" Now I ask myself, "What kind of activity can I design so that the students will have to think about the learning objectives I am trying to address, and provide evidence of having learned them?"

In traditional teaching, we lead students through lessons in which they often have no idea why they are doing what they are asked to do. In effect, the teacher is telling students, "Trust me, someday you'll see why we did this, and someday you'll thank me."

In a learner-centered lesson, teachers often create compelling "opening activities" that build on students' previous knowledge and creative curiosity, thus intrinsically motivating them to engage in discovery. This allows students to see the relevance of the lesson and focus on the "what" we want them to accomplish and often the "how." In other words, the learner-centered teacher focuses on helping students understand the key question or problem of the activity and challenges them to figure out how to achieve it.

Once we think students understand what they must accomplish, we give them choices on how they wish to achieve the goals and how they wish to demonstrate their learning. We turn them loose, but we immediately begin to scaffold. This means we first check on those students who are most likely to struggle with our directions. But we are available to all students, and we work the room to make sure each student, or group of students, is on track. We assist and scaffold, as necessary.

Challenge Students

When you enter a learner-centered classroom, you will see students working individually and/or in small groups. If the teacher is speaking, it should be to outline directions or explain an activity that will challenge students to give evidence of what they have learned. However, we also see teachers occasionally give "mini-lectures" followed by having students "pair-share" their interpretations of the teacher's information or something else to give evidence they have understood the teacher's intent. It can be effective to ask a student, "Please tell me what you think you just heard me say." However, the tone and approach should be such that it is clear to the students that your purpose is not to "catch" them being inattentive, but rather to see if you have adequately communicated your intent.

In a learner-centered classroom, an observer should be able to approach any student and that student should be able to tell you what he is doing, why he is doing it, and what the next step could be.

In a traditional classroom, the students expect the teacher to tell them what to do, when they are to do it, and when they have done enough. It is very telling when a teacher feels the need to leave detailed instructions for a substitute and asks the substitute to conduct a fairly easy lesson, rather than continue the one begun the previous day. Colleague Jack Drury of *Leading Edge*, an educational consulting firm, tells teachers, "If you are teaching effectively, the best instruction you should be able to leave for a substitute is, 'Ask the students what they should be doing and support them as they continue their work.'"

Learner-centered classrooms intrinsically motivate students. Students engage because they see the tasks as relevant and meaningful to their personal needs and interests. Most traditional classrooms, on the other hand, rely on extrinsic motivation, reward, and punishment to encourage students to complete learning tasks. And the tasks usually bore most students, especially the higher-performing ones.

 Strategy 5: Motivating Students to Go to the Books

Niagara University Professor Paul Vermette is an expert at encouraging students to seek out, on their own, books and other resources they might rebel against if they were assigned. He told us the story of how he managed to encourage a group of middle school students to study a chart on the digestive process that had been posted on a board in front of the class. Vermette's objective was to have the students sufficiently engage with the chart so they would understand and remember the seven steps in the digestive process.

"In groups of three," Vermette said to the students, "please agree on a favorite amusement park ride that the three of you would be excited to ride. Have one person in your group draw that ride through the digestive system as it is outlined on the wall over there." In small groups, the students excitedly began discussing their favorite rides. They then approached the chart to study the digestive process.

 Strategy 6: Another Example of Getting Students to the Books

The teacher places students in groups of two, three, or four, depending on the size of the class, and gives the following instructions:

> We are about to study the similarities between the way Canadians and Americans celebrate Thanksgiving. Write two journal entries: one as it might have been written by a Canadian, and one by an American. Be sure to include a detailed menu for the day in each entry and a description of activities throughout the day and evening, as well as who would be at the dinner table and why.

This is an engaging assignment that relies partially on knowledge students already have and partially on knowledge they have not acquired yet. The teacher casually reminds the students of the reference materials that are available to them in the classroom—books, computer programs, etc.—before setting them on their task. High school teachers might adapt this activity by challenging students to reflect on the origins of Thanksgiving and the treatment of Native Americans by the pilgrims (Flynn, Mesibov, Vermette & Smith, 2004a).

How Do We Know a Classroom Is Learner-Centered?

We strongly encourage the use of assessments to determine whether a classroom culture is learner-centered.

The 24-item Likert scale is one example of an assessment teachers might use. Please rate each of 24 items using this scale:

1. Never, 2. Hardly ever, 3. Sometimes, 4. Often, 5. Almost always

___ Upon entering the classroom, are students welcomed with warm, friendly greetings?

___ Do you begin class in one of these two ways, either of which is acceptable: either posing a question, activity, problem, dilemma, or some form of thought stimulator that challenges students to think critically and creatively or having students get right to work as a continuation of what they were doing the previous time in this class?

___ Do students and you treat each other with an acceptable level of respect, and do you respect each student to the degree you expect from the student? Do you and your students appear to genuinely like each other?

___ Do you demonstrate behaviors that show happiness, interest in students, humor, and caring?

___ Are there opportunities for students to make choices about individual learning activities? Are you open to student suggestions?

___ Do you focus on each student's strengths (assets vs. deficits) by allowing options that enable students to work in their strong intelligences as often as possible? (In a typical school, students are too often directed to work in areas of their weaker intelligences.)

___ Do you utilize school and community resources? For example, why not let an art class decorate the lobby instead of having teachers or custodial staff do it?

___ During student interaction, do students treat other students respectfully?

___ Do you ask questions of students that require higher-level thinking and/or which relate to their lives? Here are three examples: (1) "In *Little Women*, how would you describe the publisher's attitude toward female writers? Toward females in general?" (2) "Theodore Roosevelt has described the presidency as 'The Bully Pulpit.' What did he mean by this? Do you agree? Can you name someone who has ever used a "bully pulpit?" If so, under what conditions?" (3) "Do you think it is harmful to smoke marijuana? There are conflicting reports in the media. How can you learn the truth?"

___ Do you seek student perceptions before sharing your own on a topic?

___ Do you encourage students to share information and complete activities in pairs or small groups?

___ Are conflicts among students settled with rationality and with little emotion/drama?

___ Do you actively listen to student comments, demonstrating understanding of their content and feelings?

___ Do you turn inappropriate or irrelevant student comments or behaviors into "teachable moments," by asking focused questions of students? For example, "A student describes a TV program as 'stupid,' perhaps being sincere, perhaps in jest. It does not matter. The teacher then asks the student, 'What specifically, do you mean by stupid?'" After the student gets more specific or evades the issue, the teacher asks the class for additional comments. Following the discussion, the teacher asks the class to "pair-share" on the question, "What does this discussion teach us about our regular use of terms like stupid, dumb, retarded, or even excellent? What impact would it have, if upon hearing terms like stupid, we each asked the speaker to answer the question, 'As demonstrated by what?'"

___ Do you focus teaching and learning activities on content, concepts, and skills that make the class subject matter relevant to their lives?

___ Do you make certain that all students understand assignment details? Are your instructions both verbal and written to accommodate different learning styles?

___ Do you conduct some form of end-of-class assessment or feedback activity that asks students to make judgments of their own learning and/or teacher effectiveness?

___ Do you require students to integrate other subject areas into their learning by using art, music, science, and physical activities?

___ Do you integrate societal, political, and social/emotional issues of students into learning activities whenever possible?

___ Do you demonstrate a willingness to grow professionally by experimenting with teaching strategies that you generally do not use?

___ Are students required to distinguish fact from opinion?

___ Are students required to use reliable original sources vs. unreliable sources and learn how to distinguish the difference?

___ Are students taught how to share their thoughts and feelings responsibly about issues studied in class?

___ Is there an emphasis on critical thinking, problem-solving, and analysis as opposed to memorization and regurgitation?

The Likert scale can be used by teachers as a self-planning tool for improving the classroom's learner-centered culture. Teachers may find it useful to choose three items they wish to work on and develop an implementation plan. They can be asked, or required, to meet with a trusted teacher every week to discuss progress. Meeting with a colleague rather than an administrator encourages greater candor. The scale can also be part of improvement plans for probationary teachers whose job performance is assessed below standards for maintaining employment. In this situation, the required weekly check-in meetings should be with an administrator.

You can find another rubric for assessing the degree to which a classroom is learner-centered by visiting www.learningcentered.org or emailing institutelce@gmail.com.

A Four-Item Checklist for a Learner-Centered Lesson

Here is a simple four-item checklist for determining whether you have planned an effective learning experience. It can be utilized as a companion piece to the Likert scale.

Do you

◆ Challenge students to think critically?
◆ Engage students with information you want them to understand and apply?
◆ Offer students choice—i.e., optional ways to address the learning objectives?
◆ Ensure that evidence for learning is demonstrated through student reflection, teacher observation, or another form of written or verbal response (e.g., paraphrasing)?

✓ **Strategies 7–11: Quick-as-a-Wink, Learner-Centered Strategies**

★ Ending a lesson with "Does anyone have a question?" often gets a minimal response. Instead, help students generate their questions by creating groups of three and asking each group to come up with one, two, or three questions. An additional benefit of this activity is that some of the suggested questions often get answered by another student in the group.

★ Give students responsibility for classroom tasks as much as possible. This may include letting students conduct parts of lessons to the degree their capabilities allow. Which responsibilities to offer students is very much based on an individual assessment of each student.

★ Stand at a reasonable distance from a student who is called upon to speak. Most individuals will only speak loud enough for the person in charge to hear.

★ Resist the temptation to ask a student to speak louder if you cannot hear them. Instead, train students to signal (by touching an ear, perhaps) when they cannot hear someone, even if it is the teacher.

If someone speaks inaudibly and no one gives the signal, ask the class why no one signaled.

★ Look for opportunities to praise the entire class, or perhaps a student who usually does not do many things worthy of praise. Or ask the class to pair up to discuss what they think they deserve praise for and share with the class. Follow with a pair-share on how they would like the praise to be demonstrated.

 Strategies 12–21: 45-Minute (or Less) Strategies

We also wish to offer some teaching strategies that require no more than 45 minutes. For a detailed explanation of these strategies, visit www.learner-centered.org or email institutelce@gmail.com.

★ Carousel
★ Challenging students to create a question
★ Concept mapping
★ Exploratory and closure activities
★ Extrinsic or intrinsic motivation strategies
★ Jigsaw
★ Learning theory activities
★ Literature circles
★ PMI activity
★ Rank-order prioritizing

 Strategy 22: Involving Students in Decision-Making

Have you ever invited your three-year-old to help plant seeds in the garden, assist as you put a toy together, or fetch tools as you make a household repair? Children take pride in partnering when they are treated respectfully and given control over a meaningful task, even if the task, for an adult, would be viewed as menial. In a classroom, students (even potentially disruptive students) often enjoy being responsible for menial tasks such as cleanup, as long as they are in charge and respected for their work (Piaget, 1973).

In reality, adults are the same way. We like to be in control. Art Momet was a progressive school superintendent who committed his school district to a shared decision-making process with the teachers' union long before there were many precedents. He was asked by the author, "Art, how come at a time when most administrators are afraid to give up any control, claiming 'I'm the one who will be held accountable,' you appear to not have concerns in that regard?"

The response, from the man after whom one of the district's schools is named, was

"I find that the more control I delegate, the more power I have."

Children love to help and they, like many of us, enjoy having control and being empowered. Ownership translates into pride which often results in attentiveness and good behavior.

 Strategies 23, 24: Examples of Significant Student Involvement

In February 2018, and again in December 2019, the authors led students in two different rural school districts through a two-and-a-half hour curriculum-development process during which the students used critical-thinking skills to design a lesson that addressed state standards, as well as student-selected objectives. This was part of a pilot program initially developed for a school in a large urban area. The authors needed only this one session. The classroom teachers, and their students, took it from there.

The February 2018 session, in rural Saranac Lake, New York, involved fifth-grade students. Middle school teachers Christina Grant and Beth Whalen organized the project in coordination with the authors. The fifth-grade class's teacher was present, along with her 28 students. The first question posed to the students was, "What topics would appeal to you and, do you think, to your peers?" Following a democratic process to determine the topic, the students enthusiastically engaged in a ten-step curriculum-development process (Kirschenbaum, 1976).

A visit six months later revealed that the students' chosen topic, "Life Skills," had been implemented into the curriculum with success, as indicated by student and teacher feedback, and plans were underway for several additional student-designed projects the following year. More importantly, the concept of involving students in decision-making in a variety of structured ways was spreading to teachers whose students were not involved in this initial process.

Two years later, the authors received a follow-up email from Grant:

> Beth and I convinced our team of six teachers to let ninety eighth graders (the whole class) create, write, and direct a school Halloween assembly. The kids created groups of writers/actors, set designers, choreographers and dancers, costume designers and makeup artists, lights, sound and video, and decorators. There were moments of greatness and teamwork, as well as tears and arguments to be navigated.
>
> Our dress rehearsal was pretty terrible, and we overcame a bunch of technical obstacles including moving the whole production to the high school auditorium at the last minute. But, in the end, it was beyond amazing. The kids blew everyone away—including themselves. They could not believe they pulled it off and in such a big way. It was truly one of the most rewarding moments in my teaching career. It will be an annual event now. 100% student-led and 100% awesome in the true sense of the word. Some of the kids had some ups and downs but, in the end, every student participated—and the kids were kind of shocked by that, as were the teachers.

In December 2019, we worked with teachers, administrators, and students in Northeastern Clinton County, a rural New York State school district bordering Canada and Vermont. Seventy-six eighth grade students participated with their four team teachers and special area staff through the same two-and-a-half-hour process designed to involve the students in the design of their own standards-based lesson. We began by posing activity-generating questions as the students, working in groups of four, discussed their answers and then shared with the larger group of 76. As in Saranac Lake, students were asked to individually identify the topic that was of most interest to them and then create a combined list of three topics within their group of four.

The topic choices from this group of 76 students were narrowed to 15, which were then posted in front of the room. Each student was given a sticker and asked to place the sticker next to the topic of the student's choice. However, before voting, students were asked to discuss within their groups whether they wanted to agree on casting all four ballots for the same topic, splitting their ballots, or letting each person vote their own choice. Chrome tablets could have been used, but having each student possess a physical ballot was kinesthetically beneficial for this age group.

The result of involving students in the design of their own lesson was instructive, as evidenced by the choice of topics selected by consensus. Life skills was easily the first choice of most of the students. Additionally, many of the other first choices folded neatly under the broader category of life skills, such as the following:

- Taxes
- Drugs and alcohol
- EMT—"Because it may save someone's life, and it should include role plays and maybe use of dummies"
- Cooking
- Mental health
- Self-defense—"Gym class should do self-defense lessons"
- Budgeting
- Survival
- Opening and managing a bank account
- How to invest

By the end of the session, students and their teachers (one in each core discipline plus music and art) had designed a standards-based unit that consisted of a topic, standards to be addressed, questions for the teacher to pose, activities, and resources that would be required. Of the 76 students who participated, 68 indicated on anonymous feedback sheets that they would want to take part in this process again and were enthusiastic about actually having their teachers use lessons from this unit in class. Here are a few of the comments from students and teachers submitted on their feedback forms:

From students:

- I liked how we were all involved with the activity because it shows WE can communicate
- It was a fun experience and very exciting to participate in
- This was a good exercise on how we can take control of our education and learn what we think matters
- I felt respected; my opinion counted
- It felt like school could actually give us things we will learn in real life
- I liked working together because it taught me how to work good with others
- I liked when we voted because it seemed interesting and competitive
- I enjoyed coming up with ideas of what kind of things we want to learn about, because I like getting to learn about what I want to learn about
- I, hopefully, might be learning about some of the topics I have been wanting to learn about for years

- Because I got my chance to come up with different things, we should learn at school
- It gave us students a chance to have a voice. We could tell our teachers what we would like
- It made me understand how difficult teaching is and how hard they work to make lessons fun
- I liked that I got to miss my morning classes

Teachers observing the process were asked, "What are your feelings and reactions to what you observed today?"

- I think this is wonderful. Some of these ideas we have had, but to see it drawn all together and how it works and can be successful is amazing. This is how learning should be in our schools and future.
- I liked how the morning was structured and it was great to see so much student engagement. I look forward to talking with my classes tomorrow and seeing what ideas they have as to techniques we can use in social studies.
- I was happy to see that our students were well behaved and actively engaged. I think that asking for their input made them feel valued. Some students still need to work on group interactions, but they identified that need themselves by citing social skills as an important topic of study.
- I feel that our students' choice of EMT/Life Skills as the most important topic reflects a value of human life since they "want to help others." I heard that phrase often yesterday morning and I find it encouraging. I shared that observation with my students and I went on to say that if they want to help others, then they must not want to hurt others, so, therefore they could focus on being kind to others.

  I also get the sense that students don't feel empowered to do things for themselves and many probably feel as though they have no control of their lives whatsoever. Living that way must be a real motivation crusher and would explain the apathy that some students exhibit
- I plan to use some of the strategies I observed at least for our final project, and next year to establish class values and class rules. I am also contemplating changing my entire eighth period class to student-designed curriculum. This is the class that scored the lowest on the first unit test, can't sit still and cannot focus. Additionally, it is my goal to include more personal connections in my lessons.

For a detailed listing of the 14 steps in the two-and-a-half-hour process utilized by the authors for this student-driven unit design, visit www.learner-centered.org or email institutelce@gmail.com.

 Strategies 25–27: Ask the Students

A physical education teacher said she had wrestled with a problem involving students for 12 years, had tried "everything," and could not come up with a satisfactory solution. In desperation, she described the problem to a few of her ninth-grade students. Ten minutes later, the students had proposed a solution that worked. "I could kick myself," she said, "Why did it take me 12 years before I thought to ask the students?"

A math teacher struggled to teach a difficult concept to her students. Finally, she called aside three of the students she thought had the potential, with some tutoring, to grasp the concept. She offered extra credit (or maybe just the pride of being able to fill the role of teacher) and asked them to design a lesson for the class and then teach it to their peers.

Another teacher explained, "When I give multiple choice questions on a test, it's incredibly valuable to ask students to explain their thinking behind incorrect answers. I struggled for years not knowing why my students routinely struggled with a particular type of problem. You guessed it. When I finally asked, the students had a simple answer for me."

Asking students to help you address a problem or to teach part of a lesson does not obligate you to accept the feedback in its entirety any more than a government official is obligated to accept your feedback on a survey form. Teacher judgment is required to assess student responses. Students are so starved for a sense of involvement in decisions affecting their education that they generally appreciate any effort to solicit their opinion, even if it is not accepted in its totality every time it is requested. And, even if the student input is not what the teacher feels she can accept, good teachers know how to reinforce student feedback with sincere appreciation for their effort.

The more students are involved in making decisions that impact them, the more they take ownership of their decisions, the more motivated they are to participate in their own learning, and the better prepared they become to enter into the real world. Sometimes the solution to a difficult challenge is simply to "ask the students!"

What to Learn and How to Learn It

In traditional classrooms, the teacher decides what students must learn and how they must learn it. However, as Ms. Amberg proposed earlier in this book, why shouldn't students be involved in determining how they will learn, as long as certain non-negotiable standards are addressed? Many educators have repeatedly experienced the increased intrinsic motivation of students when they are involved in the design of a lesson. For example:

 Strategy 28: Teacher Sets the "What"; Students Help Decide "How"

A teacher walked into her classroom and wrote "Communications and the five senses" on the whiteboard. She then said to her students,

> I am announcing that we have to study the five senses and their connection to communications. Ordinarily, I would also decide how we have to learn about this topic. However, as long as you learn about communications and the five senses, I am open to how you choose to do so.

She then outlined specific objectives of the lesson, and criteria for students to address, but allowed the students to submit proposals for how they would learn about the topic. One student chose to spend three hours on a Saturday morning at a local mall wearing earplugs while wandering from store to store and interacting with customers and store employees. He then wrote a three-page reflection on his experiences.

By giving students a choice of how to address the standard (in this case, "communications"), the teacher was increasing the probability that students would select a method of exploring the topic that was meaningful to them and, hence, more intrinsically motivating. While "communications" was selected as the example in this situation, the same principle would apply with any standard the teacher might want students to address. Focus on what the student needs to learn and allow the student latitude in how to learn it. The student will often select an option for learning that is more authentic to him than what the teacher might assign. Or the teacher could offer students more than one option from which to choose and make the options specific to a list that the teacher initially feels more comfortable with.

When a student goes beyond the requirements (what Professor Vermette has labeled "hidden homework"), the student has become intrinsically motivated as a result of a well-designed activity that the student has collaborated on with her teacher.

 Strategy 29: Hidden Homework

Another example of a learner-centered lesson (one that motivates students to do "hidden homework") is from a third-grade teacher who filled a plastic bag with water and had the class record the time it took from when they placed it in a freezer until it was frozen and then subsequently thawed. She named the bag of water "Glop" and suggested students might want to try timing the Glop at home and might even want to see if changing the size of the bag would alter the time required for freezing and thawing. She suggested but did not assign the experiment. One of her third-grade students reported that he had spent the better part of the weekend freezing and thawing different-sized "Glops" and timing them. Using what he had learned about charts earlier in the year, the student actually charted the results—"hidden homework!"

Not every student will go beyond the teacher's requirements on any particular assignment. But that is OK. If students find an activity to be fun, interesting, or challenging, they are more likely to exceed the teacher's expectations regardless of whether their work is accomplished in class or as homework. And the times when a student, excited by the nature of an activity, invests more time and effort than is required by the teacher, are the times the student will take the most pride and receive the largest boost to their self-esteem. In the design of a lesson, teachers should ask themselves, "What can I ask of the students that will motivate them to walk the extra mile to do well on the task I assign?"

While extrinsic motivation (the grade, "because I said so," or a threat to call parents) may sometimes be required to get many students to complete an assignment, a task students find challenging and which offers options is more likely to allow for intrinsic motivation to take over at some point. Teachers will know when intrinsic motivation has taken over when a student is doing one thing more than he knows he must do to achieve the grade he wants and/or to satisfy the teacher. Intrinsic motivation has taken over when the student goes beyond satisfying the teacher to satisfying him or herself.

 Strategy 30: Motivating by Assessment of Effort

A strategy the authors have often used is to emphasize to students that their grade on a particular task will be based solely on effort, as long as they try their best. Because students have spent a career in schools learning that the right answer gets the highest grade, it is not always easy to convince students that the effort, not the end result, is what is important. However, it is worth a try when you believe that if you can engage your students, the learning will follow—and if you do not intend the lesson to be for purposes of high-stakes assessment. It would also be a meaningful activity to decide with students what evidence would demonstrate "effort."

 Strategy 31: Personalized Learning to Individualize Instruction

"Personalized learning" is a recent popular trend in many parts of the country that can be defined as an approach in which students have a choice over their learning based on interests and needs, flexible pacing, and/or access to differentiated content based on learning needs. The concept—though valid—is, unfortunately, being co-opted by "for-profit" companies that are trying to corner the market. All too often, these for-profit corporations are prescribing and regimenting a formula for teachers to personalize learning. Of course, this is oxymoronic since standardizing personalization implies that there is only one way to personalize learning. The key to the personalizing process is offering options to students and respecting the teacher's expertise in negotiating the individualized expectations and goals of an assignment with each student.

Teacher Kendra Bush in Denver, Colorado, has designed her own form of personalized learning. She trained with a company that appears to have struck an appropriate balance between providing guidelines without limiting the teacher's ability to personalize the company's process, which allows her to address all her expectations for meeting student needs. Ms. Bush's students' test results have been exemplary for two years, and the district has now asked her to come out of the classroom and do staff development for other teachers.

The key to Ms. Bush's success is having students choose the topics for their work. Ms. Bush uses rubrics that outline expectations for student work. She meets personally with as many as 25 students, once a week, to help each student set goals for the next few weeks and to assist them in assessing how well they have achieved those agreed-upon goals. This is a worthwhile process for helping students develop responsibility for their own learning. Here's an example: In a course on writing, the rubric may indicate that a student must have three kinds of supportive data to support each conclusion. During the meeting with that student, Ms. Bush might ask the student to review that part of the rubric and then ask the student to indicate where the data is in their writing. If the student can only point to two instances of supportive data, the next question would be, "What does this suggest for one of your goals for next week?" This may be an oversimplification. However, the point is that the rubric guides the student's self-assessment, and the conference allows the teacher to scaffold by helping the student understand what has and has not been accomplished thus far.

Where does Ms. Bush find the time to supervise the entire class and meet individually with every student weekly? According to Ms. Bush, "The students are working, independently and in small groups, on topics they choose, so most are able to work for long periods of time with little or no assistance from me or by just calling me over with a question or two before they resume their work. Therefore, I have more time to help individual students than I ever had when I taught using a more traditional model." Ms. Bush adds, "Of course, I also walk around to look over shoulders and make sure the students are on task even when they don't call for my assistance."

 Strategy 32: Assigning Classroom Roles to Students

One of the authors was observing teacher Tim Bedley, who had put a student in charge of conducting the class in Bedley's California room. The student was assigning roles from an activity Bedley had culled from the internet. Students would learn geography and history by enacting a play about historical figures in various parts of the country. The student in charge would call out a role; for example, "Who wants to be George Washington?" As someone volunteered, the student class leader would write that person's name on the other side of a tongue depressor labeled with Washington's name.

For 40 minutes, the student conducted the class while Mr. Bedley sat in the back of the room, rarely having to intercede. The student filled this role of class leader for the week. If you think, "This wouldn't be possible in my class because of a few students I could name," you may be right. On the other hand, you may be underestimating your students.

It is well established that having roles for students builds self-confidence and contributes to classroom decorum. It is also especially worthwhile for children who grow up while living in poverty. As previously mentioned, students even enjoy roles that put them in charge of cleanup, attendance taking, and other positions that might draw an "ugh" from children if they were ordered to fulfill them.

Many teachers have five or six roles that they rotate students through during the school year, and this can be very successful. Mr. Bedley does it differently. He assigns every student a role in the class, and he has as many roles as there are students. However, he may only rotate every student through a handful of these roles. He views filling roles like you would view a theatrical production. Not everyone is suited to be on stage, or build the sets, or oversee the props; consequently, he handpicks a few students to be class leaders as one of their roles. Where needed, he will give special tutoring to the class leaders, or, of course, any other students in roles that may require a little extra knowledge or ability. This is not to suggest that this is better than limiting a class to five or six roles and circulating every student through them throughout the school year. Either way can be successful. This is just an alternative way to consider.

The following is a list of 32 class roles Mr. Bedley assigned during a year in which he had 32 students in his class:

1. Bathroom Drinks Monitor
2. Class Organizer
3. Computer Timer
4. Consensus Faces
5. DJ
6. Envelope Collector
7. Excel Papers
8. Flier A
9. Flier B
10. Greeter
11. Human Resources
12. iPad Manager
13. IT
14. Levels
15. Librarian
16. Line Boss
17. Lost Recess Monitor
18. Patriot
19. Payroll
20. PPE Equipment
21. Phone
22. Planner Collector
23. Pocket Chart Monitor
24. Redo Police
25. Song Reader

26. Stamp Master
27. Store Clerk
28. Substitute
29. Tardy Police
30. Ticket Sampler
31. Tutoring Manager
32. Volume Police

For amplification on each of these roles, go to www.learnercentered.org or email institutelce@gmail.com. For additional information, see Flynn, Mesibov, Vermette, and Smith, *Captivating Classes with Constructivism*, Chapter 9 (2004b).

Having witnessed an entire class where Mr. Bedley was able to sit in the back of the room and rarely say anything, we posed the following question, "How do you decide what you will do in class and what you will *assign to students*?" Bedley said, "The only things I do are those which aren't reasonable to expect of students!"

It seems appropriate to conclude this section with a quote from Anthony Cody, a middle school science teacher, coach, and mentor for many years in Oakland, California ("Moving Beyond the Classroom: The Growing Role of Teacher Leaders," 2018):

> When I can go into a school and see teachers and administrators having deep discussions about what they teach, why and how they teach it, and how and why they assess it, that will be the true sign of significant, meaningful reform, because as a result of those discussions, meaningful, transformative educational reform will result—where we'll see kids and teachers enthusiastically engaged in learning and teaching.

COMMONSENSE CONCLUSION

One does not learn to be independent and responsible by having everything done for them.

9

Motivation Is Derived from What Students find Interesting, Relevant, or Just Plain Fun

Mr. Wabash spent half an hour attempting to explain a difficult science concept to his 11th-grade student, Bobby Orr Richard. He tried drawing charts, referring to pictures in the textbook, even involving another student in the discussion who understood what Mr. Wabash was trying to convey to his pupil.

Almost ready to give up, Mr. Wabash recalled that Bobby was an ardent hockey fan and, in fact, excelled on his high school team. In a last-ditch attempt to help Bobby grasp the elusive concept, Mr. Wabash drew a picture of a hockey rink on a sheet of paper and strategically placed six players around the rink. Then he said, "Bobby, suppose you were a defenseman, guiding the puck up ice, and…" He drew a detailed analogy between a hockey rush up the ice and the concept he was trying to teach Bobby.

When Mr. Wabash concluded his analogy, Bobby looked up at him and said, "I get it. Why didn't you say that before?"

There are many ways to motivate students, but teachers tell us they have had great success with these three:

1. Making the subject matter relevant
2. Offering fun, interesting, or challenging lessons and activities
3. Designing activities that are likely to yield student success experiences

DOI: 10.4324/9781003284697-11

Making the Subject Matter Relevant

"You've got the dream, but not the drive." This line from the song "Beauty School Dropout" in the musical *Grease* perfectly highlights the issue: Teachers need to tap into students' inner drive in order to engage them. If the student has a personal goal or interest that she perceives will be advanced by studying a mandated topic, intrinsic motivation may take hold. Relevance is critical to personal meaning and learning. If the lesson does not connect with a student's personal interests, it had better be just plain fun, or at least interesting enough to command the student's attention.

 Strategy 33: Bring in Guests Who Can Authenticate Content Relevance

The following example demonstrates how a fourth-grade teacher created relevance and motivation for a student who showed no interest in math. When the teacher asked why she was uninterested, the student replied, "I want to be a travel agent, and what use do travel agents have for math?" To create personal relevance for that student, the teacher invited a local travel agent to class and then began the Q and A by asking, "What, if any, uses do you have for a knowledge of math in your work?"

Dan: When I plan a learner-centered activity, my foremost thought is, "How can I make the content relevant to the needs and interests of each student?"

Offering Fun, Interesting, or Challenging Lessons or Activities

Unfortunately, it is not always the case that a teacher has the time and ability to help a student make the connection between what is being taught and what the student may need later in life. An easier strategy is to make an activity just plain fun—or at least interesting.

 Strategy 34: Play-Doh Activity

A Play-Doh activity can work at any grade level, right up through university students or teachers at a workshop.

Step 1

Place students in pairs or small groups and give each group assorted colors of Play-Doh in small containers (Play-Doh is inexpensive at retail stores).

Step 2

Ask students to use the Play-Doh to mold a physical object or idea related to the lesson content. For example, "Replicate with Play-Doh what you think you would see if you viewed, from afar, a battle between the British and the Americans in 1777." Or, "Create a representation of the digestive system with food flowing through it." Or, "Reproduce what you think is the most important math formula for students to know." Or, "Create a symbol representing the moral from the novel *The Red Badge of Courage*."

Step 3

Once students have had sufficient time to create their Play-Doh replications, have them visit one display at a time and guess what they are seeing. After the guesses are complete, the presenting group explains what they have created.

Some secondary teachers often dismiss the Play-Doh activity as better for younger students, but they soon find that their students are equally well motivated when given the chance to apply their creative juices. University students love this activity, as do teachers when it is used at a professional development session. For example, we have asked groups of three to six teachers to replicate what they think a learner-centered classroom might look like. The challenge put to teachers is, "If you walked into a room and your gut reaction was, 'This is a learner-centered classroom,' replicate with Play-Doh what you would be seeing." Teachers, like students of any age, dive into this activity with enthusiasm. They enjoy the chance to engage socially and academically with their peers while thinking about and discussing the session content.

Image by Afzal Khan. With permission

One teacher described, with surprise, how her students reacted the first time she conducted a Play-Doh activity:

> The higher-performing students were slow to get started. I think they were so used to getting their high grades that they were reluctant to engage until they could assure themselves that they would do well on this new type of activity. The average students jumped right in and loved working with the Play-Doh. The slower learners asked a lot of questions about my expectations before they were ready to begin the task. Probably they are so used to investing themselves in schoolwork only to discover they were not following the instructions and their time had been wasted, that they needed to be sure they understood what they were expected to do. However, for the first time all year, every student, once they got started, became fully engaged and I saw ample evidence of student learning.

Math teacher Nicole Freeman teaches in a large urban area and has her own way of utilizing Play-Doh to motivate student learning: "I use Play-Doh in my high school geometry class to help students identify sizes and shapes. Students in small groups make models (cone cylinder, prisms, etc.) and then compare and contrast. I add cross-sections in with a piece of floss. It's always a hit."

✓ Strategy 35: Gallery Learning

A way of making math fun and challenging is what progressive California educators Tim Bedley and Brian O'Connor call "Gallery Learning." Students are individually spaced around the room at consecutively numbered whiteboards or large sheets of newsprint. The teacher, in the center of the room, can view all of the students' work and can instantly create groupings by calling for "one and four" to work together, or "one and two," or "five through eight." Problems are given to be solved. Peer assessment is easy, and students are encouraged to admit if they are unable to solve a problem or think they may not have the right answer. In fact, the teacher leads applause when students acknowledge mistakes or ask for help.

This kind of approach helps students think about wrong answers as just another step in the continuous improvement process, rather than as a sign of failure. Similarly, Jenny Morrill emphasizes to her fifth-grade students that it is praiseworthy to share mistakes and ask for assistance and that there is no such thing as failure. This is an important concept. Thomas Edison, when asked if he was discouraged by the long string of failures he experienced while attempting to invent the light bulb, reportedly said. "Each unsuccessful attempt brought us one step closer to success."

Let's give Daniel a round of applause for sharing his work and asking for our assistance.

Image by Afzal Khan. With permission

Designing Activities That Are Likely to Yield Student Success Experiences

Two oft-repeated axioms are "success breeds success" and "growth leads to more growth." Why is it essential for schools to provide growth and success experiences for students if they want meaningful learning to occur? The nature of learning is that students are confronted with information they must reconcile with their prior knowledge. As they struggle to make sense of what teachers are challenging them to understand, learning occurs. However, learning only occurs if students accept the challenge to reconcile new information with their prior knowledge. An alternative to accepting this challenge is to give up.

Students who experience little success inside or outside school are likely to choose the alternative of giving up rather than rising to the challenge of learning anything new. This is particularly true of students who were raised in poverty, have been the victims of structural racism, or have a learning style that does not align with the usual classroom. These students need the encouragement that comes with successful experiences if they are to try to do the work teachers expect of them. Subsequent chapters include examples of teachers designing activities guaranteed to afford students success experiences.

Strategies 36, 37: Culminating Events to Motivate Student Engagement

Culminating events can be an excellent way to motivate student engagement. As part of an initiative organized by the authors many years ago, students from four districts across the state convened at a museum in the capital city to display work they had accomplished in their classrooms. Upon arrival, one teacher exclaimed, "I've taught for 25 years and been very traditional. But having experienced the enthusiasm and excitement of my students on the four-hour bus ride, to motivate students to actively engage, I realize I have to build more authenticity into my lessons."

Another example is placing exhibits of student work throughout a local mall for an entire weekend. An agreement can be worked out on a district or county-wide basis. Mall managers are often willing to participate because it brings in customers and positive publicity. In addition to parental involvement, it brings schools publicity that has nothing to do with budgets or other financial matters. Teachers buy-in when it is explained that the exhibits can be student work produced during the year and not necessarily designed for the exhibit.

COMMONSENSE CONCLUSION

Students, like any of us, are motivated to engage in a lesson when they perceive it to be one of the following: relevant to their lives, interesting, challenging, something at which they can succeed, or just plain fun.

10

Teachers Are Classroom Coaches

Rachel Kruze headed to class after early-morning softball practice. She was pleased with herself because her hitting had improved substantially after Coach Gutman had observed her holding the bat too high and given her an extra 15 swings in the batting cage.

As she entered Room 224, Rachel was immediately handed a 12-item, short-answer quiz to assess how well she had learned to speak in public. She was frustrated. "I can express myself very well," she thought to herself. "But I have trouble remembering the seven rules for giving a good speech. Wouldn't I learn more if I just gave a speech and had Mr. Gutman let me know what I did well and what I didn't do quite as well?"

Reference is often made to "teacher as coach." It is becoming more common to hear that teachers should go from being "sages on the stage" to" guides on the side," similar to sports team coaches. Let us expand this to *also* include theatrical directors as coaches.

When coaches first meet their players, do they start them off with a long lecture, or do they send them onto the field to see what they can do? Effective coaches often break their teams into small groups for initial drills and then teach through interventions. A typical coach's comment might be, "Do you think if you'd crouched lower, he could have gotten by you?" Or, "Were you ready for that pitch?" A play director might ask, "Would you try to empathize more with this character you're playing by remembering a time you were very sad?"

DOI: 10.4324/9781003284697-12

When a play director first meets the cast, it does not take long before the director hands out scripts and begins a read-through. Throughout play rehearsals, isn't the teaching done through interventions? Director comments like the following are common: "If you faced the audience more directly when you delivered that line, do you think you might have been heard more clearly in the balcony?"

In performance-based courses such as art, music, physical education, and technology, it is natural to have students perform and to teach through interventions. The challenge for teachers of core discipline subjects is to design activities (performance tasks) that call for students to learn through demonstrations. This allows the teacher to see what the student knows and thinks so she can then successfully teach through interventions.

A traditional opening lesson in a core discipline class usually goes something like this:

- ◆ Overview of the course
- ◆ Announcement of discipline policy
- ◆ A few questions requiring individual students to offer brief responses
- ◆ The start of a yearlong process of lecture-driven teaching. Occasionally, this involves opportunities for students to work on activities related to the lesson; however, this is often through worksheets or tasks that are focused on memorization of steps as outlined by the teacher, rather than creative thinking by the students

In this traditional process, we tell students what we want them to know, test them to see if they have learned it (mostly through short-answer essay questions that check more for memorization than higher-level thinking), then we tell them more of what we want them to know, test them again, and so on.

The teacher-as-coach approach requires teachers to create experiences for their students so that they can use these experiences as learning activities. For instance, if the teacher wants to teach about philosophers and ancient Greece through engaging students in a mock trial of Socrates, it requires that teachers prepare the activity and commit sufficient class time to its enactment. Many teachers are reluctant to learn how to design such an activity or to "give up" the necessary class time.

Happily, the good news is that anytime we can encourage teachers to try learner-centered activities, the teachers usually love the results. The questions teachers have when learning to embrace this approach are usually ones like, "How do I increase my use of learner-centered activities and still teach the curriculum?" Or, "How will this affect their test scores?" And, "Isn't it too time-consuming to use learner-centered activities?"

The answer to this last question needs to be looked at in two ways. If a learner-centered approach is new to you, then yes, learning and integrating it is time-consuming! When you first learned to change a car tire, or bake a pie, or do anything that was unfamiliar, didn't it take a lot longer the first few times? There is a learning curve. But teachers who have stayed with learner-centered strategies long enough to gain experience eventually find that they can cover more curriculum in a learner-centered classroom than a traditional one. Since it will take a while for anyone who was trained to teach traditionally, and has taught that way, to gain the experience necessary to feel in control of a learner-centered classroom, the key is to not try to convert your classroom overnight. Teachers who are proficient with learner-centered strategies got there slowly. They tried learner-centered activities that were not too ambitious or time-consuming, so if they did not work well the first time, it did not destroy an entire lesson. The most proficient learner-centered teachers gained their expertise gradually.

Keep in mind that a teacher cannot become a coach unless there is an activity in which students are engaged and through which they can be coached.

It is not that coaches do not give lectures. They do—for example, with teachable moments that are often called "chalk-talks." However, the lecture is connected to what the coach has seen in practice or during a game. Teachers can lecture in a learner-centered classroom, but the lecture should be short and related to something the teacher has observed during a learning activity, and it should be followed by a pair-share student discussion or some other process for checking student understanding.

This also does not mean we are eliminating any need for or focus on memorization—of course, it can be important to memorize certain things. But a teacher acting as a coach would actively engage students with the information she wants them to know, understand, and apply. In the November 1998 issue of *Education Leadership*, devoted entirely to articles on constructivism, Harvard professor David Perkins cites research showing that we memorize better when we are actively engaged with what we need to memorize.

For 25 years, our Institute for Learning Centered Education conducted a one-week summer conference that attracted approximately 300 people a year. Each spring, in mid-May, we would hire a university student to coordinate the registration process, including speaking by phone with registered participants and organizing lists of registrants for different activities. By the start of the late July conference, the student assistant had memorized many of the 300 names of the attendees without making a conscious effort. If we had handed the student a list of 300 names and asked her to memorize it, what could be a more boring task? We venture the reader can think of times you were engaged in an activity and memorized many names, terms, or items without consciously trying.

We learn best when we are actively engaged with information; in fact, if we are teaching someone else, we are likely to have memorized the gist of what we are teaching almost by accident, simply through our preparations to teach. Doesn't this argue for designing activities in which students teach each other that which the teacher wants them to learn?

Engagement Must Precede Explanation

Too often in education, the explanation of what we want students to learn or how we want them to learn it comes prior to engaging students with the information. The sequence in a typical course is to teach through explanation (i.e., lecture) and then have students complete worksheets or assignments, followed by a test. If there is one thing we encourage teachers to accept as a near absolute, it is this: Once you have engaged students with a launcher, bell-ringer, anticipatory set, icebreaker, or whatever you do for a few minutes to start a lesson, NEVER launch into a lecture except to briefly outline directions for student engagement!

In performance-based activities, engagement precedes explanation. The coach or theater director almost immediately puts the players on the field, or the actors onto the stage, and teaches through interventions. We suggest this should be true for every type of course.

 Strategy 38: Contrasting Traditional and Learner-Centered Teaching Practices

Suppose you wanted students to learn six different types of leaves and their characteristics. The traditional way of teaching would be to provide students with a handout that lists the six types of leaves with a few characteristics of each, then inform the students they will have a test next Tuesday in which they will be expected to be able to demonstrate knowledge of the six kinds of leaves and the characteristics of each. The test would consist of many short-answer questions and one essay question.

By contrast, in a learner-centered classroom, two teachers partnered their tenth- and third-grade students, distributed laminated samples of leaves from six different trees, and asked each pair of students to categorize the six types of leaves by common characteristics. Some student groups chose size, others shape, others color or texture.

After asking each group to view the categorizations of the other pairs, and sharing the reasoning behind them, the teacher listed the names of the six different trees and some of the characteristics of each and asked the students if they could match the leaves at their desks to the tree names she listed. This activity made students think about the sizes, shapes, and colors of different leaves and correlate this to the names and characteristics of each tree. It also demonstrated the value of partnering students from two significantly different age groupings in situations where they could work as equal participants. It increased student motivation because younger students admire older students, and older students enjoy being mentors to younger children.

 Strategy 39: Another Example Contrasting Traditional with Learner-Centered Practices

You can explain to young students how to multiply by tens and then have them practice with a worksheet. Or you can put students into small groups with a cup in front of them containing ten pieces of elbow macaroni. Have them combine their macaroni with that of another group and ask, "Can you figure out what ten, two times, adds up to? What does two times mean?" Then have them combine the 20 macaroni in their cups with a third group of ten, and so on.

After the students have played with different combinations of tens, you can give the same lecture most teachers might have begun the lesson with, but now you can refer to the "engagement" students have just had with the information. And won't the fun of playing with macaroni increase students' motivation to listen to what you have to say? The students now have a frame of reference for understanding—and taking interest in—the information you will impart in your lecture.

COMMONSENSE CONCLUSION

At all levels of a sport or performance art, coaches are really teachers. These people, whose jobs are at stake, find that the best way to teach is through intervening during practices and performances. The same strategies can be effective in all classrooms.

11

Critical Thinking Is the Main Focus for Student Learning

Esteemed author and professor Jacqueline Grennon-Brooks (The Case for Constructivist Classrooms, 1993, Schools Reimagined, 2021) *put this author through a conference activity that made an indelible impression. "She put us all at tables of eight with a bowl of water and a bowl of Gobstopper multicolored candies on each table. She asked us to play with the Gobstoppers in the water, then she had us walk around to view the different patterns formed by the candies on each table.*

"When we had all returned to our seats, she approached one table, looked a participant directly in the eye, and asked, 'Do you think if you had started with the yellow candy instead of the orange, it would have affected the pattern you ended up with?' Without awaiting a response, Ms. Grennon-Brooks turned and started to walk away. Then she stopped, turned back, and asked this same participant, 'Did my question cause you to THINK?'

"Immediately, the participant raised both hands to the sides of the head and said, 'Oh my goodness, yes.' Ms. Grennon-Brooks smiled and replied, 'Then I've done my job.'"

A teacher, hearing this story, added, "Whenever a child learns critical thinking, somewhere a conspiracy theory dies."

Professor Vermette, whom we spoke about previously, once told us, "After 25 years of teaching, I have come to the conclusion that my only role is to challenge my students to *THINK*."

Implicit, of course, is that Dr. Vermette intends his students to *think* about what he is endeavoring to have them understand and be able to apply it to the real world.

DOI: 10.4324/9781003284697-13

The wisdom in these words should be a guide for every teacher. "Am I challenging, even forcing, my students to think about what I want them to learn? I cannot control the conclusions they will reach, but if I get them to think critically and creatively, I have accomplished a significant share of my goals. If I actively engage students in meaningful activities, I can see and hear what they are thinking, which allows me to assess their learning and try to guide their thinking development."

Image by Afzal Khan. With permission

Recently retired psychology professor Ed Boyd pointed out, "One can be a thinker without being a critical thinker … critical thinking requires an ever-increasing abandonment of egocentrism and the acquisition of the ability to see something from others' perches."

So, what does it mean to be a critical thinker? According to the *Merriam-Webster* dictionary, critical thinking is "disciplined thinking that is clear, rational, open-minded, and informed by evidence." Wabisabi Learning suggests six reasons why critical thinking is an important skill to develop in students ("Six Benefits of Critical Thinking and Why They Matter," n.d.).

Why Is Critical Thinking an Important Skill?

1. **It encourages curiosity.**
   To this end, critical thinkers ask:

   ◆ What is happening? What am I seeing?
   ◆ Why is it important? Who is affected by this?
   ◆ What am I missing? What is hidden, and why is it important?

- ◆ Where did this come from? How do I know for sure?
- ◆ Who is saying this? Why should I listen to this person? What can they teach me?
- ◆ What else should I consider?
- ◆ What if …?
- ◆ Why not?

Effective critical thinkers do not take anything at face value. They never stop asking questions and enjoy exploring all sides of an issue and the deeper facts hiding within all modes of data.

2. **It enhances creativity**.
   Among many other things, critical thinking promotes the development of abilities such as reasoning skills, analytical thinking, evaluative skills, logical thinking, organizational and planning skills, language skills, self-reflective capacity, observational skills, open-mindedness, creative visualization, questioning ability, and decision-making.
3. **It promotes problem-solving ability.**
4. **It is a multifaceted practice.**
5. **It fosters independence.**
6. **It is a skill for life, not just learning.**

James Pelech, Ed.D., professor and chair of the Education Department at Benedictine University in Lisle, Illinois, and author of three books on constructivism and critical thinking, emphasizes that critical thinkers never cease questioning their assumptions. Pelech also cites the creation of disequilibrium as an effective strategy for prompting students to think more deeply about a topic. For instance, if a student alleges that slavery was the only issue that caused the Civil War, a teacher might ask, "How would you respond to someone who claims that states' rights was also a significant issue?"

Pelech also suggests activities that require students to compare and contrast, hypothesize and predict, or demonstrate personal relevance to their lives outside of school.

Many great educators have cited the importance of teaching children lifelong learning skills. John Dewey, however, probably said it best: "Education is not preparation for life; education is life itself." Educators want their learners to succeed both in and out of the classroom. The idea is to make sure that once they leave school, they no longer need us. In essence, our learners must become teachers and leaders. The point is that they *never stop being learners*. This is what it means to be a lifelong learner and a critical thinker.

It is ironic that for decades, almost every survey of the corporate sector has demonstrated that what potential employers want most in prospective employees is someone who can think critically and work collaboratively.

There is a connection between the two. When we work with others, any one person can provide the challenge to our thinking that causes us to reexamine our perceptions. How does a child learn to effectively collaborate and think critically when the only model she experiences is the teacher working alone and teaching students who are expected to work in isolation?

Schools Must Teach Children How to Discuss an Issue

Critical thinking requires an ability to stick to the issue when engaging in discussion or debate. Among the many things we should have learned from the accusations and counteraccusations during the 2020 election campaign is the importance of teaching children how to identify, and utilize, relevant arguments during a discussion. The authors believe this is so important that we offer a suggested approach later in this chapter.

 Strategy 40: Posing Questions to Challenge Students to Think Critically

In a learner-centered classroom, students are taught to think critically. They are challenged with questions that require critical thought. If the teacher preaches, students are being taught to accept what they are told. However, when the teacher poses a challenging question, it forces students to think about whether they agree and why or why not. That is the simple secret to teaching critical thinking: ask, do not tell.

Image by Afzal Khan. With permission

Strategy 41: Another Example of Using Questions to Spark Critical Thinking

On the one hand, a teacher can tell students, "George Washington never told a lie." The students listen, take note of this fact, and memorize it for the test.

Or the teacher can ask, "Do you think it can be true that George Washington never told a lie?" "How do we define 'lie'?" If he did tell lies at times, would this make him an ineffective president?" "How do we find the facts?"

We mentioned before that there is a shift toward learner-centered classrooms, but that we are not there yet. Classrooms are demonstrating positive changes; however, these changes are often limited by (1) the standardization movement, which requires students and teachers to use a factory-model/assembly-line approach aimed at producing higher standardized test score results and (2) the amount of training and experience a teacher must have with learner-centered strategies to feel comfortable using them more than occasionally.

We recognize that local teachers and administrators have no control over standardized tests. In light of this, the reader will find countless examples, in later chapters, of how teachers can utilize learner-centered practices to address required standards and to teach what is worthwhile beyond what the tests expect students to do.

 Strategies 42–47: Examples of School-Wide, Learner-Centered Strategies

Rochester, New York's School Without Walls (SWW) is an example of a high school that has successfully created, implemented, and advanced a learner-centered culture. SWW opened its doors in 1971 as one of many nationwide humanistic alternatives to what were considered highly structured, traditional high schools. The idea was that instead of being a place that inhibited authentic learning, SWW would instead be one that modeled the works of Dewey, Rogers, Postman and Weingartner, Kozol, and other educators and researchers. One reason for its remarkable survival is that SWW's founding teachers were committed to participatory decision-making. Among its other key learner-centered elements are the following:

★ Advisory groups that revolve around a key student-selected curricular issue, such as Criminal Justice or Love and Relationships.

★ School-wide "decision-making," through which advisory groups meet (sometimes in "town meetings") to explore, problem-solve, and make decisions on classroom, school, community, and national issues.

★ "Community service" during which all students engage in service to nonprofit organizations in the community for two hours per week—during school time—while the staff meets to discuss students and school issues and to participate in professional development.

★ "Evaluation as a learning experience" in which students and teachers participate in quarterly, individual evaluation conferences, as compared to the standard grades game of "Wad-Ja-Get?"

★ "Senior Projects," in which all seniors are required to complete yearlong, in-depth projects on a topic of their choice and are assessed by a committee of six that includes two teachers, two students, and two community members.

★ Performance-based assessments in place of the New York State (NYS) Regents Exams. This variance for approximately 30 NYS schools (NYS Performance Standards Consortium), which use common performance-based assessment rubrics and guidelines, was approved by New York State's Board of Regents in 2005. Individual schools interested in pursuing membership to the consortium should initiate a conversation with consortium coordinator Ann Cook at cook.ann@gmail.com.

So, if classrooms are changing for the better by becoming increasingly learner-centered, what is the need for this book? Think about how much more rapidly this change could become a reality that benefits ALL students—including the current generation—if schools made the design of learner-centered classrooms the highest priority instead of trying to bring about changes that are superficial or have little chance of being implemented. The change to learner-centered schools is not expensive, and failure to expedite the process will continue to be costly in terms of what students could have learned.

✓ Strategy 48: An Example in Seventh-Grade Math

We teach students to think critically by challenging them to analyze—to figure out how to accomplish a task or solve a problem. It is through problem-solving that we learn to think critically. Learner-centered environments require lessons that challenge students to think critically and creatively, not just to listen and regurgitate ("Twelve Solid Strategies for Teaching Critical Thinking Skills," n.d.).

Assigning a specific problem is one of the best avenues for teaching critical thinking skills. Leave the solution, or answer, open-ended for the broadest possible approach.

This is the essence of asking essential questions requiring the discovery and synthesis of knowledge through critical thinking.

Here is a specific example, from seventh-grade math:

Knowledge:
What is $5 - (-4)$?

Understanding:
Create a model
to show why $5 - (-4)$ has to have the same answer as $5 + 4$.
(Assessment on Flipboard by Mark Chubb)

Teacher (now administrator) Brian O'Connor was facilitating a group of teachers when the author noticed he had written on a whiteboard:

$$3\frac{1}{4} - 2\,3/16$$

Mr. O'Connor explained to the teachers at his presentation,

In the past I would have tried to teach my fourth-grade students how to solve this equation before asking them to try it. However, I recently tried a different approach. With no preparation, I asked for a volunteer to come up front and attempt to solve the equation. One young lady came front and center and, after a few minutes, she had scratched out the following:

$$\frac{1}{4} - 2\,3/16\,1111$$

Then she provided the correct answer.

The significance of this was not that she had the right answer. The significance was that, as with Gallery Learning, discussed in Chapter 9, her thought process was on display for the teacher. He could now inquire as to the meaning of 1 1 1 1. If the answer were incorrect, the teacher could discuss her work using the student's frame of reference rather than, as we often do, using his own, which can be difficult for someone else to understand.

The changes advocated by the authors are beginning to occur, but not fast enough. If you had entered a typical classroom 30 years ago, it is likely you would have observed a teacher standing in the front of the room talking while students sat in rows, listening and or taking notes, and expected to remain quiet. Clearly, the average classroom now finds students at least *more* at the center of the lesson than was the case previously. The challenge is for teachers to become proficient at addressing mandated standards and preparing students for standardized tests while simultaneously utilizing learner-centered, social-emotional best practices. It is not easy, but it can be done. Since teaching effectively is never easy, why not do it in a way that maximizes student learning?

Using Project-based Learning to Challenge Students to Think Critically

 Strategy 49: Scaffolding at Different Grade Levels

Here is an example of how to scaffold project-based learning for varying levels of difficulty. At the beginner level, the teacher can start the entire class on a problem posed by a school issue, current event, or curriculum topic. One curricular example for middle school students might be: "What are the conditions that societies need to have in place to prevent atrocities like the Holocaust from happening?" After dividing the class into groups of three or four, and giving each a different set of resources to use, the teacher directs the groups to determine roles and expectations for each member. As students set upon their work, the teacher visits each group, questioning, encouraging, and suggesting resources. Each group may approach the problem differently, with some having more difficulty getting started and sharing information. Supportive teacher interventions are critical. However, teachers must realize that if one of the ultimate goals is for students to become responsible for their own learning, they must have the opportunity to develop that skill and learn from failure.

A more advanced strategy is for the teacher and class to list several problems that various groups faced during the COVID-19 pandemic or as a result of climate change. The teacher instructs students to choose which problem they wish to focus on and form small groups to investigate the resources provided or needed. Each group then creates possible solutions and shares them with the entire class. The teacher may invite a representative from a local medical or environmental organization to hear the presentations as well.

For teachers who have more flexibility with their curriculum, allowing students to choose individual issues to explore can result in even more dramatic learning results. This strategy can also integrate multiple subject disciplines. For example, a student searching for methods to increase teenage self-esteem could be encouraged to use art as a way to both express a solution and develop their artistic skills. Obviously, this method requires a multitude of resources and perhaps a different schedule for students and the teacher. Student-teacher conferences, either individually or in small groups, are important for support and encouragement. Students may also require longer work periods each week or even time for interning with an organization that focuses on their chosen topic.

The aforementioned is a realistic example of project-based learning that is being modeled in Big Picture Learning schools throughout the United States and by NYS Performance Standards Consortium schools. Jacqueline and Martin Brooks also provide many examples and constructivist-based research to support a problem-based curriculum in their 2021 book *Education Reimagined*.

 Strategies 50–53: Examples at Early Grade Levels

Here are a few examples, from veteran teachers, of projects that can be used at the earliest grade levels:

★ "Have students choose an animal to research over the course of several weeks. Help them prepare an informational report to present to the class" (Julie Saunders, kindergarten teacher).

★ "Read students some examples of persuasive letters, and model how to write one. Ask them to think of a topic they could write about while trying to persuade someone. Finally, assign them to write a persuasive letter to someone about their topic" (Angelo Premo, second-grade teacher).

★ "Have students develop a proposal to persuade the local government to improve a community space. Students can suggest ways to upgrade the space and investigate what it would take (local bylaw requirements, budgets, stakeholders, etc.). Completed projects can then be shared with local government leaders and community stakeholders" (Christina Luce, technology and early elementary teacher).

★ "For math this year, I had students choose an animal they would want to have as a pet. First, they researched the associated costs (one-time, monthly, and annual) and created a budget. This gave them great practice with adding and subtracting decimals. Then, they had to design a play area for their pet with at least five different elements (pool, lawn, etc.). Students had to find the area and perimeter of each element and then research the costs to fence it" (Kendra Bush, elementary teacher).

Strategies 54–58: Quotations Can Challenge Students to Think Critically

Do you enjoy reading relevant quotations interspersed with content? Many people do—and this includes children. In fact, people pay $10 to $20 for a book that contains nothing but quotes. Ask students to interpret conflicting quotations and how each statement could apply to their lives. Let them react in pairs or small groups. They will have fun; it will sharpen their critical thinking skills, and you will learn more about how each student thinks. For instance, you could ask them how someone could reconcile "a stitch in time saves nine" with "haste makes waste."

Or, "What did Oliver Wendell Holmes mean when he said, 'The most stringent protection of free speech would not protect a man falsely shouting fire in a theatre and causing a panic'?" A discussion on the meaning of Holmes' quote could be followed up with a discussion of whether there are limitations to the first amendment regarding free speech. "Does free speech mean one can say anything at any time about anything?"

Or what was meant by "Justice should not only be done, but should manifestly and undoubtedly be seen to be done," as spoken by Ireland's Lord Hewart the then Chief Justice of England nearly 100 years ago in the case of *Rex v. Sussex Justices*, [1924] 1 KB 256.

This activity could also be a warm-up activity for a faculty meeting. Try it using one or more of the previous quotations or find your own. Make sure to allow teachers, in small groups, to share their thoughts about how to apply the activity to their classes—and allow for sharing with the entire staff. It can be good professional development and doesn't need to take more than ten or 15 minutes from your meeting.

If you want to give students an even greater challenge, ask them to create their own book, or several pages, of quotes related to something important they are studying or interested in.

The following is another learner-centered activity to motivate students to think critically while still preparing them to address required standards. What we call "ranking" or "prioritizing" is an easy-to-design but infrequently used activity. Like the also under-utilized Play-Doh activity, asking students to rank order, or prioritize, a list can be used effectively to teach standards-based activities. As the authors work with teachers in their classrooms, the ranking and the Play-Doh activities are among the most popular ones teachers utilize—once they know about them.

Strategies 59–64: Rank-Order Activity Examples in Different Disciplines

Social studies: Provide students with a list of inventors or presidents and ask students to rank them in their order of importance to society with written reasons.

English: You can do the same thing with authors, books, parts of speech, or anything that can be ranked in order of priority.

Math: Have students rank formulas, or even mathematicians, by order of importance.

Science: As with the other subjects, have students rank formulas, scientists, chemicals.

Art/music: Rank artists or musicians in order of quality of work, importance to society, and/or acceptance by society.

Physical education: Rank athletes by quality, contributions to society outside of their profession, or health consciousness.

After giving students time to research and complete their rank orders, teachers can increase the degree of development for thinking, communicating, and listening by having students meet in groups of threes to share their lists and reasons. Students can then be asked to re-order their rankings based on any new information they learned in their groups. Finally, they can share with the entire class any changes they made and why.

Here is some feedback from a teacher who tried the ranking exercise for the first time in a second-grade math activity:

> **Why did you choose this particular activity for what you wanted to accomplish?**
>
> I asked the students to think about the ways of charting data that they studied in math (survey, tally chart, picture graph, and bar graph) and rank order them from easiest to hardest to use. I chose this activity since the students have knowledge with collecting and recording data in their classroom, as well as the pre-teach math class. I wanted to see what their reactions were to the various techniques and what I still needed to review and support, based on their responses.

> **What evidence did you observe of student learning?**
>
> Students were actively engaged, really thinking about their choices, and were changing their choices as they discussed with others

or with me. Students were able to explain why they chose their #1 and #4 choices and support it with details about the data collection method. For example, some students said they picked picture graphs as their #1 because they like to draw pictures and show data using those pictures. Others picked tally chart for #4 as the hardest because they don't like to use tallies, counting by fives is hard for them, and they get confused counting. Other students said surveys are their #1 as they think it is easy to go around and ask people a question to collect data. Some selected picture graphs as their #4 because they think drawing pictures is hard for them or the pictures they need to draw are too difficult.

What would you do differently the next time with this same activity?

Now that the students understand how the prioritizing activity works, I think that they would spend less time trying to understand what is being asked of them and more time thinking about their reasons why they selected the numbers they did. I may also want to think about whether to have all students work independently or place all students in groups to be able to discuss.

 Strategies 65, 66: Fun Activities to Encourage Critical Thinking

To challenge students to think critically, build an activity around this quote from Grantland Rice, a renowned sportswriter from the first half of the twentieth century:

"When the one great scorer comes to put his mark upon your name,
   he cares not whether you won or lost, but how you played
the game!"

Ask students to discuss the contrast between Rice's quote and a philosophy espoused by football coach Vince Lombardi: "Winning isn't everything; it's the only thing."

Here is an activity that may motivate students, or children at home, to think critically. It is fun while simultaneously addressing racism and stereotyping. Ask Alexa (Amazon) or Google to play the Smothers Brothers song, "Crabs Walk Sideways and Lobsters Walk Straight." You can print out the lyrics as well as play the song to start a discussion. Among the questions to pose could be, "Can you think of how this song reflects the way some people treat others in America?" Certainly, middle and high school students are capable of understanding and debating the relevance of the lyrics to relations among people. Maybe even children at a younger age.

Advice to Marsha Hunt from Her Husband

Marsha Hunt, still alive at 103 as of this writing, was a movie star in the 1940s, blacklisted in the 1950s, and a humanitarian well into her 90s. She was married for 40 years until the death of her husband in 1986. Asked about the most valuable advice she received from her husband, she quickly replied, "He never told me what to think—he told me to think!"

COMMONSENSE CONCLUSION

Learning is experiential. If activities are designed to help students build on past experiences, and actively think about how those experiences connect with new information, students will learn to think more critically. It is the teacher's job to challenge students to think about how new information can connect with what they already know or think that they know.

12

Advisories, Journaling, and Conferencing Are Essential

Jacob's mom was surprised at her son's response when she asked him about the best part of his school day: "I like my 45-minute advisory three times a week," he replied. Jacob explained that during the advisories, he meets with 15 other students and Mr. Cook, and the students suggest topics to discuss. He keeps a journal once a week and can write about anything he wants. "Sometimes," he told his mother, "Mr. Cook will meet privately with me to discuss something in my journal, but it's just him and me because he keeps our journals confidential."

When his mother asked what they discussed in his advisory today, Jacob responded, "We prepared for each of us to conduct a parent-teacher-student conference in which we will have to present our portfolios and discuss the progress we've made on the school's standards since the last conference. Then we were asked to write a short essay stating which character in To Kill a Mockingbird, *we are most like and why. We were then paired off and asked to share our essays and invite the other student to tell us which character they think their partner is like and why."*

We attribute the success of the previously discussed Rochester City School District's School Without Walls to many factors, including a curriculum driven by student interest, an emphasis on critical thinking and creative problem-solving skills, performance-based assessments, classroom and school-wide decision-making, and learner-centered pedagogy. However, we also cite three additional elements as being critical for student growth and development: advisory groups, personal conferences, and journaling, which are all directly related to the key component of "student-teacher relationship building."

DOI: 10.4324/9781003284697-14

Let us explore what these three key elements look like in actual practice and why they are so essential to the success of any school. While School Without Walls is a secondary school, the concepts are relevant to lower grades as well as universities.

✓ **Strategies 67–69: Real-World Examples of Advisories, Journaling, and Conferencing**

Advisories: Rather than being assigned a traditional "homeroom" by the high school administration, 15 ninth-grade students meet with a randomly assigned teacher for an hour each day in an "advisory group." The same advisory assignment takes place with all other students in the same grade level.

Sheela, a ninth-grade student, listens for her name to be taken for daily attendance and then the morning announcements by a student. Today, a Monday, is reserved for "Decision-Making," during which students brainstorm classroom, school, district, neighborhood, national, or global issues they wish to discuss, and they generate proposals for the class or school to vote on. On this day, they agree to deal with the issue of homeless people who "hang around" her school. After an intense discussion on student-generated solutions, three students, including Sheela, agree to write a proposal on giving free meals to the homeless for advisory group approval and circulation to the entire school for a vote.

On Tuesday, Sheela's class is committed, along with several other ninth-grade advisory groups, to hear a community agency speaker present and discuss "sexual assault" with her class.

On Wednesday, her advisory group debriefs the "sexual assault" presentation and agrees that it is a serious school issue that needs more discussion; it is agreed to have it be part of the proposals for Monday's "Decision-Making" time. Tuesdays and Wednesdays are reserved for their advisory curricular emphasis, "Teen Issues," which they decided upon as a group in September. This includes discussions, activities, guest speakers, films, debates, book discussions, moral dilemma activities, and individual and small group research projects, which often lead to discussions and proposals. Students earn English and elective credit for successfully completing the "Teen Issues" class, through which writing, listening, media literacy, research, critical thinking, and creative problem-solving skills are emphasized.

On Thursday, Sheela participates with two other advisory students in a triad, where each student spends five minutes sharing a personal decision-making issue or problem they have with academics, athletics, other extracurricular activities, or with family or friends. Sheela shares that she has a very difficult time getting up each morning for school. The triad groups' other two members, bound by confidentiality, offer several suggestions. Sheela agrees to try putting her alarm clock on the other side of her bedroom so she will not hit the "snooze button" several times before finally getting up. She will try this solution over the week and report to her triad members on the next Thursday.

Fridays are reserved for journal writing, reading, research for Monday's Decision-Making agenda, and for "personal conferences" with their teacher. Sheela will be working on the "Homeless Proposal" with three other students.

Personal Conferences: Personal conferences can take place with any student, K–12. Teachers who use this method may use 15- to 20-minute blocks during an advisory or have assigned times before or after school or during lunch, once or twice per month.

In Katie's case, a fourth-grade student in a rural elementary school, she is meeting with her teacher during her assigned time for 15 minutes during Wednesday's lunchtime. She and her teacher are having lunch together in her classroom while the rest of her classmates are having lunch in the cafeteria. After some initial conversation about how much her teacher enjoys Katie's art projects, the teacher asks about the journal in which Katie shared her fear about going home on certain days. Katie begins to cry and shares that her mother's boyfriend has been abusing her. Her teacher hugs Katie and tells her that she will get Katie help. After reporting the incident to the school social worker, a Child Protective Services worker meets with Katie to secure protection and deal with her family.

Journaling: Each day, following lunch, Kevin's sixth-grade class is required to write in their journals. Kevin and his classmates have been told by their teacher, Mr. Martin, that they can share anything they like with him in their journals. However, if they do write something that indicates they are in danger, he is bound by law to report it to Child Protective Services and their parents.

Mr. Martin has also stated that the journals are each student's personal private property and that no one may read another student's journal without their permission. Each day, four assigned students submit their journals to Mr. Martin for him to review and comment upon in writing that evening. This spreads out the number of journal entries Mr. Martin must review each day.

On this particular day, Mr. Martin gives the students three open-ended paragraph starters to help focus on specific issues. The sentence-starters are: "When I have an important test coming up, I feel…," "I feel this way because…," and "I think the tests the state gives us…" Kevin is not a good test-taker, but is a good writer, and shares his fear of being labeled a "failure" by his test score. Mr. Martin, after reading Kevin's concerns, meets with Kevin to assure him that the state tests are not an accurate measure of any individual student's success or intelligence and that Kevin is a "great" student. He also asks Kevin if he thinks other students may feel the same way about the state tests and wonders what he might do as a teacher to help students deal with "test anxiety." After his conference with Kevin, Mr. Martin decides to introduce "mindfulness" exercises to his class to deal with their test stress.

DAN: The teacher/advisor of a 15-year-old student shared a journal entry with me; it revealed that the student was contemplating suicide. We were able to immediately have her meet with our school social worker. She continued to meet with that social worker and graduated two years later.

Status of Advisories, Student Conferences, and Journaling in Schools

There seems to be little argument that elementary or K–6 schools have fewer barriers to instituting advisory time, journals, and student-teacher conferences than secondary schools. The fact that many K–6 schools schedule their students with one teacher for a major part of the day creates more scheduling flexibility. However, the reality of pressure on teachers to ensure higher standardized test scores, along with mandated standardized curricula and pedagogy, are omnipresent and can deter creative teachers from instituting more social-emotional, skill-building processes in their classrooms.

None of this, however, reduces the importance of advisories, personal conferences, and journaling in support of student learning. These processes may not be mandated, but they should be treated as if they are. Despite the obstacles, all that is required to create and implement these essential strategies is the mindset, creativity, and courage to make it happen. The relationship between teacher and student (and the student's perception of how much the teacher likes him or her) is paramount.

 Strategy 70: List Benefits of Advisories, Conferencing, and Journaling

For middle schools and high schools, teachers are encouraged to form a team with members from each subject discipline; create a proposed schedule for implementing advisories, journals, and personal conferences; and devise a list of the benefits these activities will yield with supporting research. Benefits could include the following:

★ Students develop as school and community citizens, with skills to think critically and act as change agents for creating a healthier society.

★ Teachers can identify student problems and issues that require school or outside agency intervention, as well as prevent long-term personal issues that negatively impact a student's academic and social-emotional growth.

★ Students develop the interpersonal and intrapersonal skills to effectively cope with teenage social issues.

★ Advisories create a dramatic decline in suspensions, drop-outs, and disruptive incidents and an increase in student attendance, engagement in academics, and positive social behaviors.

 Strategy 71: Engage Young Students in Metacognition

It is never too early to start children on journaling. As soon as they are old enough to write simple sentences, start a sentence for them and ask them to complete it. For example, "Today I am feeling…," or "Yesterday I…," or "I feel that…," or "I wish…" You can assure them that anything recorded in their journals will be kept confidential. If students are not old enough to write, ask the questions verbally to the entire class and take down their responses.

 Strategies 72–78: Additional Strategies for Advisories, Conferencing, and Journaling

★ End-of-class journals: Leave the last five minutes of each class for students to write something about their experiences in your class, during the school day, or over the past weekend at home. Their writing can be kept in their notebooks or in a separate journal that you collect each day or at the end of the week for review.

★ Write positive comments and ask clarifying questions on student journals and writing assignments. Be descriptive by telling what you liked about the content and style of their writing. Make inferences about how they may have felt. Tell them how their writing makes you feel.

★ As much as possible, incorporate issues that are relevant to your students into your curriculum and integrate the skills that the standards or tests focus upon to justify the unit. Exceed the district or state standards by having students learn to write and present proposals to the school, school board, or town officials on teen issues or other social issues related to the school environment or social justice.

★ Try to arrange at least one personal conference with each of your students each month, or minimally, each semester. Prioritize those students who seem to express problems through their journals.

★ Model and teach interpersonal skills, such as active listening, sending "I-messages," being nonjudgmental, and asking clarifying questions. An "I-message" focuses on the feelings of the speaker rather than the characteristics the speaker attributes to someone else. For instance, "When you ignore me in front of other students, it makes me feel that you don't respect me."

★ Arrange for at least one guest speaker per month to address the class about teenage and other societal issues. Have students write about how the topic related to their own lives and what they would like to do about the issues discussed. Have students send their writing to the local newspaper as editorials or guest essays.

★ Have students write to a local legislator about an issue that concerns them. Usually, they'll be reinforced by a response, even if it is a form letter. In fact, the nature of the response, or lack thereof, can lend itself to an interesting discussion about politics and politicians' responses to constituents' concerns.

COMMONSENSE CONCLUSION

If your school is lacking advisories, personal conferences, or journaling, make their implementation a priority. These are low-cost/high-benefit items. They may involve some minimal restructuring of the class or school schedule, but they are worth prioritizing compared with other things we spend time on in schools that may have questionable or little value (Sparks, 2019).

13

Music and Art Facilitate Learning in All Disciplines

"This morning," Evelyn told her mother, "our class learned a song about the president's job." "That's wonderful," her mother exclaimed, proud because her daughter is in a class with other special education students and doesn't frequently have a chance to boast about her work in school. "Oh, and Mom," Evelyn continued enthusiastically, "here's a picture Melissa and I drew of the president making a speech in Pennsylvania. Do you know what it was about? I do!"

Attention math, science, English, and social studies teachers: If you want to reach more of your students, increase your use of music, art, and multiple intelligences as vehicles for learning in your discipline (Vermette, 2002).

According to Marie Allsopp of Purdue University,

> The power of using music and emotions to engage students' attention, stimulate learning, and increase retention is often overlooked. As a faculty member, I look for ways to make class enjoyable, pique student curiosity, and incorporate meaningful exercises to engage students with course content. The use of an attention-grabbing activity can increase student participation and improve short and long-term retention.
>
> (Howell Major, Harris, and Zakrajsek, 2015)

In addition, novel information that stimulates emotions and curiosity also improves recall and retention (Fenker and Schutz, 2008).

DOI: 10.4324/9781003284697-15

Why Is the Use of Music or Art an Effective Way to Reach ALL Students?

If a child has weak auditory skills or is weak in linguistic and/or mathematical-logical intelligence, chances are this is a student who is a potential dropout and probably a C-student at best, even though their overall intelligence may equal or exceed that of students with higher grades.

Also, this student, in a traditional classroom, will not learn as effectively as they could in a learner-centered classroom. No amount of in-class remediation, especially if it mimics traditional teaching styles, is likely to help. Some children experiencing failure may be strong in musical or spatial intelligence (which may translate to being gifted artistically). One of the authors is probably weaker than anyone reading this book when it comes to ability with art or music. Yet, if he is not being evaluated on his ability, he can enjoy participating in a sing-along or drawing a picture, even though he cannot draw a straight line with a ruler. The point is that when a teacher uses art or music as an integral part of a lesson, they can often capture the attention of every student in the room.

According to Ron Berk, there are three potential learning outcomes for using music in the classroom:

◆ Increased student engagement and concentration
◆ Increased student enjoyment, attendance, and love of learning
◆ A positive atmosphere/environment resulting in more positive student behavior and fewer suspensions

---

✔️ **Strategies 79–85: Use Art and Music to Support Student Learning in Core Subjects**

★ Building art into a lesson is easy. Anything you can ask students to do verbally, you can ask them to represent artistically. At the start of a lesson, instead of going around the room and asking students, "What's one thing you know about _____," ask them to draw a picture of one thing they know about it. To add some humor, have them exchange pictures with a partner and ask the partners to share what they think the picture represents and then share with the class what they learned from their partners. Of course, if you ask students to reflect their thoughts artistically, it must be about a topic or event they know something about. For an assessment activity, instead of a short-answer-essay test, give students the option of producing a piece of artwork or a collage that addresses what they are expected to have learned during the lesson.

★ Music usually has a positive effect on attitudes. Have music playing as students enter the classroom. We typically start with our musical preferences and then use the prospect of student selections as an incentive, particularly if students complain about our "dated" choices. Students can be allowed to sign up for a day on which they will choose the music.

★ Ask students to select a song that reflects the message or theme in a class lesson. Have the students play the song to the class, explain the connections they see, and entertain other students' questions.

★ Ask students, in groups of three or four, to design a CD or DVD cover with ten songs listed that relate to a specified decade. Set criteria depending on the discipline(s) and your learning objectives. For instance:

a. Two of the songs have to reflect significant events in (math, science, social studies, literature, art, music, etc.) from a specific decade. The events must be from the specified decade, but the songs can be from any era and only have to reference the event.

b. Two of the songs must reflect individuals who had a significant impact during the chosen decade, or two of the songs must reflect the culture of the decade.

c. You could also set criteria for wording to go on the jacket/cover.

★ Another example is asking students to create a poster or bumper sticker that sends a message about an issue they feel strongly about. This could include ideas such as designing a school poster that advertises a book on a common teen problem, designing a bumper sticker promoting flu shots in the fall, or challenging students to create a campaign for convincing the public that carbon emissions are an imminent threat to our way of life.

★ At the end of a lesson, ask each student to name and describe a song that they believe connects to the topic being explored by students. Or they can write a song, develop a rap, or create a video or a podcast that connects to the topic.

★ Music can connect to physical education as well. Since movement is critical to brain functioning, the teacher could ask a different student each day to volunteer to lead the class in a five-minute exercise to break up the routine. The volunteer chooses the exercise or can ask the teacher or another student to select it, and music can be played in the background. The student can also be offered the opportunity to select the background music to be played during the exercise activity.

Students whose best skill set involves music or art may go through an entire scholastic career without being the one other students rely on in a small group setting or who has the good answer when the teacher poses a question to the entire class. But when art or music becomes the main vehicle for a lesson in math, science, social studies, or English class, it enables students who rarely have the opportunity to shine. Connecting to this student's interest can lead to their ongoing engagement with the class, and with the teacher, on a much more personal level.

All that is required to integrate music, art, or physical movement into lessons is a new mindset. Get your creative juices flowing and think about it.

COMMONSENSE CONCLUSION

Integrating music, art, and physical movement into instruction in the academic disciplines helps to assure learning for all students. Why do we allow students with talent in music, art, or physical education to go through their entire scholastic career without ever putting them in a position where they can be recognized for their talents to the same degree as students with good verbal skills or the ability to memorize for tests?

14

Students Need a Vision

Image by Afzal Khan. With permission

Picture these situations:

- ◆ *A student in poverty to whom hunger is no stranger*
- ◆ *A student living in a crime-ridden section of town whose primary concern is getting to school and back home without being threatened by gangs*
- ◆ *A child from a middle- or upper-class family whose father is not in the picture*
- ◆ *A child whose mother has an addiction or mental health problem*
- ◆ *A child who regularly experiences racial, religious, gender, or ethnic bias*

DOI: 10.4324/9781003284697-16

What chance is there that these students have the luxury of thinking beyond the next day? What kind of a future do any of these students envision for themselves, if in fact they believe they have a future?

A teacher cannot always be a savior. There are just too many factors that affect whether a student raised in poverty can break the cycle or a student with little family support can overcome this handicap. But a teacher can help students think about the fact that there is life after schooling, and a teacher can open students' minds to the kinds of opportunities that many students, particularly those raised in poverty, may not be aware exist.

Here is a headline from the Los Angeles Times in 1990:

Millionaire's Scholarship Offer Pays Off for Students in Harlem: Spurred by Eugene Lang's vow to pay college tuition, 90% of P.S. 121's Class of 1981 has finished high school

Thanks to Eugene Lang's impulsive promise at a grade-school graduation, 90% of the Class of 1981 at East Harlem's P.S. 121 has now graduated from high school. Half of them went on to Bard, Swarthmore, Barnard, and other universities, spurred by the millionaire's vow to pay the college tuition of each of the 61 students if they got high school diplomas. And around the country, others copied Lang's largesse.

(Neff, 1990)

In his book *Man's Search for Meaning*, Austrian neurologist, psychiatrist, and Holocaust survivor Victor Frankl asserted that one of three characteristics shared by many survivors was having a vision of what they wanted to do with their lives when the horror of their experience ended. Frankl writes that man's search for meaning is the primary motivation in his life and not a "secondary rationalization" of instinctual drives. Frankl pointed to research indicating a strong relationship between "meaninglessness" and criminal behaviors, addictions, and depression. Without meaning, people fill the void with hedonistic pleasures, power, materialism, hatred, boredom, or neurotic obsessions and compulsions (Simon, 2020).

In essence, Lang and Frankl both recognized the importance of having a vision of what one's life can become. Many children raised in poverty or without solid support at home tend to live day-to-day, focusing on instant gratification or survival rather than thinking of the future. If children do not have positive role models, they are often unaware of opportunities that exist in the outside world or of the need to envision a future beyond the next day (Anda, 2020).

Football coach Pete Carroll encourages his professional athletes to create a vision for themselves. Carroll suggests that "A vision is different from a personal philosophy." In a *New York Times* article, he asks his players "to think about what it truly means to excel, whether it's winning a football game or just being a better person."

Art teacher Jason Hubbard was a self-described cutup in school until, as a middle school student, he was informed by a teacher that he had college potential. "Until then," according to Jason, "I'd never even thought of college as an option. From that moment on, my studies took on an importance in my life to the point that by the time I was a high school senior, my friends were referring to me as the class nerd."

While we acknowledge that a teacher cannot be a savior, many successful people who faced hardship as children credit a teacher with making a significant impact on their ability to emerge from their circumstances despite the challenges that confronted them. Jason is just one example.

What does it mean to have a vision for your future? According to the Earl E. Bakken Center for Spirituality and Healing at the University of Minnesota, "Your life purpose consists of the central motivating aims of your life—the reasons you get up in the morning. Purpose can guide life decisions, influence behavior, shape goals, offer a sense of direction, and create meaning. For some people, purpose is connected to vocation—meaningful, satisfying work."

 Strategies 86–95: Help Students Create a Vision for Their Future

★ Ask students to name three possible things they would like to do when they finish their schooling. In groups of two or three, have students share, so through listening to other students they grasp the wide variety of possibilities that exist. Preschool is not too soon to begin with an activity like this, and 12th grade is not too late.

★ Ask students to ask someone at home to name three possible career options. Then share the options with the entire class and create and post a master list of career options.

★ Read, or have students read, stories of people who succeeded despite childhood disadvantages. Have students write what they would have to do with their lives to achieve this kind of success.

★ Ask students, "What would you like to do when you finish your schooling? Think about what you would need to do to qualify for this kind of work. Then write a paper or prepare a verbal report on one thing you will need to learn in order to qualify for your choice."

★ Create vision boards with your students. A classroom vision board is a collage that reflects student goals and aspirations. An example could be pictures and/or words depicting firefighters, doctors, planes, a nice home, and someone listening to music. It can include women in traditionally male occupations and people of color in professions that currently lack diversity.

Danielle Knight, a curriculum resources designer, EdTech enthusiast, and high school special education teacher, writes,

> A hot topic in education now is growth mindset. We are trying to teach our children to never give up, to keep going despite the many hardships and setbacks they may face. Creating a vision board and displaying it somewhere that they can see it daily is an excellent reminder to help them stay focused on what they really want in life and to do whatever it takes to achieve it. They will be constantly reminded of why they are doing the things they do every day and the pride and happiness that will come as a result.
> ("Why Teachers Should Create Vision Boards with Their Students," n.d.)

Growth mindset refers to a learning theory developed by Dr. Carol Dweck. It revolves around the belief that you can improve intelligence, ability, and performance through hard work and the belief that failures are an opportunity for learning.

Additional ideas:

◆ Beginning at an early age, take students for a walk or drive through a college campus. One author's child took swimming lessons at a local college at age two and went to computer camp from age six to eight. Just being on a college campus serves to demystify the college experience for children as they grow older. It is important for schools to bring students to college campuses, particularly if there are no universities in the immediate vicinity. For children living in poverty, it may be their only opportunity to see what's possible after high school graduation.

◆ Post a list of career options in the classroom and make it a work in progress throughout the year. Encourage students to add one career option a week.

◆ Invite former students to speak to your students about their experiences in college, in a career, or in a temporary job.

◆ Each week select a career option (or ask your students to agree on one) and have your students do some research into the necessary qualifications, aspects of the job that may not be self-evident, training, challenges, and difficulties. Help them to the degree their age level requires.

◆ Propose to school or district administrators that at some point before graduation, every student should experience a half-day-per-week internship in a position that most closely coincides with their visions. The internship should be credit-bearing, be supervised by an organization manager and school counselor or advisor and require weekly written reports. This could also be a graduation requirement.

Let Us Not Ignore the Unhappiness of Many Children

Do you have fond memories of your years as a young child and then a teenager? We hear many people say that their growing-up years were stressful, anxious, nervous times. While there certainly must be many people with fond memories of growing up, teenagers in particular often struggle with their identity, peer pressure, and a feeling of loneliness—"No one truly understands me." The rising number of teen suicides nationwide offers evidence of this.

Schools can help students overcome the obstacles to surviving childhood. Just helping students see that they are not alone and that others share their feelings can provide meaningful support. Utilize school assemblies and class discussions to let students know that it is not uncommon to have feelings of being overwhelmed. Share stories like this from a friend who spoke of the most meaningful thing his father ever did for him when he told him, "Many of us struggled to get through to the age of 20, or older, but it does get much better as you get older." What about an assembly in which several adults share what they endured in their most formative years?

COMMONSENSE CONCLUSION

We need to recognize that many of our students have been so absorbed in surviving one day at a time that they have not been able to think about what opportunities are available to them or what they might want to do with their lives in the future.

15

Introverted (or Quiet) Children Require Special Strategies

Billy asked his friend Belinda, "How come you hardly ever say anything in class, but when you and I are alone or working in class as a pair, I sometimes can't get you to stop talking? Belinda replied, 'I'm not sure, except that when we are working together or in a small group, I'm more comfortable.'"

A teacher overhearing Belinda's comments said to a colleague, "You know, I went through 19 years of coursework, starting in kindergarten, and I rarely said anything in class. It's not that I never had anything to say, but I'm not one to shout out my thoughts or to compete with students madly waving their hands. Teachers just didn't give me the opportunity to speak in ways I could feel more comfortable. Besides, what's wrong with being shy about speaking in front of big groups?"

Perhaps one of the most neglected areas of school reform was publicized by Susan Cain in her 2012 book *Quiet*, which details Western culture's strong preference for extroverted individuals over introverted ones, and specifically, how schools are not meeting the needs, interests, and learning styles of introverted children. Research indicates that approximately 50% of our students are introverted and generally prefer to work independently or with another student whom they trust. Among other things, they also prefer lectures, reading silently, playing musical instruments, doing individual projects, and reflective thinking.

Introverts often tend to be labeled as shy, loners, quiet, antisocial or withdrawn, sensitive, empathetic, and often, creative. However, we live in an extrovert-desired society. Who does not want their child to be outgoing, lively, talkative, socially engaging, and popular? That is what our schools—and even most parents—generally desire as student outcomes.

DOI: 10.4324/9781003284697-17

As a result of our efforts to teach introverted children to become extroverts, we are in many cases shaming them and diverting them from their natural inclinations, which could be causing a severe reduction in self-esteem. Think about the impact of that on academic learning! What is wrong with simply accepting and valuing introverted children's personalities as they are, and individualizing the activities and expectations we have for them?

That is not to say that we, as educators, cannot gradually encourage introverted children to take some risks to engage with extroverted children so that all children can experience and learn to value each other.

 Strategies 96–101: Engaging Introverted Children

Teachers can begin to meet the needs of introverted children by

★ Reading Susan Cain's book;
★ Telling introverted children, in private, like Mr. Rogers would, that "I like you just the way you are";
★ Using more "pair-share" activities, which give introverted children the opportunity to be vocal while not having to risk sharing with a large group;
★ Prearranging small groups that will have sensitive extroverted children in the groups as support for introverted children;
★ Showing sensitivity to both introvert and extrovert needs when assigning roles to students for group activities (for example, do not assign an introverted student to be the "reporter" to the entire class until they have expressed to you that they are ready for that role); or
★ Encouraging introverted students to think about the possibility of learning to play a musical instrument, to take art lessons, or to engage in some type of one-on-one community service to build their self-confidence (for example, tutoring a younger, introverted student).

 Strategies 102–109: Actions for Parents to Consider

Cain encourages parents to look for supportive schools and teachers who fit certain criteria. She suggests considering whether the school and/or teacher

★ Prizes independent interests and autonomy of students;
★ Conducts group activities in moderation and uses small, managed group activities;

★ Values and integrates kindness, empathy, caring, and good citizenship into the curriculum and classroom culture;

★ Insists on nonthreatening classrooms and hallways;

★ Hires teachers who can demonstrate their support for these criteria;

★ Creates curricular and extracurricular activities that meet student interests;

★ Strongly supports anti-bullying programs; and

★ Connects with parents to support each child's interests, growth, and development.

COMMONSENSE CONCLUSION

Meeting the needs of introverted students has often been neglected through cultural, school, and teacher expectations. A new school and teacher mindset can change this dynamic—one that may be harming as many as 50% of our students.

16

Educators Can Make Use of Lectures and Be Effective

A college professor is recognized worldwide for her research demonstrating that learner-centered practices are best practices. Yet two-thirds of her colleagues in the education department continue to teach traditionally and even mock her for fear that if her beliefs spread, they might have to change the way they teach. The percentage of professors in other departments who ignore her research is even higher and their mockery even greater.

Isn't it ironic that support for learner-centered teaching has come primarily from iconic university researchers such as Jacqueline Grennon Brooks and Martin G. Brooks, Charlotte Danielson, Linda Darling-Hammond, Giselle Martin-Kniep, Jay McTighe, Fred Newmann, Diane Ravitch, and many others—yet many education departments are still placing little emphasis on learner-centered teaching competency? And, given that many researchers advocate for learner-centered practices, isn't it also ironic that many university professors, in all curricular areas, continue to primarily use lectures (Allen & Forman, 2019)?

The authors frequently conduct workshops with university professors and interact with them in a variety of forums. We are often challenged by professors to explain whether our emphasis on learner-centered strategies is intended as an indictment of the way many of them teach.

Are professors who lecture ineffective? There are two equally valid responses to this question: "Not necessarily," and "It depends." For anyone who teaches at any level, it is essential that they know their subject matter. Equally important, however, they must know how to communicate their

DOI: 10.4324/9781003284697-18

subject matter to students, who must then be able to apply that information or skill to the real world. Not all lecturing is contrary to learner-centered education practices. The main considerations when determining whether a lecture is appropriate in a learner-centered environment are as follows:

- ◆ The audience: Is there reason to believe they want the information that will be offered?
- ◆ Can the information be articulated in a few minutes, recognizing there is beauty in brevity?
- ◆ Does the information relate to experiences common to those in the audience?
- ◆ Is the information presented to the audience in ways they can find relevant and relatable?

One of the authors presented at an annual Lilly Conference in Bethesda, Maryland, attended primarily by university professors. His presentation on *Making Students Want What You Want Them to Learn* attracted the largest turnout of more than 39 breakout sessions. At the conclusion of the 75-minute interactive presentation with 64 participants crammed into an overcrowded conference room, a young lady approached him and said, "I want to thank you so much. I just got my doctorate. I have been teaching at the university for three years, and this is the first time in my scholastic career that I have been able to take a course on how to teach."

Most universities do not require a professor to have had any training courses in how to teach. If their research credentials are promising (publish or perish), or they have name recognition that attracts students and funding to the university, they are qualified to be employed at the university level.

This does not at all mean that professors cannot be good teachers. While it may not be a job requirement, many have trained or taken courses on their own, and some are instinctively good teachers. Unfortunately, however, many professors equate talking and telling with good teaching.

The authors stand behind the research that for a lesson to be effective, there must be learner engagement with the information, whether the teaching be in preschool, elementary, middle, high school, or higher education (Dewey, 1938).

However, that engagement can occur in the classroom or outside of it. Universities increasingly offer students opportunities to travel abroad, go on extended field trips, and take on internships. When these outside experiences are discussed and reflected upon in class, the necessary engagement for significant learning is occurring.

Strategy 110: Use Field Trips to Bring Content to Life

Former third-grade teacher Christina Luce, currently a technology director for her school, says, "My geology professor took us out on field trips pretty regularly to actually see what he was talking about. Hands-on learning experiences were a requirement for my initial field of study for sure. I took physics twice. The first time it was a disaster. The second time I loved it. I had a professor who emphasized the magic of physics. He always incorporated some kind of demonstration into the lecture. It was super engaging. He probably would have given Bill Nye a run for his money."

There is a significant difference between K–12, where students often have little choice in the courses they take, and college or university, where students are usually at a school that they have chosen based on alignment with their interests. This is an important distinction because, at the university, students are more likely to be taking a course in a subject area that they enjoy or believe they need to take to address their career aspirations. So, even if a lecture is dry and provides little opportunity for engagement with the information being imparted, students can be intrinsically motivated to engage with a lecture because they believe they may be able to apply the information to a job, internship, or hobby.

How much do you recall of high school lectures? Few of us can recall anything we were taught if there was no immediate engagement with the information (Silberman, "Crisis in the Classroom," 1967). You either use it or lose it. If there is no engagement with information, then this saying probably reflects reality.

Strategy 111: An Activity to Use with Future and Current Teachers

To demonstrate the value of engaging students with the information they need to learn, there is a workshop activity the authors have conducted many times, most often for student teachers but also for classroom teachers and university professors. Here are the steps:

STEP 1:

Participants are at tables of three to six people.

STEP 2:

Participants are asked to list, "What should a teacher be thinking about and looking for when conducting a group activity with students?" A group volunteer lists the suggestions so all group members can see them.

STEP 3:

Participants at each table are given a large sheet of newsprint and multiple-colored markers, and are asked, as a group, to either put their responses into an artistic design or to prepare a performance: for example, a poem, skit, rap, to perform their list.

STEP 4:

Participants at each table hold up their artistic design and explain it or give their performance.

STEP 5:

Participants at each table are given a list of responses to the question they just addressed. It is an intentionally incomplete list of not more than six items. Participants are then asked to compare their list with that of the workshop leaders and to have a reporter ready to share anything on one list but not the other, and to comment on whether they believe it to be a valid entry.

Without fail, this activity generates enthusiasm, smiles, and active engagement from all participants. Those with artistic ability or performance skills find themselves in the unique position of being leaders in their group. Those, like the authors, with understandable reluctance to expose their inability to draw or perform, enjoy being part of a group where they can participate without having to lead.

Most significantly, all participants, because of their enjoyment of the activity, think a lot about the question they are addressing. Do you think participants would have given the same critical thought if someone had given a 30-minute lecture on the role of a teacher? Once this activity concludes, there is still an opportunity for the professor or teacher to summarize and process out the anticipated lesson.

COMMONSENSE CONCLUSION

Lectures can be effective learning processes if they are short, offer reference to an activity or event that has previously occurred, and combine with some form of immediate interactive student processing.

Section Three

Is There Room for the Affective Domain?

A few decades ago, social-emotional learning strategies were met with, "We don't need that "touchy-feely stuff"; now professional development focusing on SEL is in demand because educators are realizing they can't reach all students with content that many students find disconnected to their social-emotional needs.

17

Content and Social-Emotional Learning Are Compatible

Mr. Greenstreet arranged his class into groups of three and then engaged them in a productive discussion of The House on Mango Street. *At the conclusion of the discussion, he asked each group to address three questions: (1) On a scale of one to five, rate yourselves as a group in terms of how effective you were at reaching conclusions. (2) When your discussion was productive within your group, what was the reason? (3) When your discussion was less productive, what could you have done to improve your ability to work together?*

After leading the groups through this self-assessment, he conducted a whole class discussion for 15 minutes. At the end of class, Mr. Greenstreet asked students to form a line starting at the door and extending from there in the order in which each student felt they had participated in the discussion.

A visitor to the class was impressed that Mr. Greenstreet prefaced every request he made of his students with "please," and also thanked students for offering their thoughts during the discussion.

The authors' vision is that all teachers will regard the following four aspects of student learning as critical ingredients to include in developing and teaching a lesson:

1. Subject-matter content
2. SEL (the affective domain)
3. Skills and attitudes of successful people, such as citizenship, integrity, and social justice
4. Student engagement and application

DOI: 10.4324/9781003284697-20

Because so much of what is taught gets departmentalized (science class is for science, math class is for math, etc.), the typical teacher's thought process goes, "I would like to spend more time on social-emotional learning and issues like citizenship and social justice, but the standardized tests are oriented toward subject-matter content, and I just don't have time for teaching much of anything else."

If teachers think they have to apportion separate class time for each of these four areas, they will always choose subject content over development of the whole child or a person who is prepared for the real world. And who can blame them? Most students, parents, and educators believe it is acceptable for teachers to venture into areas of citizenship, social justice, opening a bank account, and check writing—but only if they can do so while still preparing students to do well on standardized tests.

There is a way to give a significant amount of time to subject content, the affective domain, and issues students will perceive to be relevant. It requires training teachers differently, training them to do what some are already doing proficiently.

Addressing SEL-emotional learning is easiest. It can be modeled by the way you greet students when they enter the classroom, how you react to their questions, and how you set expectations. Integrating social justice issues requires not only a new mindset but also some creative thinking.

SEL Increases Content Retention

It is a positive development that the field of education is making far greater use of social-emotional strategies than in the past. As recently as 15 years ago, if someone mentioned the affective domain, the reaction from many educators would have been, "You mean that touchy-feely stuff? I have not got time for that. Too much curriculum to cover." In contrast to this reaction, which reflects an attitude that existed for most of the twentieth century, schools are now clamoring for professional development on social-emotional strategies.

DON: When I was athletic director at a summer camp, I could have taught some of my campers more about adverbs and adjectives in ten minutes than I could have taught the youngsters of the same age in my English class a month later.

The difference was the rapport I could develop with the children in the camp environment.

While it is fortunate that there is more of a focus on SEL practices, it is unfortunate that the reason for the change is not so much a recognition that the role of schools should be to produce well-rounded students, equipped with the skills and attitudes necessary to become good citizens, but rather the ability to maintain decorum in the classrooms. It has become so difficult that there is recognition, out of desperation, that students can no longer be motivated to sit still and listen, take notes, and take tests. A few years ago, as part of an experiment in five major cities, students were paid money to get good grades! (Hammond, 2016).

There is growing awareness that students have to be motivated to pay attention the same way adults do, but not with money—instead, with information presented in ways that interest and involve students and respect their need to feel respected (Kohn, 1999).

Parents and Students Want Lifelong Learner Outcomes

While it is positive that educators are gravitating toward using the affective domain to develop rapport with students, and learner-centered practices to engage them in the learning process, the irony is that state and federal mandates are heavily weighted toward subject-area content and standardized tests. The result is teachers and administrators are inclined to focus student learning primarily in math, science, social studies, and English language arts. This severely limits the time teachers believe they can take to explore the affective domain or content such as citizenship, student rights and responsibilities, and other societal issues that directly affect young people.

But learning in the content areas is not what parents want most for their children. Ask parents what they want for their children upon graduation from high school or college and you get responses similar to the following:

◆ Lifelong learners
◆ Good citizens
◆ Respected and respectful individuals
◆ Solid value systems
◆ Qualities such as honesty, character, empathy, and integrity
◆ Ability to earn a living

In the early 1990s, the New York State Education Department (NYSED) initiated a program it labeled "Standards of Excellence" (see math, science, technology standards, New York State, 1994). As part of this program, NYSED sent staff members throughout the state to conduct meetings with parents, community members, and professional educators. The purpose was to form committees that would identify outcomes the community wanted from its high school graduates. The question that was posed to community groups across the state was, "What are the outcomes you would like for your children upon graduation from high school?" This was to be the basis for the redesign of the state's schools. One of the authors was tutored in this process by a staff member at NYSED and sat in on many of these community feedback sessions.

The aforementioned outcomes popped up on almost all lists from anywhere in the state. Only occasionally was content in a particular subject area mentioned. Unfortunately, as with many state education department initiatives, there was no follow-through. In fact, after two years of gathering feedback from parents, teachers, and community groups across the state, the initiative was abandoned. Instead, NYSED promulgated its own set of standards, totally ignoring the input generated at the community gatherings it had organized.

School districts will focus on what states mandate. They will interpret what the state is mandating through the content on the standardized tests it administers. In New York State, newspapers publish the results of each school's test scores. Many school boards evaluate their administrators on how well their students do on these tests, and many administrators evaluate their teachers on how well their students do. And everyone must answer to parents when standardized test scores go down.

Beginning in the mid-'90s, New York State introduced its own set of standards and, in addition to the familiar disciplines, it included a category it labeled the "Career Development and Occupational Standards" (CDOS). This was a good idea. However, if you ask teachers or administrators today if they can tell you what "CDOS" refers to, you will likely not find one in ten who can identify the term. The ones who can are sure to be veterans with more than 20 years' experience or possibly special educators.

Why? Because the assessments turned out by the state, intended to measure student success by the state's standards, did not include questions related to the CDOS standards. Teachers teach to the test because they are held accountable for their students' results. Students study what will be tested because they know the test results will carry the greatest weight on their grades and futures. The fact that most standardized tests are not accurate assessments of what they purport to assess is still an issue, and this is addressed in a later chapter on standardized assessments.

Imagine if schools were required to teach students about character, citizenship, social justice, and other issues related to becoming a good citizen.

And imagine further if tests assessed for student learning on these topics. Imagine still further if instead of short-answer essay questions, students were given performance assessments with tasks that require them to demonstrate what they understand and can apply to the real world, not what they can memorize.

President John F. Kennedy is reported to have said he hoped he was an idealist with no illusions. Not being idealists WITH illusions, the authors do not expect the system to change any time soon. However, to quote another well-regarded individual, Mark Twain, "It is better to shoot for the moon and wind up on the fencepost than to shoot for the fencepost and wind up on the ground."

It would be an illusion to think that in our lifetimes, schools will place as heavy an emphasis on the affective domain, critical thinking, social justice, ethical conduct, and good citizenship as on the content subjects. However, there are many ways that teachers can integrate the aforementioned topics into the subject content they are teaching without taking time away from the content they are required to teach.

To Summarize

1. Students are overwhelmed with content they are required to memorize for standardized and local tests.
2. Students will not give their complete effort and attention in classes just because we tell them it will help them after they graduate. Some students do not place a high priority on graduation.
3. Teachers are overwhelmed with content they are required to teach and tests they must prepare their students to pass, which detract from teaching competencies of lifelong learners that parents and students want.
4. Teachers cannot, and will not, sacrifice teaching the content that is mandated. Therefore, SEL, and focusing on character, social justice, respect, integrity, and other important qualities of a good citizen will only happen when teachers learn how to design lessons that address mandated content while simultaneously using activities, skills, and issues that students can perceive as relevant to their daily lives.
5. To motivate students intrinsically, lessons must be perceived as interesting, fun, and/or relevant. Teachers who appreciate the value of the affective domain have the key to opening student receptivity to lessons from which they can learn mandated content.

COMMONSENSE CONCLUSION

Teachers will continue to have to choose between teaching subject-area content or more relevant and important issues until they learn how to address mandated curriculum by integrating meaningful issues and skills into their lessons.

18

Let All Students Know They Are Liked as Individuals

The Classroom Culture Sends a Message to Students

Ms. Archer checks off student names on her roster every time she compliments them or asks them a personal question such as, "How did your soccer game go?" or "Is your brother OK after his long illness?" She begins classes every year by telling her students, "You will work hard in this class, but I will only ask you to do your best, and I will give you all the help you need whenever you need it." When Byron came to class on crutches, Ms. Archer asked him where he could sit most comfortably. In private, she asked him if he would need an extra day to complete the previous assignment since his injury caused him to miss a day of school.

Why is it that in almost everything we want to do with children, we lower our expectations to a reasonable level, but where school is concerned, we expect far more of children, expecting them to endure what we would endure as adults? We assume they will do what we ask just because we are the adults, even though there are few tasks adults will undertake unless we understand why.

If you want an adult to engage with something, they need to either believe there will be value in it at some point in life, or it has to be just plain fun, or at least enjoyable. Yet, adults expect young students to sit quietly for hours and engage their brains when we talk about things that are of little interest to them and use learning strategies that would not engage the average adult. It is often difficult for children to understand why something the teacher wants them to learn is actually necessary. If children believe the teacher truly cares about them, aren't they more likely to be responsive to a lesson led by the teacher?

DOI: 10.4324/9781003284697-21

Telling children, "Someday you will see why you need this; someday you'll thank me," just does not make a difference with most students, as far as motivation to engage. We can compel students to be physically present, but we cannot compel them to open their minds. Eric Jensen has stated, "Students don't care what you know; they want to know that you care!" (2011).

The parent of a high-performing fourth-grade student explained why she transferred her son to a private school: "My son John had complained that his teacher didn't know anything about him, and he didn't know anything about his teacher. Then, in November, this teacher referred to John as Ronald. Now anyone can momentarily forget a name," the parent continued, "but it was apparent to my son that the teacher had never known his name, cared to, or cared about him as a person. He asked if he could go to a different school and that is why we transferred him to a private school where we hope he will have a teacher he can respect." This is not an argument for private schools. It could easily have happened in reverse.

Students react best to teachers they believe care about them. It is part of our job as educators to convince students we care about them. To do this, we have to genuinely care about each student. We cannot fake it. They will know! In fact, students who believe that their teacher "likes" them as individuals will demonstrate the most positive social and academic engagement (Ryan, 2016).

There are many ways to show students the teacher cares about them. One way is to take the time as students enter your room to ask about what they did the day before, or to compliment them on something you have heard about them, or just greet them by name. During a class, you can ask students to write down three things about themselves that others probably do not know. You can start by sharing three things about yourself (that are not too personal) so they will have an example of what you want from them. This can start or continue the process of both of you learning about each other.

Raising the Bar

Recently, we interviewed 30 teachers from a school with a staff of 43. Separately, many of these teachers told us that the school held students in poverty to the lowest standards and students whose parents were teachers (presumably not in poverty) to the highest standards. Why? "We expect them to perform better."

This is ironic. Think of any movie or book about a school that was successful in improving student learning. In many films, the scene is usually set in an area of poverty where resources are scarce. Ironically, the key leader (principal or teacher) often raises standards and makes it more difficult for students to achieve. The reason their story was worthy of publication was because the students who previously had failed to achieve lower standards were suddenly able to overachieve.

How factual are these stories? Each might lead the reader or viewer to believe that simply raising expectations for students will magically cause students to achieve at higher levels. This belief is simply not factual. You do not get high jumpers to leap to greater heights simply by raising the bar, and you do not get students to improve their achievement levels simply by increasing the challenge.

The other typical factor in these books and movies is that the leader who challenged students to greater effort combined the educational challenge with a significant amount of time developing a rapport with the students and convincing them, through actions, that she truly cared about them as people. The high jumper will be able to clear the higher bar only if there are changes in the methods of training—if support, encouragement, and resources are provided. In schools, the extra support that enables students to achieve a higher standard is knowing that the teacher cares.

We all have limits in terms of what we can achieve at present and what we can achieve with the best training and resources. We all know that a five-foot, 300-pound individual will not be an effective high jumper. Mass and gravity rule. All the encouragement and caring in the world will not make a difference to someone with these characteristics. But a caring teacher will have reasonable expectations for this individual or gently counsel them to lose weight or try an interest area more likely to generate enjoyment and success.

 Strategy 112: Convincing Students the Teacher Cares about Them

How do you demonstrate to students that you care? Here is a ten-minute activity we recommend every school staff undertake. Ask staff members, individually, to write three things they already do that demonstrate to students that they care. Then collect the responses, eliminate duplications, and reproduce the list for every teacher to use as a checklist. An effective addition to this activity is to have teachers meet in groups of three and have teachers share their lists and respond to clarifying questions by the other group members.

The value of this professional development activity is as follows:

★ For the teacher who never gave a thought to showing students she cares, it creates an awareness and gives her an instant checklist of suggestions from which to draw.

- ★ For the teacher who acts instinctively, it creates a consciousness that will lead to even more efforts to demonstrate caring.
- ★ For the teacher who has always consciously sought to demonstrate caring, it provides a checklist of ideas, some of them new. This kind of teacher is always on the lookout for new ideas.

 Strategy 113: Involving Students in the Same Activity

A school superintendent, observing her staff being led through this activity, speculated, "I wonder what students would say if asked this same question about teachers?" So, a fifth- and a seventh-grade teacher volunteered to ask their students what convinces them that a teacher cares about them as an individual. The responses from students were significantly different in some respects from the teacher responses. Teacher responses, while valid, focused on single events, such as a pizza party or a recognition day, to demonstrate to students that they care. However, the two sets of student responses were indicative of what impressed students even more:

- ★ "A teacher saw that I was hungry and gave me a snack bar."
- ★ "My teacher saw that I looked worried, sat down with me, and asked me if something was bothering me, and 'actually listened' as I talked."

 Strategies 114, 115: Additional Activities Related to Showing That Teachers Care

- ★ Put all school staff, nonteaching staff included, through the aforementioned activity, asking them to list three things they do to let students know they care about them. Then distribute the combined list of responses to every staff member. Do not ignore the impact of your nonteaching staff in convincing students that the school cares about them.
- ★ Early in the school year, even the first day, encourage all classroom teachers to ask their students to write a sentence or two describing one thing a teacher has done that convinced them that the teacher cared about them. (If they cannot think of anything, you might ask them one thing a teacher has done that led them to believe the teacher did not care about them and instruct them not to mention the teacher's name). If the students are too young to submit a response in writing, the teacher can pose the question verbally and record responses as a whole class activity.

Recently retired Professor Ed Boyd, who taught in the psychology department of the State University of New York Canton College, was chosen, just prior to his retirement, as a recipient of the Distinguished Faculty Award. Boyd was a professor who cared about his students. *North Country Now* reported the honor as follows:

> "Once Professor Boyd learns your name, his goal is then to know you," wrote Applied Psychology student Stacie G. Hale, class of 2020, in her letter of support to the council. "He works to learn about who you are as a person, what career might suit you, and even how your child's musical recital went. He cares deeply for every single student who walks through his door."
>
> (May 7, 2020)

Obviously, this chapter focuses on the importance of social-emotional-intellectual learning and letting students know that you, as their teacher, care about each of them as individuals. Presently, professional development related to SEL is in high demand because educators are recognizing that students need to feel connected to their teacher before they will open their minds to what he has to offer.

Image by Afzal Khan. With permission

 Strategy 116: Demonstrating the Significance of the Learning Environment

One of the authors taught a college-level course for 22 years. He had access to two rooms: one was ideal for learner-centered activities, with comfortable chairs, movable tables, and lots of room, while the other, across the hall, was a typical classroom that could squeeze 30 students into desks with built-in chairs set up in rows. As students would arrive for the first class, they would be directed by a sign to the traditional classroom. As they entered, music would be playing and the chairs, as much as possible, would be arranged in a semicircle. Name tags and markers would be on the professor's desk and, without speaking, the professor would point toward the name tags as students entered the room.

Before even introducing himself, the professor would go around the room and ask each student to respond to the question, "What did you first notice as you entered the room a moment ago?" Almost all responders would cite either the music, the seating arrangement, or the name tags.

Then the professor would go back to some of the students who cited the music: "What went through your mind as you heard the music?" Responses varied from, "It was nice," to "This class may be different," to "I was surprised." Those who noted the name tags said they thought it meant there would be more interaction than in most classes. One student said, "I feel like I'll get to know my classmates better at the end of the first class than I do after an entire semester in some other classes." The students who noticed the seating arrangement said it signaled that there would be a lot of class discussions and a more relaxed atmosphere, both of which they liked.

First impressions of a classroom's culture are important!

How frequently is the previously described classroom model seen in K–12 classrooms or in professional development sessions for teachers? What is preventing it from becoming a norm?

 Strategies 117–122: Strategies of Some Winning Leaders

The job of a college or professional sports coach is contingent on winning, often at all costs. The ideal educator, on the other hand, is focused on developing children's academic skills, character, and ethical behavior. Yet, a few winning coaches, and all outstanding educators, have one thing in common: they understand the importance of creating a culture and environment that conveys the message "I care about you" to the people they are expected to lead.

With the disclaimer that there is much about college and professional sports that the authors would not want educators to emulate, here are a few of the more exemplary approaches allegedly employed by some coaches. We trust the reader will see the transference of these strategies from sports to education as the practices of successful people in all fields and not as an endorsement of a particular sport or coach.

Hayden Fry is credited with reinvigorating the University of Iowa football program between 1978 and 1998. The recently deceased coach once said, "I'm the kind of coach that always tries to have fun, in practice and on game day. We tried to be demanding, but knew it had to be fun. The most important thing was the mental aspect."

Tony Dungy is a former professional football player and coach in the National Football League (NFL). As head coach of the Indianapolis Colts from 2002 to 2008, he became the first African American head coach to win a Super Bowl (2007). According to Dungy, "The secret to success is good leadership, and good leadership is all about making the lives of your team members or workers better."

Dabo Swinney's Clemson University Tigers won the National Championship in 2016 and 2018 and were runners-up in 2019. Clemson has won or challenged for the national college football championship almost every year since he became head coach. Coach Swinney has been cited for his positive approach toward his players and his efforts to create a warm, friendly culture. One recent recruit said he chose Clemson, in part, because it is "the type of school where they try to make it as much like home as possible."

Eddie Robinson earned an unprecedented 408 college football victories to set the National Collegiate Athletic Association's (NCAA) benchmark for wins in Division I. Coach Robinson, an African American, retired with an overall record of 408 wins, 165 losses, and 15 ties. "Coach Rob did a lot more for us than teach us about football. He used to come through the halls early in the morning with a cowbell, waking us up for class and for church." According to Everson Walls, former Grambling and NFL cornerback "Eddie Robinson was a great mentor to us all. He was a dynamic coach with a phenomenal record, but he was much more than that as a leader of young men, a great American and an example of character and integrity."

Bill Parcells won two Super Bowls with the New York Giants. It was said of Parcells that he treated his players the same by treating them differently. He knew which players needed a stern approach and which required more pats on the back.

Pat Summitt is perhaps best known for winning more games than any other NCAA Division I basketball coach, male or female. She spent 38 years as the head coach of the University of Tennessee women's basketball team, the Lady Volunteers, winning eight national titles and

1,098 games. Tennessee also made 31 consecutive NCAA tournament appearances under Coach Summitt. Among her inspirational quotes, she has said, "If I was renowned as a tough coach, I also wanted to be a caring one." She also has said, "I think I can help others just by my example."

✓ **Strategies 123–125: Physical Contact Options to Demonstrate Caring**

Offering students a hug to express caring or comfort has become less of an option for teachers as the years have passed, particularly as students move up from preschool. From fear of accusations of molestation to health concerns, the ways teachers can demonstrate affection for their students has become limited.

Here is how some teachers have handled the challenge of using physical contact in a way that does not lead to a criminal complaint or lawsuit. Some of these may not be relevant while the effects of the COVID-19 pandemic are with us.

★ One middle school teacher greets every student at the classroom door at the start of a period with a special hand-to-hand, arm-to-arm signal that she devised. If a student does not want to participate, they can just walk by her into class, but few ever do.

★ Another teacher has a large sign on the door with four columns, each headed by one of the following: hug, high five, knuckles, none of these. As students approach the door to begin class, they point to one of the four options and the teacher complies.

Everyone has his own style and it is important to be authentic. What is authentic for one person may not be for another. The main idea is to find ways to develop an individual rapport with as many students as possible. A person's rapport with a child is the handle that opens the door to the child's mind, feelings, and willingness to confide.

Bob Lewis was principal of Fox Road Elementary School in North Raleigh, North Carolina, in 2019. Principal Lewis's school, in a low-income neighborhood, received front-page notice for a significant increase in student achievement. One of the North Raleigh School District's goals was to create a positive, fun environment for students and staff in each of its schools.

Fist bumps are part of the daily ritual for students arriving at Fox Road Elementary School (as were hugs and handshakes prior to the COVID-19 crisis). Fox Road's "Gauntlet of Love" has teachers and staff line the entrance and hallways to greet the 420 students as they arrive for another day of classes. It's part of a culture of caring that principal Lewis credits for helping the high-poverty school double its passing rate on state tests over the past seven years.

"We strongly feel that the relationship piece is central to what we do," Lewis said in an interview. "As a staff we greet our kids in a way that is affirming the one-to-one piece, that they have real meaning in our lives and that we're there for them. It's a way of saying to them that school is a safe place, school is a good place" (Hui, 2019).

✅ Strategies 126–135: Strategies to Create a Warm, Safe Classroom Culture

Teachers make their classes more inviting and able to meet social-emotional needs through the use of the following:

- ★ Interactive bulletin boards
- ★ Positive calls to parents
- ★ Sunshine cards listing positive actions students take
- ★ Greetings at the door or the start of a lesson
- ★ Relevant, compelling discussion topics
- ★ Relating social-emotional issues to characters in literature
- ★ Available books for students on social-emotional issues
- ★ Using Emojis (which is particularly relevant for today's children)
- ★ Keeping an eye on sad children and giving them more attention
- ★ Asking excited kids to share what they are excited about

An administrator's form for observing a teacher will include the following questions if the objective is to encourage teachers to create classroom environments conducive to learning:

- ★ As you enter the room, is it welcoming? As demonstrated by what?
- ★ Does the room inspire critical thinking and creativity? How?
- ★ Were the students involved in developing the norms and rules? Are they displayed?
- ★ Do students help solve violations of classroom norms and rules? How?
- ★ Are there celebrations of success? How?
- ★ Is the room well-organized and clean? As demonstrated by what?
- ★ Is individual and/or group success defined as giving forth maximum effort?
- ★ Does the teacher listen actively? Do students show indications of active listening skills?

John Hynes coached the New Jersey Devils hockey team for five years through December 2020. During the press conference announcing his hiring in June 2015, Hynes said his first goal would be to get to know his players, what they need, and what they should expect from him and his vision for the club. "I think what goes into winning is across the board, whatever level," Hynes said. "It is connecting with people. It's having solid structure and a plan and trying to maximize the group you have."

The use of sports analogies in this chapter may risk leaving the impression that the authors endorse the win-at-all-costs philosophy of many in college and professional sports. This is not so. Scoring high on standardized tests is education's version of winning. The authors strongly argue against the nature and extent of these tests, so there is certainly no intent to exalt the significance of winning and competitiveness in education. The reason for quoting winning coaches is to point out that there are certain qualities that leaders in all aspects of life hold dear and that to create a culture and environment that demonstrate caring is simply sound policy for a leader in any field—and teachers and administrators ARE leaders.

COMMONSENSE CONCLUSION

If we would only ask ourselves when viewing a room upon entering, "How invited and comfortable would I feel if I entered this room for the first time and was asked to spend considerable time here? What messages would the appearance of this room send to me?"

19

Teaching Good Citizenship Prepares Students for Life and Raises Student Achievement

Image by Afzal Khan. With permission

Students Need to Be Taught How to Participate in a Democratic Society

At some time in every teacher's career, a student has challenged a teacher's directive with, "You can't make us do that, it's a free country!"

DOI: 10.4324/9781003284697-22

Students need to be taught about their rights as well as the limitations and responsibilities of those rights. Three world-renowned schools, the School Without Walls, Central Park East, and the Ithaca Alternative School, each build in time during the week for students to participate in democratic forums. Central Park East founder and first principal Deborah Meier recently told the authors that in helping students learn about democracy, it is important to teach them appropriate ways to resist authority. "I always reminded teachers that it is not their job to eliminate resistance to authority. Instead, they need to turn resistance into a learning experience."

DON: Ithaca Alternative School founder Dave Lehman told me many years ago that you do not teach students how to participate in a democracy by telling them about it. "You teach them by having them do it."

DAN: Every Friday morning for 90 minutes, School Without Walls students were involved in "Decision-Making" that involved classroom, school-wide, neighborhood, city, state, national, and world issues. I recall one class proposing to the students and staff that due to the increasing number of assaults at bus stops, they would recruit the city mayor, a police officer, and a self-defense expert to discuss strategies at a town meeting with the entire school. Students voted to approve the proposal and a rich learning experience evolved for our students.

Good Parents Raise Their Children to Be Good Citizens

The following are excerpts from a February 9, 2020, article by Matthew Futterman, New York Times sports columnist, sharing discussions he had with Jeff Shiffrin, father of the Olympic skier, Mikaela Shiffrin: "I told Jeff a story of how at a lunch a few months back, Mikaela, who had come by my New York office with a half-dozen others, had been the only one to help me carry the trays of sandwiches and salads. When lunch was over, the gold medalist started clearing everyone's plates and throwing them in the garbage. Again, she was the only one doing this. Jeff chuckled and took a sip of his drink. 'Hearing stories like that about Mikaela is so much better than watching her win a gold medal,' he said."

Futterman ended the article relating another occasion when he and Jeff were at a party at U.S.A. House, the social headquarters for the American team. "Neither of us really wanted to be there. We were cold, it was late and loud, speakers booming with music for the younger set. The Olympics were nearly over, and we were both pretty exhausted, but we both had an obligation to be there for the same reason. We had to keep an eye on his daughter, then an 18-year-old budding celebrity enduring all the pressures and pitfalls that come with that.

"In fact, we didn't (need to keep an eye on her). There was not much chance of Mikaela Shiffrin doing anything that was going to make headlines. So when we drifted to a quieter spot to kibitz, I mentioned that I was impressed with the gold medal, but more taken with this thoughtful kid, self-conscious beyond her years, able to speak in long paragraphs rather than sound bites, unafraid to admit her fears and very aware of her good fortune. 'You have no idea how much that means,' he said, 'This stuff,' he gestured to the seemingly glamorous event unfolding nearby and all the attention being heaped on his not-so-little superstar, 'none of it matters.'"

Jeff's daughter had obviously been taught, and now modeled, the qualities of "good" character. But what about the too many children who do not receive this kind of education at home? Despite the trauma and emotional turmoil many preadolescents and young adults experience in their lives, few schools spend significant time on helping students develop citizenship, character, and social-emotional skills.

The pressure of mandated high-stakes standardized testing, curricula, and even pedagogical mandates prevent many schools from engaging students in meaningful discussions and activities to encourage them to explore the values and behaviors that make up the qualities of good character (Abeles, 2011).

Unfortunately, too many of the people making the decisions about what our schools should look like are people with doctoral degrees who got to their level of influence and salary by listening to lectures, writing lengthy research papers, and getting high grades on standardized tests. They often think everyone should go through the same educational process they experienced. Too often, they believe that content learning in math, science, social studies, and English are so important that they do not allow time in a curriculum for student development with citizenship, character, social justice, and social-emotional issues. How to open a bank account or write a check is considered good to offer only if there is room in the curriculum for a business course, but they are considered digressions from the main purposes of education and are usually sacrificed if they interfere with core discipline content, graduation requirements, test preparation, or budgetary concerns.

DAN AND DON: We acknowledge that there are excellent, well-rounded people who have earned doctoral degrees and contribute to the improvement of our educational systems. Some of them are among the researchers touting the ideas being proposed in this book. We do not propose to disqualify people from positions of authority in the educational process who have earned a doctorate. We do, however, strongly advocate that all education leaders reevaluate the mandated content and skills that students need to become effective, responsible citizens in a complex, diverse, inequitable society. Until they do, songwriters like Simon and Garfunkel will continue to sing about "all the crap I learned in high school," while some students with graduate degrees who have not learned to think critically will continue to espouse baseless conspiracy theories.

Image by Afzal Khan. With permission

 Strategy 136: Teaching the Importance of Respecting Those with Whom You Must Work

To prepare students for the real world after schooling, Professor Vermette has a simple activity that he uses the first time he is about to introduce group work to a new class of students: "Turn to the person next to you and shake his hand. While holding the shake, first one of you, then the other, repeat after me: 'I do not have to like you, but I will work with you and I will respect you.'"

Upon hearing this activity described at a workshop, a veteran teacher arose and, smiling, said, "I learned that from Dr. Vermette twenty years ago and I use it all the time." Another teacher shared an experience she had with a former student, five years after he had graduated, who told how he had said that to a fellow construction worker who would not give him the time of day. According to the student, "He didn't instantly take a liking to me, but he did stop the sarcasm and we were able to work together for the first time."

In the movie *A Beautiful Day in the Neighborhood*, Mr. Rogers, as played by Tom Hanks, is asked, "What is your major objective when you work with children?" To paraphrase Mr. Rogers's response: Children have a lot of issues that cause them stress. I just want to help them address their issues. We believe that public schools can effectively integrate Mr. Rogers's logic and emphasis into all K–12 school curricula.

✅ Strategies 137–145: How to Integrate Social Justice Issues into Mandated Curriculum

The following are examples of lessons on citizenship, social justice, and/or social-emotional goals that experienced learner-centered teachers were successfully able to weave into the required curriculum.

★ A middle school staff agrees that class periods will be shortened every Monday by ten minutes, and the first hour will be used for school-wide decision-making, during which school, neighborhood, community, or national issues will be discussed, explored, and acted upon through class proposals. One sixth-grade class decides that the school needs to clean up the litter around the school every Monday morning and proposes that each class rotate that responsibility. The entire school votes on the proposal, and it passes. Another class initiates a proposal for the entire school to engage in sexual assault prevention training.

★ After reading *The Red Badge of Courage*, a ninth-grade English teacher directs students to brainstorm the values that they believe are most admirable in people, and she posts them as students respond. She then directs students to list the three values from this brainstormed class list that they believe are most important to them and to give two reasons for each of their choices. Students are then placed in groups of three where they must practice the skills of active listening as they share their lists and reasons, and then as a group narrow their list down to the three most important values. The teacher then asks groups to share their lists with reasons and to present why the task may have been difficult. Students then write an essay on how the main character demonstrated these values or how it would have changed the story if the character had not done so.

★ A fifth-grade teacher directs her students to list "20 Things I Love to Do." She then asks students to draw several vertical columns for checkmarks, with the first column labeled "With Friends," and the other columns labeled "Helps Others," "Good Feelings," "Learn Something New," "Costs Money," "Involves Family," "Last Time I Did It," "Involves Technology," and "Involves Physical Exertion." She has the students place a checkmark next to any of their "20 Things ..." that meet the criterion. After the students are given time to review and think about their responses, they are asked to write about what five conclusions they can reach about themselves and what changes they would like to make in their lives. Their teacher collects the assignment, does not grade it, but writes positive comments and clarifying questions on each student's paper.

★ School communities (teachers, administrators, students, and parents) can conduct problem-solving activities to identify the citizenship skills, values, and character and well-being traits that they believe are important for all members of the school community to develop. Once these skills and traits have been identified, discussions occur in each group to identify activities, instructional units, speakers, all-school activities, etc., for making the identified values, character, and citizenship and social-emotional skills a meaningful part of the school.

★ As preventative or reactive activities, teachers can conduct "moral reasoning" activities that focus on issues of character and citizenship that many students will encounter. For example, students could be presented with a moral dilemma involving one student seeing another student shoplift. In groups of three, students will brainstorm alternative responses, list and evaluate the advantages and disadvantages for each alternative, come to a consensus on an action with reasons, and then present their decisions to the class. The teacher acts as the facilitator, asking the groups questions, such as, "Who gets hurt, and who gets helped with this decision?" "Which solution do you think is the fairest and why?"

★ Since one of the main traits of individual well-being is having positive relationships with others, seek to build friendships among students—especially among those who are more introverted. Select a few students to help you form friendships with the shy students. Teach these helpers how to approach the other students with sensitivity.

★ Assign small groups of students to investigate selected Constitutional amendments that have a direct impact on their lives. Have each group research an amendment and demonstrate to the class some of the societal issues that these amendments deal with.

Ask students to "rank-order," write about, and present which of the amendments are most important to them.

★ Teach students Maslow's Theory of "Hierarchy of Needs" by dividing the class into five groups and assigning each group one of Maslow's needs: physical, safety, love and belonging, recognition, and self-actualization. Have each group research the specific need they are assigned with the understanding that they will have to teach other students about it. Direct each group except one of its members to go to a different table. The new groups will now have a member representing each of Maslow's needs. The teacher directs representatives of the lowest Maslow need, physical, to teach the other members about that need. After a set time limit, the student assigned to research safety presents to her group, and so on, until each of Maslow's needs has been presented. Following the presentations, a discussion of what happens if the needs are not met is led by the teacher. Students are then asked to return to their original groups and create at least three strategies that could be used in the school to assist students and teachers in having Maslow's needs met at the school.

★ Direct each student to interview a family member and two other adults in their neighborhood or family on what they think is the neighborhood's most important problem and the reasons for their choice. As an entire class, have each student share and post their top choice and reasons so others can view them. Divide the class into small working groups of two to four students, and have each group decide on one of the problems and create their own solution. Follow this by having each group present its plan to the class. Direct each group to modify its plan based on class feedback and prepare for a "Shark Tank"–type presentation to an invited local legislator.

COMMONSENSE CONCLUSION

Parents and students are clear: They want children to learn the skills and attitudes to be lifelong learners who can become successful and happy citizens. For this to happen, we need to teach our students how to participate in a democratic society.

20

More Activities to Start the Year or to Use Any Time

Mr. Dundy greeted his 23 students on the first day of class and asked them to help him set rules for appropriate behavior. He had his own list of ten rules, but he did not share it with the class. As students called out suggestions, Mr. Dundy recorded them in view of everyone. After 15 minutes, the student list included eight of the items on his list, a few additional items that he could accept, and one item that was a lot harsher than anything he would have required.

He then shared the two items on his list that the students hadn't suggested and asked if anyone thought either was unfair. No one voiced an objection—it was Mr. Dundy's experience that none would object because, in his words, "Students are so starved for involvement in decisions that affect them that they rarely object to anything I want to add. If they do, I might ultimately insist on adding my items. After all, it's a negotiation process. If students propose eight of ten items as classroom rules, they'll have ownership."

These activities could easily fit in the chapter on placing students at the center of a lesson. However, when utilized early in the year, they help to establish a favorable climate, and this renders them of even greater value when addressing the affective domain. They also convey a message to students: "I like you; I care about you as a person; I am not just someone who knows it all and is going to stuff information into your head."

DOI: 10.4324/9781003284697-23

✅ Strategies 146–153: Start the School Year with These Activities

While the following activities are ideal for the start of a semester or school year, they can be effective at any time. In fact, if class is not going so well, some of these activities later on in the year might rescue the course for the teacher.

★ Almost immediately, the first day of class, create student interaction as a means toward introducing students to each other and the teacher. The purpose is partly to create a safe and nurturing environment for learning. Based on their experiences in other courses, your students have probably begun your course expecting to be bored with lengthy lectures—surprise them!

Pair students and ask them to share three pieces of information: name, favorite hobby, one personal goal for this class. Thirty seconds might be allotted for each student to share. After a minute, ask students to partner with another student and share the same three pieces of information. Repeat with different partners three or four times.

Prior to the last pairing, alert the students that they will be expected to introduce their next partner to the entire class by sharing their names and the unique features of that individual.

★ In a learner-centered classroom, there will be a lot of planned chaos. Students should be excited by activities, and there will be noise from meaningful discussions and students enjoying their work. You will need a way to bring the class to order quickly when you want to process out the activity, give a prompt, or have another reason for calling the class to order.

Use a signal that everyone recognizes, and teach them that it means they should cease work and focus their eyes on the teacher or classroom leader. For example, "When I raise my hand, you raise yours and cease talking." With this signal, even if some students have their backs to the teacher, they can see the hands of their peers raised and get the message. To ensure students will not raise their hands and keep speaking, you might consider asking them: "Pretend there is a string tied from your hand to your mouth. When you raise your hand, the string closes your mouth."

Some teachers not only insist on silence when all hands are raised but also, "I want all eyes looking at my eyes." Important: Do not begin to speak until there is absolute silence or all eyes are on you—whatever you have set as the requirement. If you start to talk over noise, you can count on always having the same level of noise to talk over.

★ Similar to the previous example with Mr. Dundy, negotiate a discipline policy with the students. This can be done on the first day of school or any time during the year. Rather than announce the classroom rules, ask students, "What do you think should be the rules for this class?" As the teacher, you will have a list of the rules you require as the necessary items for a discipline policy. The list will be as short as possible, but it will not be shared with the class at this time. Your objective is to create two separate lists. You will then ask the class, "What do you think are ways we should expect each other to behave?" Also, "What do you think you have a right to expect of me?" Students can be asked to respond individually, in pairs, or in groups no larger than four. They are given time to think about, discuss, and then record their responses (or you can create a list from students' verbal responses).

You then add anything to the list that is on your original list that has not been offered by students. We know of one teacher who added only one behavioral expectation to every class list: "Everyone is responsible for their own behavior!" The list can then be posted for reference throughout the year. If students are too young to record responses, this process can be done verbally with the teacher taking responses from the front of the room and listing them where all can see.

★ For a learner-centered activity, Jack Drury suggests that teachers can lead students to a consensus on what constitutes a Quality Audience. Ask the class, "If someone in our class is behaving appropriately while listening to someone speak or present, what would he be doing and not doing?" Discuss this in pairs and be prepared to share qualities that can be heard or seen." Once a class list is created of appropriate behaviors of members of a Quality Audience, it is negotiated for acceptance with the class, posted, and referred to during the year whenever necessary. For instance, a tenth-grade teacher observed two students talking to each other while another student was addressing the class. The teacher simply walked toward the posted list of qualities, hand-signaled for the attention of the two students, and then pointed toward "listen while the teacher or other students are talking," and that solved the problem. Nothing had to be said.

★ Create a series of getting to know you questions like, "What do you like best about school?" "What name do you like for teachers to use when calling on you?" "What's your favorite kind of learning activity?"

★ Ask students to describe the most satisfying learning activity they have experienced from elementary school. From last year? Outside of school?

★ Try an inside-outside circle. Put four to six students in a circle facing outward. Put the same number of students on the outside of the circle but facing inward so that they are each face-to-face with a student on the inside. Review or teach them the art of active listening. Pose a question similar to the questions referenced above. Give students anywhere between 40 seconds to a minute (depending on the complexity of the question) for one student to respond to the student opposite. Then allow the same amount of time for the other partner to share. After each of the students in each pair has shared with the other, ask students on the inside circle to stay put while those on the outside move to their right to face another student. Repeat the process. If there are time constraints, it is not necessary to continue until everyone on the outside has shared with each person on the inside circle.

Some teachers have used this activity as an icebreaker, but it can also be used throughout the year to engage students in discussions of subject content. Just pose questions that require students to think critically about whatever they are being asked to learn.

★ As suggested in Chapter 11, teach students how to engage in discussions as active participants and listeners. Reinforce your guidelines each time you conduct a class discussion so that students learn to use listening skills, seek to understand before trying to be understood, distinguish fact from opinion; cite multiple sources to support an argument, and avoid irrelevant arguments.

COMMONSENSE CONCLUSION

Good activities can contribute to student learning, as well as their overall happiness with the way they are learning.

Section Four

Do Students Find School Relevant?

Classroom Tasks Must Be Meaningful and Authentic
9/11 and COVID-19: Opportunities for Student Learning

Information to be learned and understood
must be perceived by students as relevant
to their lives, or they will be unmotivated to
engage in teacher-designed activities.

21

Classroom Tasks Must Be Meaningful and Authentic

As the students entered the classroom on January 7, 2021, several were talking about the insurrection at the U.S. Capitol the day before. They were eager to engage in a discussion or some kind of activity through which they could express their viewpoints and learn more about the event. Ms. Bryan quickly took attendance and started the class by saying, "I know many of you are interested in discussing yesterday's news, and we can spend about ten minutes on that. Then it'll be back to covering the curriculum. We've got to get you guys ready for that state exam!"

The students were visibly enthusiastic when Ms. Bryan announced they would be discussing the events of January 6. However, when she said the discussion would be limited to ten minutes, there was a collective sigh from the students, and one in the back of the room whispered to her friend, "WOW, ten whole minutes for us to discuss, and she'll probably talk for eight of those ten."

According to the University of Wisconsin's Fred Newman (Newman, 1997):

1. A task is authentic when it has personal or public value for the learner.
2. A task is authentic if the student is motivated by something other than a grade (or reward) from the teacher or a desire to please his/her parents.

Each definition provides guidance to teachers for designing authentic, meaningful learning activities. For example, students writing a letter to the editor or

DOI: 10.4324/9781003284697-25

a legislator on an issue they feel strongly about is both meaningful and authentic because it has personal value for the student. Another example is having secondary students select a publication to write to and then write and submit their articles to those publications. What additionally makes a lesson "authentic" is if students are using the same skills and content that would be used in the real world. This is what gives a lesson personal or public value to the student.

The second definition often affords teachers an easy guide to building authenticity into a lesson. It encourages teachers to think in terms of who the audience can be for a student product or process: classmates, parents, community or town board members, a legislator, an administrator, or another teacher who can be asked to stop in to view student work or a performance demonstration. Even when students work as part of a pair or small group, they often feel compelled to raise the standard of their work out of concern of disappointing others.

Can "worksheets" be made relevant to student needs and interests? It depends on whether they allow students to focus on content and skills that align with their interests and whether students find the work sufficiently relevant and motivating.

Strategies 154–157: Examples of Authentic Tasks

★ Students conduct an environmental study of the community and submit findings to a local town board.
★ The school chorus or band performs for parents and community members.
★ An art class creates an exhibit of worldwide holiday celebrations for display in the school lobby.
★ Students share portfolios of their work with parents or a community member.

These are examples of authentic, real-world tasks that have the potential to generate personal AND public value for students. Helping students identify "authentic" audiences is also a valuable student learning experience for developing compassion and empathy skills.

Strategies 158–160: Real-World Data and Audiences Beyond the Teacher

★ High school students plan the school's annual senior trip and use actual data from AAA maps, hotel prices, and meal charges. The experience is even more "authentic" if students actually take the trip, but either way, there is a large degree of authenticity because they are working from real-world, not hypothetical, data.

★ First-grade students create real-world posters or drawings that the teacher indicates will be displayed for visitors to see during parents' night.

★ Visitors (parents, other teachers, other students, the principal) visit a class to view a project or see a performance, discussion, talk, or another kind of student exhibit. Thus, students are motivated by reasons other than a teacher-assigned grade.

✅ Strategies 161–168: Authentic Tasks that Challenge Students to Think Critically

The following authentic tasks can be the basis for the main activities of a lesson or unit. Notice how each task will require the learner to think critically and to make dozens of decisions. Each decision requires the learner to synthesize past experiences with new information in order to determine the next steps of the task.

Students can be asked to do the following:

★ Create a project for a science fair.

★ Prepare a booklet of math problems for people to solve that will be distributed throughout the school, the community, and even elsewhere in the world. In the 30-minute video "Good Morning Miss Toliver," this award-winning teacher can be seen taking her students on a walk through the streets of a city as the students identify problems they can design for inclusion in their book. This would work equally well in a rural setting with students walking out the doors to the school and circling the playground and grounds surrounding the school. On their walk, students might discover right angles on tree branches and quadrilaterals in the fencing surrounding the school and athletic fields and come up with all kinds of inventive problems they could design around objects and sightings in their surroundings.

★ Create an experiment that demonstrates something students have learned in science or designed themselves, which can be presented before a few parents who will come to school to be an audience.

★ Conduct a student-run class: It is best to set aside two days for this lesson, so you will want to select content that is important for students to learn. Divide your students into groups and assign each group a lesson to teach the rest of the class for a specified amount of time. For an English class in which everyone has read a particular story or novel, each of four groups can be assigned one key element—conflict, character, plot, or setting—to study and then teach to the rest of the class, focusing on how that element impacts the outcome of the story.

★ Display student work for viewing by other students, parents, and/or community members. For example, one teacher displayed at a local mall more than a dozen games that students had built. Specific elements of science, social studies, math, foreign language, or English had to be addressed for the successful completion of the game. When asked how she could be certain the student games would result in meaningful learning, the teacher responded, "I distributed criteria that needed to be addressed, and I required students to submit a detailed proposal before I would provide the resources and permission for them to proceed."

★ Make, bake, or analyze and present something using only the resources that would have been available at a certain point in our history.

★ Write a letter that someone living in a free or slave state in 1863 might have written to a friend: Ask students to be prepared to read their letters to a few parents who will come to class and who may ask them to respond to questions about what they wrote.

★ Create in small groups a recipe for a Thanksgiving dinner item that could have been made and served in 1808. You could then prepare the food for students to take home, or to eat as a class lunch. You can end the activity with the students sharing their recipes. For even greater authenticity, you could have the class create a cookbook the students could take home.

A Significantly Underutilized Format for Designing an Authentic Activity

To design authentic learning experiences for students, one class can be an excellent audience for another. Teachers often reject such partnering because they mistakenly think they need to have common planning time with another teacher and/or the same students in each class. When teachers of two different classes, often at different grade levels, partner on a task, students are motivated because

1. They have an audience other than the teacher for a grade,
2. Older students love to mentor younger students,

3. Younger students look up to older students, and

4. Students want to perform well in front of their peers.

✅ Strategies 169–172: Getting Two Classes to Be Audiences for Each Other

Here are some examples of utilizing two classes to create authentic learning experiences. Notice that each could be planned in one five-minute telephone call and none requires the partnering teachers to have the same students:

★ A sixth-grade class read stories to a kindergarten class, and the kindergarteners taught a dance step to the sixth graders.

★ A fourth-grade class and a second-grade class created a booklet on Native American culture. Each fourth grader was teamed with a second grader to write a chapter or part of a chapter for the booklet, or to create an illustration about the story. The fourth-grade teacher said, "I knew this would be a success even before the classes had met when I saw how excited my fourth graders were to hear that they would be mentoring younger children." Whether a pair of students is assigned an entire chapter, a page, one drawing, or just a paragraph can be tailored by the teacher to the perceived capabilities of the students in each pair so that not every student has to be assigned the same workload. The key, according to Vermette, is not to pair two students with such divergent abilities that the higher-performing student will not benefit from the partnership and the other student will not simply tag along.

★ An art teacher and a grade-level teacher teamed up to create an illustrated story. The grade-level students began by writing the story, and then the art class added illustrations. Then it went back and forth as each group contributed to the editing process. This has been successful anywhere from kindergarten to 12th grade.

★ An 11th-grade science teacher allowed students to volunteer to skip their Friday labs to instead teach the content of the labs to fourth-grade students.

Equalize Learning Opportunities by Offering Options

One way of maximizing the degree of "authenticity" for every student is to have options so that every student can address the teacher's learning objectives in a way that is suited to their individual strengths. Options can include allowing students to write an essay, give an oral report, or create a diorama, poster, or some other method that relies on artistic or musical initiative.

Options are critical to increasing the chances every student will learn, and they are essential if the activity requires an assessment. If a student understands major concepts in a physics course, but a test question requires the learner to demonstrate understanding by drawing a concept map, then the assessment is as much about the student's knowledge of concept maps as it is of knowledge of the physics material. When students are required to write an essay response to a question, is this an assessment of their knowledge in history, or science, or reading comprehension, or does the student with better writing ability have the advantage? In fact, doesn't it penalize the student who might be able to demonstrate knowledge with a concept map or verbal explanation but is a poor writer?

A lesson can also have increased authenticity for students if it relies on commonly-known national or global events. Following 9/11, few teachers built lessons around that tragic—and rare-in-a-lifetime—event. COVID-19 provides opportunities for linking lessons to an authentic event that everyone is sure to be aware of. See examples in the chapter on COVID-19.

✅ Strategies 173–175: Assign Students to Work with Resources in Their Local Environment

With a little creative thinking by the teacher, it is relatively easy to link almost any lesson to authentic events of which students are aware. And, to add authenticity to a lesson does not require that every student use the same information at the same time. Consider the following for instance:

★ Measure the length and width of a sofa in your home; then measure the width of the nearest doorway to that sofa. Bring those statistics with you tomorrow, and we'll use them in a math lesson.

★ Or for students who may never have ventured more than 20 miles from their hometown, instead of a math problem involving London and Paris, try something they can connect to: "It is five miles from McDonald's to our school. The speed limit is 30 miles an hour between there and here. Assume it will take you seven minutes to place your order for an Egg McMuffin and depart McDonald's from the time you arrive there in the morning. What time do you need to arrive at McDonald's in order to arrive at school by 7:30 am for the start of classes?"

One More Example

We are spending a lot of time discussing authentic learning because we believe it is a critical aspect of a successful learner-centered classroom. Here is another example of an authentic task verses a more traditional one and how the learner-centered approach is more likely to result in greater student learning.

> Traditional Teacher: Imagine you are a teacher who is trying to assign an authentic (real-world) task, but you came from a more traditional teaching background. You intend to ask students to prepare a project for a science fair coming up in two months. You begin with a ten-minute lecture explaining the rules and procedures for having a proposal accepted. Students sit quietly. A few are attentive, but most are bored, lost in their own thoughts of anything except the information you are attempting to impart.
>
> Learner-Centered Teacher: As an alternative, you skip the opening lecture and immediately inform the students you would like them to develop, individually or with a partner, a proposal for submission to a science fair. You state emphatically, "You will not be graded on the quality of your proposal, provided you exert maximum effort on this activity and provided your proposal addresses a few criteria I will distribute in writing and post on the wall."

Then ask each student to list or orally state their three major hobbies or interests. Having heard from each student, you now ask students to take ten minutes to think of something they might want to propose for the science fair. As you hear from students, you do some coaching for those students having difficulty coming up with a good idea. "You two like hockey—what if you worked together to design a board or electronic game about hockey that will demonstrate something related to the speed with which a round object can be propelled along an ice surface?" Or, "You like to read by yourself. What about a resource list of books and articles related to topics that are required learning in science at our grade level? I can provide you with a curriculum outline for any grade level you choose."

After the students have each selected an idea for their proposal (it may take more than one class period), you announce, "You are doing so well on this project and I am proud of you. Therefore, for the time and effort you are putting in, I want to make sure you have a good chance of having your proposals accepted for display at the science fair. I will distribute in writing, and go over verbally, a list of the rules and procedures you will need to follow to give your proposals the best chance for acceptance."

You then give the exact same lecture that the teacher in the first example (traditional teaching) would have given at the start of the lesson, but now the lens for listening that the students will use includes the idea they have invested their time developing. The students now have a frame of reference for understanding, and being interested in, the information you will impart in your lecture.

Continuum of Authentic Tasks

A task or project is not simply authentic or not authentic. There are degrees of authenticity, which the graphic that follows attempts to capture. No project or task has the same degree of "authenticity" for every student. What excites and motivates one student may not have the same effect on another. The goal for the teacher is to achieve as high a degree of authenticity for every student as possible.

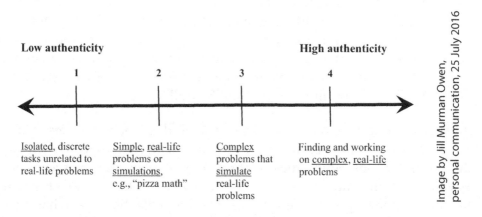

Image by Jill Murman Owen, personal communication, 25 July 2016

Tasks become more authentic on two dimensions: (1) their complexity (e.g., use of higher-order skills) and (2) their similarity to real-life problems.

Few classrooms solely use tasks on the far right of the continuum. Many teachers who are committed to authentic instruction simply try to use tasks that are to the right of the middle of the continuum, recognizing that some tasks will be more genuine and complex than others.

Checklist for Designing an Authentic Task

1. Do students have options for approaching a task? As mentioned, options are important because what is authentic for one student may not have the same degree of authenticity for another.

2. Do the options allow students to function in their areas of strength (i.e., strongest multiple intelligences)? The question may arise, "Shouldn't we encourage students to work on their weaker intelligence domains?" Students are often in the position of having to learn in ways that require them to utilize their weaker intelligence domains, particularly those students whose psycho-linguistic skills are weak. This is because teaching styles vary considerably among the instructors a student is exposed to. It is therefore highly probable that all students spend a share of their school day having to function in their weaker areas of intelligence in order to accommodate the styles of some of their teachers.

   Given that perspective, we need to allow students to function in the domains where they are strong if we want them to experience success and be motivated to learn. This is best accomplished by offering choices in how to address assigned tasks.

3. Does the task provide students with real-world data and challenge them to solve a real-world problem?

Here is an example of what you could call "the ultimate authentic task." Try preparing students to conduct a parent-student-teacher conference in which the student discusses with the parent and teacher the skills and knowledge he has improved since the last conference. There are ideas online for student-run parent conferences that can be found through a simple Google search for "student-run parent conferences."

COMMONSENSE CONCLUSION

The more authentic students perceive a lesson to be, the more likely they will work independently for longer periods of time, which gives the teacher time to coach/tutor individual students or small groups. When a teacher individualizes instruction, it demonstrates respect for students which, in turn, generates student respect for the teacher.

22

9/11 and COVID-19

Opportunities for Student Learning

Ms. Lazio says to Mr. Spade in the school faculty room, "COVID-19 is a terrible tragedy for so many people, but it does give us a chance to make school really relevant for our students. How many events occur where you can count on every student and every parent to be impacted?"

"I'd love to include it in a lesson," Mr. Spade responds, "but I haven't got time to add anything to the curriculum. And besides, the SATs are coming up."

"Can't you teach what you have to teach and build your lesson around COVID-19? Wouldn't that be motivating for students?" Ms. Lazio persists: "Can't you teach about chemicals by having your students research the chemical composition of the vaccines? Think about it!"

The tragic 9/11 terrorist attacks on New York's World Trade Center and Washington's Pentagon building are perfect examples of how most teachers and administrators denied their students a critical "teachable moment." After 9/11, the authors interviewed many teachers, asking whether they spent much class time challenging their students to think critically about this significant event in the lives of every American and many world citizens. Few teachers devoted more than a period or two to this world-changing event—usually to class discussion at the secondary level—and where time was devoted, it was largely for the purpose of allowing students to vent and pose questions. This had value, but few teachers actually created activities that would have students think critically and learn anything from such a historic event.

It became clear to us through our interviews that most teachers, with little resistance from their administrators, believed they had "to get back to the

DOI: 10.4324/9781003284697-26

mandated curriculum" rather than integrate the event into lessons that met students' social-emotional needs, as well as society's needs.

COVID-19 and 9/11 may be the only events since the assassinations of the 1960s where educators can anticipate that every student and every parent is aware of what has happened. These tragedies had a rampant impact throughout the nation's public schools, homes, and public institutions. Will educators ignore COVID-19 as they did with 9/11 when some students had burning questions about terrorism, the role of religion, politics, government response, war, motivation, Afghanistan, Palestine, and Israel and all students needed to learn more about these related topics? Even the youngest children are aware of COVID-19 to some degree. While the questions a teacher might pose to students at a lower grade level will be far less sophisticated, some time spent in class discussion, with opportunities for small group interaction, can be a valuable learning experience for every child.

There is an obvious dilemma for teachers and education policymakers who want to meet the needs and interests of students and society, versus assuring that students have all the content information to pass end-of-the-year, high-stakes exams. A solution to the problem is to integrate COVID-19 into a lesson on content you are mandated to teach. Think of the increased motivational factor if students are using activities focused on COVID-19 instead of hypothetical situations that many have never experienced and find unreal, such as, "The train leaves Paris …," or "How many pineapples can fit in …?" The double "bang for the buck" of this approach is the value students will gain from studying this historic happening in depth.

Unfortunately, many teachers may only see the blending of mandated content with an out-of-school event as taking extra time from an already jam-packed school year. And few have the requisite experience to design such a lesson in the first place.

☑ **Strategies 176–184: Teaching about COVID-19 as Part of the Mandated Curriculum**

The following are ideas that will enable teachers to teach students about COVID-19 without taking a moment of time away from the required curriculum:

★ Science classes could be asked to research and explain why it usually takes up to 18 months from the onset of a disease until a vaccine is developed and approved for distribution. Students could also investigate how that time frame was reduced for COVID-19

vaccines, some of which took less than a year to produce and receive Federal Drug Administration approval.
★ Social studies teachers could have students study other periods in history by comparing this pandemic to other crises of similar dimensions, such as the influenza pandemic of 1918–1919.
★ In math, statistics of reported cases relative to deaths could be converted into percentages.
★ In an English class, where reading or writing is the goal, an entire curriculum could be designed around the pandemic.
★ Students could be asked to review the restrictions placed on residents in many states and discuss or write about, how music, art, and physical activity were utilized to pass the time when people were quarantined and only allowed out of their homes for essentials or for solitary physical activity.
★ Younger students can simply be asked what they know about the COVID-19 pandemic and how they feel about it.

An Activity for Students to Share Experiences

STEP ONE: Individually, ask students to think about, and write down, their most vivid experience during the worst of the pandemic. At the very youngest grades, this can be done as a verbal activity. The questions to be posed are as follows:

◆ Why did you choose this experience as the most meaningful?
◆ What did you learn from this experience and how did you learn it?

STEP TWO: Put students in groups of three; ask students in each group to share their responses to both questions. Allow approximately two minutes for each student to share; then announce when it is time for the next student in each group to share with his group.

STEP THREE: Ask students to agree on one story from their group to share with the entire class. However, set these ground rules:

◆ The student whose experience is chosen does not report out to the class; one of the other two students shares the experience.
◆ The third student explains why the student whose experience was described felt it was meaningful and what was learned from it.

STEP FOUR: If time allows, the teacher asks follow-up questions to challenge the students to think more deeply about the impact of COVID-19 on the students, the community, and the world.

STANDARDS ADDRESSED

- ◆ Ability to articulate verbally
- ◆ Writing skills
- ◆ Creative thinking
- ◆ Decision-making

Standards from any discipline can be addressed by changing the questions that are posed

An Activity for Students to Develop Questions

STEP ONE:
Explanation
Explain to students, and/or distribute in writing, that there are three levels of questions:

A. Factual, meaning who, what, or where, and when questions that give specific facts.
   Example: *How many battles were fought during the Civil War?*
B. Conceptual, meaning those that describe how and why something happened:
   Why are there more divorces now than 50 years ago?
C. Value and moral questions, which focus on importance and what is right or wrong:
   If two people each shoot someone with the intent to kill, why is the punishment for murder much harsher than for attempted murder, even though the intent of each shooters was the same? Is this fair?

STEP TWO:
Group Work
Direct students to work individually to create a question for each category, followed by having them work in groups of three to share their questions and agree on which of their nine total questions are most important. Have each group share and list them on the board.

The following might be some of the class's most important questions:

1. What caused the virus?
2. Was the United States ready to deal with it?
3. What should be done to help us if another pandemic strikes?

STEP THREE:
Responding to Questions
Rotate each group's questions to other groups and allow five or ten minutes for each group to formulate responses to the questions it received. Then have each group, in order, read one of its questions and its response. Continue around until all questions have been addressed, but just one at a time per group. After a group shares its question and a response, ask the rest of the class if they agree and, if not, why not. Try to get students to answer all the questions but intercede when necessary. You could also turn this into a game. Software is available for Jeopardy and for other games.

An Ambitious Activity

The following activity will be ambitious for all *except* the teacher who is experienced and comfortable with learner-centered teaching.

Here is how to get maximum student learning by creating a unit around the COVID-19 pandemic:

1. Decide that you or your school will spend a reasonable amount of time on the critical event—for example, two weeks or a month.
2. Decide that to meet the exam preparation for students, your class will use the expeditionary model of an "intensive" week or two devoted entirely to exam prep in exchange for the time spent on the world event.
3. Use the curriculum development model to develop the critical unit of study as
   ◆ An individual teacher,
      ◆ A subject-specific or interdisciplinary group of teachers, or
   ◆ With your individual classes.

Please go to www.learningcentered.org for the entire 14-step curriculum design model in an easy-to-apply format for use with any student group.

COMMONSENSE CONCLUSION

When schools do not address life-altering events and issues, it reinforces the belief for students that schools are irrelevant to real life and therefore boring and meaningless.

Section Five

How Do We Test What Students *Should* Be Learning?

*Assessment Practices Drive Instruction
Standardized Tests Directly Impact
What Teachers Teach, What Students
Learn, and How Students Learn*

With traditional testing, we teach and stop the
learning process to test; then we resume
teaching until it's time to test again. With
performance assessment, the assessment
continues and enhances student learning.

The real value of a rubric is that it provides an effective way
to assess a strudent's performance as opposed to using a
short answer/essay test which primarily assesses a student's
ability to memorize. Hence a typical standardized test may
assess a stuent's ability to memorize but not reveal much
about their ability to understand and apply what they have
learned.

23

Assessment Practices Drive Instruction

Myron asks his mother, "Mom, how many different kinds of conflict can be in a story? His mother asks him, "Do you know why it's important to have conflict in a story?"

"Mom, just tell me how many kinds of conflict there are. The short-answer test is tomorrow, and all I need to know is the number of conflicts that could be in a story. I don't need to be able to explain my answer."

Assessment drives instruction! Rightly or wrongly, students study for tests because of the impact they know tests will have on their grades. Teachers are too often judged on the test results of their students. Good teachers are constantly utilizing many forms of assessment in determining what students are learning and how best to improve instruction. Hence, because of the importance of assessments in driving instruction, it is critical that education professionals scrutinize the effectiveness and validity of all methods of assessment.

The problem with many tests, standardized and teacher-designed, is that they focus too much on memorization and regurgitation and insufficiently on student understanding and ability to apply and create. Standardized tests are also culturally insensitive to many students of color and immigrants, and they often focus on information that is irrelevant to students. Lyrics from two songs that were popular more than 50 years ago are indicative of the attitudes of many students toward schooling, then and now: "When I think of all the crap I learned in high school…" (Simon and Kirschenbaum, 1971) refers to all the content students are required to memorize and then regurgitate for tests that heavily influence grades, which, in turn, subsequently affect

DOI: 10.4324/9781003284697-28

post-secondary or job opportunities. From the perspective of many students, by the time they graduate from high school, they will already have forgotten much of what they had been required to memorize. Also, if students learn to be resourceful, they can recapture previously learned content with a quick Google search. For instance, if a high school graduate cannot recall the names of certain minerals or authors, or the name of the 20th president, or the person who said, "Give me liberty or give me death," they can access this information if and when it becomes relevant to their lives. Memorization of generally irrelevant facts has never served as a useful skill or useful knowledge base unless students are going to appear on Jeopardy.

Another lyric that sums up many students' attitudes toward schooling was introduced to the public by Mary Martin in the 1954 Broadway show *Peter Pan*: "I don't want to go to school just to learn to be a parrot."

As discussed throughout this book, there is a place for short-answer-essay questions because there are some things students should memorize. There are many other forms of assessment, however, that are often more reliable indicators for more critical skills, such as what a student knows, can apply, and can create. Yet, these assessments are too infrequently relied upon.

The Correlation between Performance Assessments and Rubrics

A *performance assessment* is any performance demonstration that requires students to exhibit their knowledge, understanding, and proficiency. Performance assessments serve as evidence of learning and reflect the following characteristics ("What Is a Performance Task," n.d.):

- ◆ Performance assessments are learner-centered.
- ◆ The assessments often use rubrics.
- ◆ Assessment is feedback, both to the teacher and to the students.
- ◆ Feedback is about student improvement; it is not about justifying a grade.

NOTE: A performance task does not require a formal assessment in every instance. Its purpose can be solely to advance student learning. However, a rubric is usually, but not always, the vehicle for a structured, more formal assessment of student performance. If a performance task is not utilized for a formal structured assessment, it still lends itself to formative assessment by teacher observation.

Often, when many teachers begin to use rubrics, they use the rubric in ways similar to how they always evaluated student work. For example, the student who gets 90% of the answers correct on a test will receive the highest rating on the rubric; the student with 80% correct responses may receive a "3" instead of a "4" and so on.

It can take a while before a teacher understands how a rubric can enable teachers to assess all expectations more accurately, as well as skills that they previously viewed as too difficult to assess. Rubrics are a significant innovation in the field of education. Without a rubric, a teacher might assess a student's ability to articulate thoughts verbally in one of two ways: (1) with a test that might ask a multiple-choice question about how often a speaker should make eye contact with a listener or (2) a teacher's "top of the head" judgment about how effectively a student articulates thoughts during a discussion with other students.

The rubric provides specific criteria. A good rubric guides the learner and is the vehicle for assessment. It takes assessment of student performance from educated guesswork to a measurement that has reliability and validity.

Image by Afzal Khan. With permission

To understand how far the teaching profession has come using performance assessments, but also how far it still has to go, think of how judges arrive at scores for diving or ice skating in the Winter Olympics. Isn't it remarkable that within a few seconds of a completed dive or a skater completing a routine, the TV flashes scores of several judges with very similar scores? The judges are working from a rubric. They have practiced scoring by viewing tapes of skaters, scoring them and their routines, and discussing any differences in their scores so that by the time of the event, the judges are well synchronized as to how they will interpret the criteria for each dive or skating routine. This process is called "inter-rater reliability." The reality is that throughout the twentieth century, before the use of rubrics became more widespread, skaters and divers were judged by diverse sets of standards, some of which were unrelated to the performance (such as the costume or swimsuit), and that had little correlation to the other judges' criteria.

At present, however, a growing number of teachers are doing the equivalent of letting the skaters get on the ice, yet judging their performances based on paper and pencil tests. It is as if the skaters were awarded medals based on their test scores rather than how they performed their routines. Reliable and valid performance assessment is coming to the field of education as teachers require students to show what they understand through a performance demonstration. But effective use of rubrics for performance assessment is proving to be a lengthy learning process for educators to accept and learn.

As discussed earlier, many teachers are still in the earlier stages of gaining experience designing rubrics to define expectations for their entire class on performance assignments. Therefore, it may be many years before we can expect a large number of teachers to design and utilize individualized rubrics for every student. But shouldn't that be a goal? While not all students can attain a high rubric rating, each student is capable of exerting a great deal of effort to grow and develop. The development of individualized rubric expectations, to meet the needs and goals of each student, appears to be a much fairer and more just system, especially when every student should be considered unique, learns differently, grows at different rates, and has a variety of ways of demonstrating proficiency.

Make no mistake: the use of rubrics to assess student performance may be among the most significant advances in the field of education in the past century. Consider that in 1995, when the Institute for Learning Centered Education sponsored its first weeklong summer conference modeling learner-centered practices, less than 5% of 150 cutting-edge educators in attendance had ever heard of a rubric. And among the 5% who indicated they had heard of rubrics, several later admitted they had been thinking of Rubik's Cubes, not assessment rubrics! However, almost all educators in attendance at the Institute's 2018 conference knew what rubrics are, and many were proficient with their use. So, while it is taking time for many educators to understand the value of rubrics for assessing performance, progress is evident.

Helping Students Understand Their Task

For students to engage in a lesson, they must understand three critical factors:

- ◆ A written statement of expectations, which is often accomplished with a teacher-designed rubric.
- ◆ Discussion and negotiation between students and their teacher on the expectations outlined in the rubric.
- ◆ Exemplars or discussions of student work demonstrating what different levels of performance might look like. However, we do not want "exemplars" to be models for students to replicate or imitate. We want them to individually create their own meaning, which will call upon their development and use of higher-level thinking skills.

Discussion Is Required to Clarify a Rubric's Criteria

A discussion of the expectations spelled out in the rubric is necessary because no two people are guaranteed to interpret directions the same way. If there is not a clear understanding of what the rubric intends, resulting student work can lead to conflicts that are unproductive and unnecessary. The rubric should define the level of quality anticipated. For example, a rubric stating, "The student will demonstrate an understanding of the three major causes of the American Revolution" is insufficient. The rubric must indicate what would constitute satisfactory demonstration of the intended outcome, by stating what the student must do to demonstrate understanding. An example might be "by completing a two- to three-page research paper that uses at least three different sources and appropriate citations."

 Strategies 185, 186: Negotiating a Rubric with Students

If the teacher chooses to "negotiate" the rubric with students, the process and outcome are much more likely to increase student understanding and ownership of the expectations. How do you negotiate a rubric with students? A straightforward way is simply to describe the assignment to the students and ask them what they think you should look for when you grade the end product. Let students work in pairs or groups of three or four and discuss their responses before sharing with the class. In other words, the negotiations accomplish the discussion part of creating a

> mutual understanding of the words in the rubric between the teacher and the student; as a bonus, students have engaged in a critical thinking activity in which they "create meaning."

The late education consultant and writer Grant Wiggins once described a lengthier, but worthwhile, process using English as an example. Distribute an essay, perhaps from a previous class, and ask students to work in small groups to classify each essay as excellent, average, or poor—with reasons for their ratings. Then redistribute the essays rated excellent. Ask the students to identify the characteristics these essays have in common. In essence, they will be creating their own rubric.

A college professor negotiated a rubric for journal entries he would require each week. The criteria he wanted to see in a rubric were (1) that the entries are relevant to the course curriculum and (2) that there is an analysis of at least one aspect of course content in each entry.

He also wanted entries to be a minimum of three-fourths of a page in length (anticipating students would ask "How long?" and not believing a student could demonstrate thorough analysis in a shorter commentary). He announced the minimum length requirement as a "task specification," a precondition for acceptance of the journal entry before assessing its quality. (See next page for the definition of "task specifications.")

Instead of sharing his list of these criteria, the professor asked the students what they thought should be in a journal entry that would have mutual benefit for the student and the professor. The students agreed upon a two-page minimum that would include some detailed analysis. The professor suggested adding "relevant to course content" and no one objected. If anyone had, the professor would have discussed it with the class and, unless he was convinced it was unnecessary, he would have encouraged the class to accept it—or he would have insisted upon it. After all, in a negotiation, the teacher has rights too.

But the truth is that when students are included in decision-making, they give wide latitude to what they accept from the teacher because most students are so starved for any involvement in decisions affecting them, they will accept from a teacher that which they might otherwise protest. Actually, the same is true of teachers when an administrator involves them in decision-making. Teachers, too, are often starved for involvement in the decisions that affect their ability to be successful in the classroom; as a result, they appreciate the administrator who gives them meaningful involvement and rarely will challenge what the administrator indicates is important to her.

✔ Strategy 187: Example of a Rubric for Assessing a Performance Task

Create a persuasive essay regarding immigration to the United States:

Dimensions	Criteria for a Score of 3	Criteria for a Score of 2	Criteria for a Score of 1
Understanding of the concept of immigration	The essay contains a coherent, functional definition of immigration, *all* parts of which relate to and support each other.	The essay contains a coherent, functional definition of immigration, some parts are not shown to relate to each other.	The essay contains a confusing definition of immigration, parts of which contradict or are in conflict with each other.
Understanding the causes of the immigration controversy	Four or more main causes are included and clearly explained.	Four or more main causes are included and somewhat explained.	Less than four main causes are included, and there is little explanation.
Persuasive essay	The writer takes clear positions and backs them up with logical arguments.	The writer takes clear positions, some of which are not backed with logical arguments.	The writer's positions are unclear. There is little attempt to back them up with logical arguments.
Compelling opening paragraph	The language of the opening paragraph draws the reader in and holds the reader's attention.	The language of the opening paragraph draws the reader in but fails to hold the reader's attention.	The language of the opening paragraph is vague.

Note: Dimensions align with objectives

The scoring tells us what is good, good enough, not good enough.
The criteria are the qualities of the dimension.
Chart by Pat Flynn with permission.

Task specifications are those things that must be fulfilled before student work is eligible to be assessed by the teacher. They are never part of the rubric because a rubric should address expectations for the quality of a student's work, not the expectations for the task.

In this example the task specifications are as follows:

◆ Read three assigned readings on immigration.
◆ Write a five-page essay.
◆ The essay must be neatly typed.

A common mistake of teacher-designed rubrics is to include task specifications in the rubric, whether the rubric is used for grading or formative feedback. Whether the task is completed on time, is the appropriate length, or is neatly typed has nothing to do with the quality of the product.

For a real-world analogy, think of a grant application (called an RFP, request for proposal). Contained in the RFP are requirements such as a deadline date for submission, maximum length of an abstract, and method of submission. These are the equivalent of task specifications. Grant readers will not review any application that fails to address these specifications. Only if these specifications are met will the grant reader review the application to see if the criteria are addressed and qualify the applicant for the grant.

In school, we need to separate the assessment of the quality of the student's product or performance from whether the task specifications are addressed. Teachers should not assess for quality until and unless task specifications are met, or they have negotiated other task specifications. For example, a student may prefer to create a podcast or a video documentary rather than the teacher's assigned task. Negotiation is something that happens in the real world, and students can understand this.

Words to the Wise

A brief perusal of internet sites dedicated to rubrics, from elementary through high school and college, yields a considerable number and variety of styles. Some focus on off-the-shelf rubrics, while others focus on rubric creation tutorials—and for good measure, there is an assortment of idiosyncratic takes on what a rubric is and what it should do. Several describe what it is about using different terms for dimensions and criteria but are nevertheless worthy of consideration. Some sites can be very helpful and thought-provoking; others can confuse, mislead, and misdirect. The key things to keep in mind when judging a rubric culled from the internet are these: (1) Are the dimensions (left column) truly and clearly connected to the lesson's learning objectives? (2) Do the criteria specifically describe the qualities that the task should demonstrate?

The sample rubric on immigration is concise and extremely practical. There are excellent rubrics for assessing teacher performance by recognized experts, but some extend from 44 to 60 pages in length. The lengthier the rubric, whether for assessment of student or teacher performance, the more diluted each element gets. Being human, we are more likely to focus on those aspects of the rubric that assess what we already do well. The value, of course, for teacher evaluation, is when the teacher focuses on those aspects of performance that are weakest, not the strongest. In a 50-page rubric, there is too much latitude to be selective.

Peer and Self-Assessment

While performance assessment often refers to a teacher assessing student work based on what students can demonstrate, it can also refer to the act of a student assessing the performance of a peer or himself. The act of assessing is a skill valued in the real world.

 Strategy 188: A Peer Assessment Process

Since the internet is filled with models for peer and self-assessment, we will simply give a single example. In 1993, one author walked into a third-grade class and observed students assessing other students' work in pairs. They had an outline of a map of South America on one side of a page and a list of South American countries on the other side, and they were working from a rubric the teacher had distributed. Overheard was one student saying to her partner, "I'd give it a B +." The partner thought for a moment, checked the rubric, and replied: "I'd only give it a C; Argentina is in the wrong place and so are several other countries." The "pair-share" process gives students the experience of thinking at a level that requires the use of specific criteria as opposed to simply giving their opinion.

As observers and critics, we would encourage teachers to use ratings that are more descriptive than traditional letter or numerical grades, such as "Exceeds Expectations," "Meets Expectations," and "Almost Meets Expectations." This approach gives reviewers more latitude to assess achievement or progress without labeling students as failures (e.g., using "Es" and "Fs").

Assessment by Teacher Observation

Perhaps one of the most neglected—but most important—forms of student assessment is teacher observation. Teachers are trained to assess student work in traditional forms, such as grading homework and tests. Teachers often seek to prepare their students for passing traditional, high-stakes, standardized, state-created tests by designing their own practice tests, both of which require little critical thinking or have little application to the real world. Hence a vicious cycle of "teaching-to-the-test" ensues in most classrooms. While teachers are continually observing students at work, their observations are usually obscured by the need to prepare students for standardized tests. Consequently, teacher observations, often gut-level and not formalized, are undervalued by administrators and parents. Teachers have observation skills, albeit in varying degrees, and these skills should be as valued in the field of education as much as doctors' and nurses' observations in the medical field.

As we move into an era where performance and thinking skills are valued as highly, or more highly, than the ability to memorize, teachers should have criteria for their observations and be required to document student reports based on observation of performance rather than test results.

 Strategy 189: Teacher Observation Assessment with Note-Taking

Important: In a learner-centered classroom, where students are doing the work and the teachers are the facilitators who observe, listen, and assess, opportunities abound for teachers to gather evidence of student learning. This documentation is also essential if teachers are to defend grades to parents and administrators without relying too heavily on test scores. Making notations on the class roster is a standard operating procedure that can provide much of this evidence. There are also helpful apps.

When a teacher "works the room" during an activity where students, whether in groups or individually, engage in performance learning, the teacher will overhear certain students discussing their thoughts, which will make it evident to the teacher whether the student clearly does, or does not, grasp the intent of the lesson. A teacher will not be able to make a notation on the roster for every student during a single activity, but over time, the teacher will accumulate data on each student. This information is more valuable for instructional improvement than a string of test scores. For quiet, introverted students, teachers can conduct individual conferences to gather evidence of growth and development.

Teacher observations are legitimate evidence of student learning, but they must record them before they forget them. Their judgments about individual student performances can be reflected in written comments such as, "Weak!" or "Excellent job!" Teachers should always follow such statements by completing the sentence starter, "As demonstrated by…" Students who receive no teacher comments should be interviewed by the teacher to determine their understanding and development.

COMMONSENSE CONCLUSION

Logic dictates students should be assessed based on how they can demonstrate what they know, understand, and can apply. But performance assessments can only replace pencil and paper tests when teachers, using rubrics and recorded observations, are able to document their assessments of student work.

24

Standardized Tests Directly Impact What Teachers Teach, What Students Learn, and How Students Learn

Myron said to his mother after receiving his test grade, "Mom, this isn't fair. I got marked off for an answer that was correct. The question was, 'How many sides does a square have: two, four, six, eight, or ten?' I answered two."

"Well, doesn't a square have four sides?" his mother asked. "Yes," Myron said, "but it also has two sides. I thought it might be a trick question since four is the obvious answer. But two is also correct, and I got marked off."

Standardized tests

- ♦ Tend to assess students on memorization rather than critical thinking skills;
- ♦ Set the same standard for all students, regardless of their differing learning styles and environments, which can range from caring and privileged to deprived and/or poverty-stricken; and
- ♦ Are often racist in their design.

Yet, the reality is that despite their significant shortcomings, standardized tests are an important factor in educational decision-making that is not likely to change significantly in the near future. Therefore, educators need to find ways to provide quality and equal educational opportunities for students until more equitable methods of setting expectations for students and assessing their progress become part of the process of educating children.

DOI: 10.4324/9781003284697-29

Teaching Effectively while Living with Standardized Assessments

One of the greatest concerns we have heard expressed by teachers, administrators, parents, and students is how to make teaching and learning more meaningful and enjoyable within this environment that assesses student learning almost exclusively through students' test scores. Unfortunately, high-stakes standardized tests drive what is taught by almost all teachers. This reality clearly compromises the desire of teachers to be more creative and flexible with standards, curriculum, pedagogy, and assessment, and to meet the needs and interests of students more effectively.

Standardized Tests Are Inadequate for Assessing a Student's Understanding or Ability to Apply Knowledge

How do you know whether a person understands and can apply what they have memorized unless you see them demonstrate what they are expected to do? Any of us can regurgitate information on a short-answer-essay test without really understanding what we are saying.

It Is Wrong to Use the Same Standard for Students of Diverse Backgrounds

Acknowledging that local teachers and administrators have little control over the preponderance of standardized tests, we must nevertheless reference the research-based conclusion that such tests are not an effective, meaningful measure of what a student has learned in any class (Koretz, 2017). Students begin a course at vastly different levels of competence, skill, and understanding. Given that, is it fair to expect all students to gain the same degree of knowledge from any class or learning experience? Of course not! Students are unique in many ways. The only fair way to assess individual student growth is to assess each student individually, based on their initial demonstration of skills or understanding in comparison to their next demonstration of those same skills—but not in comparison to any other student since they are unique and should not be expected to attain the same results (Kohn, 1999).

Standardized Tests Are Racist

Dr. Amy Wells, American Education Research Association president, states that the current use of high-stakes standardized assessment and curriculum is structurally racist and blatantly discriminates against students of color by teaching and testing about curricula that are racially biased and culturally irrelevant, and in the process harming millions of students (Wells: "The Inconvenient Truth About the New Jim Crow in Education," AERA Keynote Address, 2019).

As a result of these testing policies, students, teachers, and schools are too often rated as "failing." This causes many parents to "opt" their children out of standardized high-stakes tests in states where this is an option. It also causes enrollment declines in teacher preparation programs, an increase in student stress, and more of a "teaching-to-the-test" approach as opposed to instructional time spent on music, art, play, and citizenship development. Finally, the evaluation of teachers based on student test scores is unreliable and invalid (Koretz, 2017).

This kind of learning environment, combined with a lack of equitable funding of schools (especially for poverty-stricken schools), the demonization of teachers for not raising test scores, and the lack of meaningful, research-based professional development for teachers to create healthy learning environments, begs the question, "What can teachers and administrators do to make classrooms more meaningful and enjoyable for students?"

✓ **Strategies 190–197: Strategies to Make Classrooms More Meaningful and Enjoyable**

★ Use creative, relevant learning units, based on student interest, but weave in test-related skills and content. For example, middle school students are usually interested in issues related to "family," "friendship," and "love." Why not create a learner-centered unit that involves interesting novels, speakers, activities, research, plays, and discussions on these topics, but include activities that have persuasive writing, vocabulary development, listening skills, and reading comprehension as learning objectives? This will help students prepare for the real world and prepare them for passing standardized tests.

★ For assessment of important skills or knowledge, use performance-based assessments instead of short-answer-essay exams that rely more on memorization than demonstrated ability. For instance, if you want to know whether students understand the need to make eye contact and use correct body language when speaking with someone, have them interview each other and assess their performance. This is a much more effective way to gauge their skills than a multiple-choice test asking, "Which of these choices is the best when you interview someone?"

★ Emphasize formative assessment processes. Formative assessment is an ongoing information-gathering and feedback process used to adjust teachers' teaching to student needs and provide students with meaningful feedback on their growth and development. The opposite is summative assessment—a final evaluation of a student's work, usually in the form of a grade.

　　Both formative and summative assessment can be used to promote student growth and development. However, the formative process has the potential for much more impact during a student's daily classroom experiences. Many teachers regularly do this by reading a student's writing assignment or listening to them read and then adjusting their instruction to improve that student's skill or knowledge development. It can also occur by simply asking a student, "What are you having difficulty with?" and then providing the kind of clarification, experiences, or encouragement the student needs.

★ Using individualized rubrics is also an effective process. For example, if the desired skill is "creative problem-solving" and a requirement is to use several resources for research, a teacher may negotiate with students how many resources a student should read and report on, the level of quality required for an "exemplary" rating, how many for a "proficient" rating, and so on depending on the student's reading comprehension and writing abilities.

★ Try short-term, planned, test-based "intensives," a strategy that focuses "intensively" on one aspect of schooling, which could be a topic or test preparation. This is an effective strategy that some "expeditionary learning" schools use in conjunction with creative, compelling learning units. Teachers may explain to students that they want them to enjoy learning as much as possible, but they must also be prepared for being tested. As a class, they will be creative, learn and have fun, but every month or so, there will be a break from the routine—it might even get called "real learning"—and intensively prepare for the tests for a week at a time. Each day during that week will be "test-prep." There is no question that this strategy is a compromise for creative teachers, but it may be one of the best ways to deal with the bureaucratic demands to raise test scores.

★ Create more meaningful student assessment processes to accompany required school or district-imposed student report cards. This form of personalized "report card" would be unique to your classroom and would focus on the skills, projects, and values that you are expecting students to develop, in addition to whatever is emphasized by the school. A teacher-developed reporting process could be a narrative about each individual student, describing what they have accomplished, how they are doing, and what they would like to see each student focus on for development. Some creative, progressive teachers also include a space for a student "self-evaluation." Scheduling individual student conferences, if possible, also adds a great deal to creating an assessment process that is a real learning experience. The idea is to create a culture that focuses on grades' causes ("What did I learn?") as opposed to the "Wad-ja-get?" grade-obsession game.

★ Develop a portfolio process that uses parents and community professionals. Have each student create a binder for all their important classwork. Each semester, organize two separate review processes. The first is for parents to review their student's portfolio, with the student explaining what each piece of work is about and what skills or content they learned. This could occur with multiple parents and student groups operating simultaneously in your classroom (e.g., at a parent-conference event).

At another time during the semester, after having recruited interested professional individuals from the community for one or more students, have the students conduct the same process with their assigned community reviewers. Reviewers could also ask each student what they think they would like to do differently in the future and submit student/reviewer-written recommendations to the teacher. Using carefully selected community volunteers can add a great deal of real-world meaning to this assessment process, and it can be intrinsically motivating for students to grow and develop.

★ Organize a support group of teachers who can share what they have done to make teaching and learning more enjoyable and meaningful. Teachers are creative and often develop and use teaching methods that others are not aware of. This can also be a great process for sharing other issues, such as student behavioral issues. You may have to start small, with only one or two other teachers, but small numbers can be effective and grow.

The Fallacies of Standardized Testing

Test scores are inherently flawed because each student is unique, with special strengths and weaknesses based on a variety of factors: their family's income, values, environment, number of books in their home, trauma, etc. A wide range of test scores should be expected in any class of heterogeneous students, and students should be expected neither to grow at the same rate as others nor achieve the same scores. Students need to be seen as individual learners and encouraged to appreciate themselves as unique without trying to compare themselves to their peers.

Also, it can easily be argued that poverty-stricken students, many of whom experience trauma, do not have the advantages of many other students, and will inevitably have lower test scores, making them victims of unfair high-stakes standardized-testing expectations.

The flaws in testing illustrate why distance runners focus more on their personal best time in a marathon, rather than where they finish in relation to other runners. A runner who has never run a marathon in less than seven hours should not compare himself to one who rarely takes more than four hours to finish. Additionally, there is much research indicating that standardized tests are racially and culturally biased, often using language and scenarios that students of color and foreign cultures have never experienced (Wells, 2019).

Similarly, when two students begin a class with widely divergent knowledge in the course subject matter, is it realistic to compare their grades on a standardized test? If there is any conclusion to be drawn, it is that comparing students, especially through standardized tests, is counterproductive to what research on individual student growth concludes. Some would argue that standardized test scores are necessary and meaningful for college entrance, even though there is overwhelming research that shows SAT or ACT scores are not good predictors for college success. In any case, standardized tests are a poor assessment indicator of what an individual student has learned.

The High-Stakes Standardized Test Crisis

There are volumes of research on how high-stakes, standardized tests are harmful to students, schools, teachers, administrators, communities, and society. Daniel Koretz, professor of Education at Harvard University's Graduate School of Education, in his recent book *The Testing Charade: Pretending to Make Schools Better* makes several recommendations that teachers, administrators, parents, and students may wish to propose to their school, school district, or state. Among Koretz's recommendations are the following:

◆ *Test samples of the school population, rather than every student.* This testing method is used with what we consider to be the "gold standard," National Assessment of Education Progress tests. Comparisons of student demographic groups can then be made, if desired, and performance results can be used to raise questions about instructional and curricular changes. Individual scores do not count, nor are they shared.

◆ *Use standardized test results only for diagnostic purposes.* Given the negative impact of high-stakes standardized tests on students, teachers, and schools, this solution would allow sample school population data to be used to raise questions about critically important skill and knowledge development for each grade level and subgroup within that school. Schools could then make plans for improvement without public fanfare.

◆ *Create realistic and appropriate test score goals for students.* If sample testing is not used, appropriate expectations for each individual student align much better with human development research and theory. This process minimizes the occurrences of what can be an inevitable consequence of some students being labeled failures, thereby decreasing their self-esteem and love of learning.

◆ *Use performance-based as opposed to "memorize and regurgitate"–style tests:* Authentic, real-world tasks or projects through which students apply skills and knowledge is a much more meaningful method of judging a student's proficiency. Using a panel of two teachers and a professional member of the community, and including Q&A discussions with individual students, provides balance and credibility to the process. Adding the dynamic of a student presentation allows for interaction, which can enhance the learning from the process.

◆ *Pilot for validity and reliability.* Any new school, district, or statewide assessment system should undergo a process for feedback, reevaluation, and modifications to the process before it is implemented on a large-scale basis.

What about the Need for Students to Be Prepared for Standardized Tests?

Conducting a learner-centered class prepares students for standardized tests without creating test anxiety and obsession. Recently retired science teacher Becky Buckingham echoes what several learner-centered teachers say: "I would spend a few weeks preparing my students for the standardized assessments and they would do as well, or better, than students who took a semester-long course to prepare for the same exams."

As stated previously, competent teachers like Ms. Buckingham do not develop their expertise in designing learner-centered classrooms overnight. They do, however, prove the point that as our education system transitions toward assessment by performance, teachers do not have to choose between effective teaching practices and preparing their students to survive the standardized-testing mania.

A learner-centered classroom prepares students to think critically, and to understand and apply skills and knowledge. For students in such a class, the preparation for standardized tests is a by-product of an emphasis on critical thinking skills. However, it does not guarantee high test scores any more than a traditional "test-prep" emphasis. In fact, research concludes that student success and test scores are strongly correlated with family income. This fact leads to the conclusion that poverty and trauma-stricken students will generally demonstrate lower standardized test scores through no fault of their own. As a result, teachers and school administrations are caught "between a rock and a hard place." Though learner-centered classrooms will help poverty-stricken—and all—students develop more effectively, poverty-stricken students will need more coaching and ongoing formative assessment than students from higher-income families.

COMMONSENSE CONCLUSION

In the real world, we are judged by what we create rather than how well we memorize—so let us approach preparing students that way too.

Section Six

What Should All Teachers Understand?

Do we want students to learn to respect
the rights of others and to view diversity
as a strength of our democracy? If so,
the process must begin in the schools; the
one common place our youth
share and the best place to reach children in
their most formative years.

25

How to Interact with Disruptive Students

Jeremy is always happy to be sent to the office for disruptive behavior—anything to get out of algebra. His classmate Cynthia could care less that their teacher has threatened to call her mother. She knows how to turn a deaf ear to her mother and that there will be no consequences.

It may be hyperbole to suggest that making lessons interesting will eliminate discipline problems entirely, but any teacher experienced with learner-centered strategies will attest that such strategies reduce the number of students exhibiting disruptive behaviors (Cornelius-White, 2007).

It Is Not Enough to Simply Neutralize the Behavior of a Disruptive Student

One disruptive student can waste a lot of teacher and student time, as well as create a pathway to an unhappy future for herself. Perhaps the biggest weakness of many schools is not having anyone on staff with the skills, training, and, especially, the *time* to work specifically with disruptive students. This is because most schools are satisfied if they can neutralize students' negative behaviors without taking the time or expense to hire someone to work with them to avoid future disruptions.

But schools end up wasting money—and the time of teachers and other students—by sending disruptive students through revolving doors of

DOI: 10.4324/9781003284697-31

suspension, retention, and return to the classrooms without having actually addressed the root of the problem. It requires specialized training to be able to address the underlying causes of a student's disruptive behaviors and to guide the student toward more appropriate behaviors. Schools need unscheduled time for someone with the skills and training to support these students. It is ineffective to simply add this role to an already overworked assistant principal or guidance counselor.

Yes, it will cost some money to hire a person, or people (depending on the size of the district), to fulfill the sole role of working with disruptive students to help them improve at managing their behaviors, but this expense is important. Money is tight all over. But considering the cost to the education of all students, including the disruptive ones, isn't it worth taking the money to hire the necessary people and to provide them with the time to address the problem of disruptive students?

Is It Justifiable to Use Suspension?

Suspension, except in the situation where the student is a danger to self or others, is counterproductive and should be an unacceptable response, especially if the goal is to help the disruptive student grow academically and socially. Is it not logical to presume that a disruptive student is probably experiencing academic difficulties and feeling hopelessly behind, which may be the cause of his disruptive behavior? And if a student is behind in their work and taken out of class for a day—or longer—isn't it likely that upon return they will fall even further behind, become more deeply discouraged, and revert to the same disruptive behaviors?

What are the best alternatives to suspension when a student is being disruptive? A few schools have conflict resolution rooms where disruptive students experience a "time-out" and can study with a qualified teacher. Others have strategies for preempting disruptive behaviors so fewer suspensions occur. In the Baltimore City School District, according to a CBS report, some classrooms begin each day with mindfulness exercises. When asked about the impact on the students' behavior, one elementary school principal responded, "We haven't had any suspensions this year, after many in the past."

It is wise for all schools and districts to seek solutions to the problems presented by disruptive students—solutions that will cost a minimal amount of money. However, the need for fully funded behavioral specialists and equitable learning opportunities for all students exemplifies why we need a massive increase of funding for public education, especially in poor, urban schools where the potential for disruptive behavior due to poverty-induced trauma is much greater. This reality is not an indictment of the students. Their behaviors are directly related to the impact of generational poverty, with conditions often caused by historical and institutional racism and classism. Their actions often get exacerbated when teachers are not trained to understand cultural differences between the way they were raised and the experiences of many of the students in their classes.

Practice Rational Detachment

When a child is two years old and reaches for the electric socket, it is easy to remind yourself, "He's just a child," and say with a smile on your face as you pull his hand back from the outlet, "I love you, but you can't do that." And you may repeat the friendly reminder several times, always smiling and speaking lovingly, as the child repeatedly tries to return his hand to the socket.

It's quite more difficult to maintain your rational detachment when the child is a teenager towering over you, screaming swear words, and making menacing gestures. Yet, it is every bit as necessary to remain cool, calm, and collected as you attempt to deescalate the situation. Nothing is more critical to successfully dealing with a child who is being disruptive than maintaining rational detachment.

Threats Often Backfire

Of the key things to consider when working with disruptive students, let us start with what might be the most important: the ineffectiveness of threats. There is such a natural tendency to threaten a child with a consequence in an effort to use fear to deter negative behaviors. Good parents, as well as caring educators, use threats—but their children survive and thrive because they are in a loving environment. You might say they grow up to be good citizens despite, not because of, the use of threats to generate appropriate behaviors. Disruptive students, often without good parenting to offset the use of occasional threats, have probably had to deal with threats throughout their childhood. They have learned to let the threats roll off their backs.

For example, one student, raised in a dysfunctional home environment, shared that she sees a teacher's threat as a dare that prompts her to respond, "Do what yah gotta do!"

> ### ☑ Strategies 198–207: How to Address Students Following a Disruptive Incident
>
> ★ Brain research tells us that there is a gap between stimulus and reaction. This means that when someone is overreacting, disruptive, in tantrum mode, etc., it is not the time to expect to have a rational conversation. The immediate goal should be to calm the disruptive student. It could be a few minutes, an hour, a few days, or longer before it is time to expect the student to react rationally in a discussion about the disruption in which she was involved.
>
> ★ Ask questions calmly, do not lecture. Students who tend to be disruptive have heard lectures many times and have learned to tune them out. Instead, encourage students to share what their desired outcome was by their behavior and how this connected or did not connect with their goal.
>
> ★ Consider, when possible, creating a student court to solve student conflicts.
>
> ★ Keep in mind that your facial expressions, body language, and tone of voice will often generate the same response from students.
>
> ★ Demonstrate to disruptive students that despite their behavior, you know they are "more than that one behavior" and that you care and like them.
>
> ★ If possible, use restorative justice strategies that meet the individual needs of students, teachers, and the school. Restorative justice encourages students to resolve conflicts on their own or in small groups and prepares them with the necessary skills to do this. Since teachers must be trained in order to use restorative justice effectively, prioritize professional development for all staff.
>
> ★ Use logical consequences that relate to behavioral causes and outcomes. For example, having a student work with a custodian to clean a room they trashed is logical, as opposed to banning the student from his favorite art class for a week.
>
> ★ Use suspensions only when the student represents a physical threat to self or others.
>
> ★ Use moral reasoning strategies as a preventative curricular strategy in English, social studies, or advisory groups to challenge students to respond to situations that may result in disruptive behavior.

In addition, all students should be aware of the school or classroom's code of conduct—they can even be a part of creating it. Students need to clearly understand what constitutes a violation of the code and what the consequences are. The process for dealing with violations should be straightforward: "You were disruptive in class, so here is the consequence—now let us develop a plan for how you can be successful." Teachers must also be trained to respond to violations without coming across as threatening—especially in a trauma-sensitive school, where consistency is critical.

There must also be a process through which students can appeal consequences they believe are unfair. This contributes to a perception of fairness and allows for consideration of unusual factors when a violation may have mitigating circumstances.

Using Critical Thinking Skills to Address Student Problems and Behaviors

For a whole class activity, small groups of students could be asked to create situations where there might be conflict involving one of their expected behaviors. Have them role-play the incident for the class and then lead a discussion of the question, "How should this conflict be solved?" This activity can lead to meaningful, cooperative class discussions on reasonable consequences and solutions.

What about when there is a behavioral problem involving a single student, or students who must be dealt with individually? A key question to ask such students is, "How do we turn this situation into a learning experience?" As discussed earlier in this chapter, brain research tells us that there must be a lapse in time between the stimulus of the event and when you can expect to rationally discuss the event with the student. To calm a disruptive student, and before attempting any discussion, try saying nothing for a while and waiting for the student to speak. It will change the student's attitude from, "Here we go with another lecture," to, "What's going on here? What did I do that I'm responsible for?"

 Strategy 208: Handling a Behavioral Incident

The following process is an example of what could take place at a meeting between a student and teacher following a behavioral incident. The teacher and student sit down, and the teacher asks the student to respond to the following questions in writing:

1. What happened? Describe in detail.
2. Who did it help?
3. Who did it hurt?

4. What could you have done differently?
5. What might happen as a result of each of the different things you could have done?
6. Which one of these options are you committed to trying should there be a similar situation in the future?
7. What will you do to ensure that you will follow through?
8. Who will help you do this? Who are you willing to ask for help, to remind you and be your advocate?
9. When will you meet with your advocate to discuss this?
10. Please sign this as a binding contract.

Following this meeting, the teacher shares the contract with the student's family and advocate and then meets again with the student to see if she is following through. Encouragement and discussion of successes and failures with the contract are part of the process. The meetings could result in a new or modified contract.

DON: Two of my learnings over a 56-year career in education:

Listening to a psychologist discussing a ten-year-old who had been swinging a bat wildly, I learned that this was probably a cry for help.

The child knew he was out of control; his biggest fear was that no one could control him at times like these. It contributed to his security when someone was able to grab the bat and help the child avoid harming himself or anyone else. Of course, if harm had come to anyone, there would have had to be consequences. It changed my attitude and approach toward children who go out of control even as I recognize that there have to be consequences for such behaviors.

I also learned that a child's brief hostility toward you may be a sign you are reaching that child. And an educator must be able to recognize when a child is testing as opposed to just being belligerent. An idealistic young lady, fresh off the campus of Berkeley College in California, joined the staff at our overnight summer camp. For three weeks she interacted with a teenage girl and commanded positive behaviors that this child did not offer to any other staff member. One day, this teenager was seen kicking the staff member in the knees and cursing at her. Veteran staff members tried to put this rebellion into perspective. They explained that the teenager had probably experienced a childhood in which she was frequently disillusioned by adults she thought she could trust who let her down. This was her way of saying, "It is easy for you to get along with me when I am behaving; let us see if you can care about me when I am not." Unfortunately, this young staff member could only think, "After all I tried to do for her, apparently it didn't amount to anything." She was destroyed as a child advocate for the rest of the summer. I can only hope she gained a perspective over time.

COMMONSENSE CONCLUSION

School mission statements love to include references to educating "all" students. However, school policies determine whether traumatized students and those displaying inappropriate behaviors are among the "all" students we are trying to educate.

26

Schools Must Be Trauma-Sensitive

"Most of the young children separated from their parents at the border got back together with them within a few months. So, what's the big deal? My father screamed at my mother and then left home for good when I was four years old, and I still have nightmares about it and panic attacks. But I'm doing fine!" said Ms. Lund, a parent, 42 years old.

Schools in one state were losing aid because parents of students receiving free lunches were not filing the appropriate forms that would entitle the school district to reimbursement. Some districts addressed the problem with a costly extra effort; they sent social workers to homes and offered other services to encourage families to complete the required forms. However, quite a few districts adopted policies of denying students a hot lunch if their families had not completed the required forms. These students, not entirely limited to those in poverty, were entitled to peanut butter sandwiches or other such cold meals.

It gets worse.

Teachers were aware that many of these students were skipping lunch rather than be singled out in front of their peers. Where they could, teachers slipped these students money to pay for their lunches to avoid embarrassment.

It gets still worse.

In some of these schools, if a disqualified student made it to the cash register with a hot meal, the cashier would take the hot items off the student's tray and, in front of the entire crowded population of the cafeteria, deposit these items in the wastebasket.

DOI: 10.4324/9781003284697-32

When teachers complained to administrators, the explanation for these horrendous policies was often that they were necessary because the cafeteria was not solvent or the administrators had no control over the cafeteria's budget.

We are not unsympathetic to the financial difficulties confronting most school districts, but some things are so onerous that they must be addressed no matter what other priorities have to be sacrificed. The public humiliation of students, for any reason, cannot be tolerated.

We share these examples not because there were a few insensitive people allowing this shaming to occur (on the contrary, this happened in some districts with otherwise strong, effective leaders). We share it to illustrate how critical it is for educators to learn what trauma is, how prevalent it is in our schools, and how devastating it is to the well-being of students experiencing it.

Adverse Childhood Experiences (ACEs) are traumatic events occurring before age 18. ACEs include all types of abuse and neglect, as well as parental mental illness, substance use, divorce, incarceration, and domestic violence. ACE findings suggest that a large part of the adolescent student population may be silently dealing with past traumatic experiences without community or professional support ("The Benefits of a Trauma-Informed School Community," 2018).

With a combined 100 years in education, the authors have come to believe that addressing student trauma is one of the most worthwhile, practical, least expensive, single undertakings for any school district attempting to improve the quality of education for *all* its students. The practices required to create a trauma-sensitive school are the same ones that will enable teachers to challenge higher-performing students and teach all students—average, below average, and special needs.

DAN: What was the biggest challenge confronting me as a principal trying to provide leadership for a learner-centered school? Given the poverty and trauma that many of our students experienced, there were many non-school factors (ACEs) that prevented some students from graduating, through no fault of their own.

A student with reasonable family support and an adequate educational background will usually survive weak educational experiences (although not without boredom and below-average learning). For students with severe trauma, the benefits of best teaching practices may be the difference between success or failure in life. However, *all* students will benefit from a teacher and school that exhibit the practices that are essential for supporting students experiencing poverty and/or trauma.

To be clear:

- Extreme trauma is most prevalent among children raised in concentrated poverty. However, it can also impact students at all levels of the economic spectrum, from prekindergarten through college and graduate school. Children raised in the trappings of wealth can experience severe trauma if they do not feel loved and safe, or if they undergo life-changing events such as parental divorce, death, or abandonment.
- There are a growing number of university students who suffer panic attacks and other symptoms of trauma.
- Extreme trauma inhibits student learning (see ACES Study—an internet search will take you there).
- Inappropriate behaviors exhibited by children in poverty are often not controllable by the student without meaningful and extensive interventions. It is not always beneficial to say, "You know better than to behave that way."
- Students whose parents have sought political asylum, or a more positive life for their families, often have limited or no English language skills and economic or social support. As a result, these students experience a high degree of trauma when enrolling in and adjusting to a new school. Apprehension, fear, feeling lost, homesickness, depression, and frustration are only a few of the strong feelings these students, as well as their parents, experience.

Not all disruptive students suffer from trauma, but a large number do. By creating a trauma-sensitive school, we are simultaneously addressing the needs of disruptive students and the many other students whose learning and/or daily living may not be infected with the consequences of trauma. Creating a trauma-sensitive school requires the immersion of a school community in ideas and strategies that will change the way we think about our interactions with all students. Addressing student trauma does not mean bringing in a single program and acting as if your school has done all it can. It does mean designing a long-range plan that includes well-conceived initiatives and reaches every staff member on a regular basis.

 Strategies 209–217: Movement, Praise, and Success Experiences Motivate Students

Does your school have a detailed plan for becoming a trauma-sensitive school? There are best practice, research-based strategies available to classroom teachers for addressing the unique needs of students experiencing poverty and/or trauma that do not require altering a lesson plan or disrupting a planned classroom routine. These strategies benefit all students, not only those in poverty or trauma. The following are examples:

★ Marlene Pickering, a child advocate who was raised in poverty, stated, "As a child in first grade, I just wished I could have been the leader in a small group, even if just for 10 minutes as the timekeeper, but the teacher always called on the better dressed or better-performing students. This increased my stress level, which was always high to begin with." Teachers should give equal opportunities to those students whose appearance, comportment, or initial attitude may not be endearing.

★ Brain research informs us that movement is important if we want students to perform at peak levels. Instead of asking her students for a show of hands, secondary school teacher April Charleson will say, "Please stand up if you…"

★ Award-winning fourth- and fifth-grade teacher Tim Bedley also generates movement in his classes when conducting a think-pair-share activity. Mr. Bedley directs his students to stand while they discuss his question and then sit when they are prepared to respond. This process gives students a chance to relax and exercise, which is particularly important for students with strong bodily/kinesthetic intelligence. It also enables Mr. Bedley to more easily identify which pairs are ready to move on.

★ University professor Paul Vermette believes that success breeds success, and he too builds on brain research that demonstrates the value of integrating movement into a lesson (Jensen, 1994). Hence, he can generate student movement while simultaneously creating a situation where he will be able to give every student a success experience. An example is a lesson in which he asks students to make a list of things they know about a particular issue or topic they are studying. For instance, he may ask them to list three things they know about effective writing, or about rocks, or about the industrial revolution. Then he will say, "Now get up, move around, and add to your list one item from the list of another student—but only *after* you are able to explain what they know about the item. Then, repeat this process, collecting at least two more items from two other students."

As he observes the students adding to their lists, Dr. Vermette notices that no student has a list of less than six items. "If you have at least four items on your list, you are doing great and can sit down," he announces, knowing, of course, the complimentary effect this will have since each student has at least two more items

> than the minimum proclaimed by the teacher. Once seated, teachers can ask for volunteers to share one new item they added and what they learned about it. This last step can contribute to the success experience since almost any response a student can offer will be acceptable if it is sincere.
>
> ★ Also believing that success breeds success, psychiatrist Bruce Perry explained how children who face adversity at home can bring anxiety to school, "where they disrupt class when feeling threatened or shut down, losing opportunities to learn." Perry has an approach "which emphasizes the therapeutic effect of small, accumulated positive experiences." Perry stated, "For instance, greeting a student in the hall, remembering her name, makes a therapeutic moment and hundreds of these moments can change a child whose life is wrought with dysfunction" (2020).

Teachers, and parents at home, can create success experiences (therapeutic moments) for students. Just remember that it is counterproductive to praise a student for something that is not praiseworthy—and you will lose credibility.

But every human being exhibits behaviors that are worthy of praise. In a 45-minute class, better-behaving students may create a multitude of opportunities to justify praise. Even the worst-behaving student may pick up a dropped book, say one nice thing to someone, or pay more attention to the teacher than usual. These behaviors are worth mentioning to that student. For example, "Alphonse, I really liked the way you were paying attention when we had that discussion in class today," is a reasonable, positive, reinforcing statement for a teacher to make to a student.

If a teacher or parent is looking for something worthy of praise, they will find it. Of course, this can be difficult with students who tend to exhibit fewer behaviors worthy of praise (and who, ironically, need praise the most). Still, "seek and ye shall find."

The previous examples are among dozens of easy-to-apply strategies that educators can use if exposed to them. However, most professional educators have experienced few, if any, of these strategies at the university level or in professional development.

Storytelling Can Be Effective

The aforementioned Marlene Pickering was raised in poverty, raised four children herself in poverty, and finally broke out of the cycle. She got her high school degree at age 30 and has since worked for community organizations providing services to those in need. To develop classrooms that are sensitive to the range of cultures, backgrounds, and experiences students may be coming from, Marlene recommends that teachers, starting at the lowest grade levels possible, use authentic stories that children can relate to. For example, "I have two mommies," or "I come from a blended family." Teachers can then use these stories as catalysts for class discussion. (In Chapter 29, we discuss concerns about students being too young to talk about issues such as the ones raised here. We maintain that many children either experience these issues firsthand or have classmates who do, so we are not exposing students to anything that is new to them.)

For examples of books and stories, along with summaries, grade-level appropriate titles, and authors, visit the following website focused on poverty and trauma sponsored by the Institute for Learning Centered Education: https://www.poverty-initiative.com/.

April Charleson is the oldest of the four daughters raised in poverty by Ms. Pickering. Ms. Charleson, a veteran secondary English teacher, shares the impact of poverty and trauma on her childhood in a book of poems about her experiences at home and in school. The following was written by Ms. Charleson about an experience when she was seven years old.

> Dad does not go out to the bars anymore,
> Which should be a good thing.
> But it's not, because now the party is at our house.
> We listen to "Bad to the Bone" and Top well past our bedtime.
> The smell of pot is in the air.
> The next morning casts a lovely glow on empty and crushed cans
> Of Pabst Blue Ribbon and Milwaukee's Best.
> "The Party Comes Home" (Charleson, 2015)

After reading this excerpt, ask yourself, "Is it reasonable to have the same expectations for homework, classroom engagement, and test scores from April as from students with reasonably strong parental support?"

Trauma Triggers

A trauma trigger can ignite inappropriate or self-destructive behaviors in a child or adult suffering from trauma. It is important for educators to recognize the signs of trauma triggers because a student exhibiting any of them may not be able to control his reactions. You made need to confer with a social worker, guidance counselor, or other professional to determine how to handle the situation.

Common triggers suggested by Maryland's Center for Mental Health Services (2013) include the following:

- The anniversary dates of losses or trauma
- Frightening news events
- Too much to do, feeling overwhelmed
- Family friction
- The end of a relationship
- Spending too much time alone
- Being judged, criticized, teased, or put down
- Financial problems (e.g., getting a big bill)
- Physical illness
- Sexual harassment
- Being yelled at
- Aggressive-sounding noises or exposure to anything that makes you feel uncomfortable
- Being around someone who has treated you badly
- Certain smells, tastes, or noises

The last example in particular ("certain smells, tastes, or noises") shows just how personal and unique triggers can be to each individual. What triggers one student may not be something that would set off, or be recognizable to, anyone else. This is why it can be unfair to seek a rational explanation for a student's trauma-induced behavior.

 Strategy 218: Teaching Second Graders about Kindness

Angela Premo, a teacher in a high-poverty, rural town, began reading poems from *Rain Falls on Sunshine*, the book of poetry by April Charleson, to her second-grade students. "I started at the beginning of the book and only skipped the poems about sex abuse," Angela told the authors. "The kids loved hearing and discussing the poems. One child saw me placing the book in my purse and said, 'Mrs. Premo, you're not taking that home with you, are you?'"

The poems led to class discussions on alcohol, drug addiction, and abuse in general. Ms. Premo had each student write down three things they learned from these discussions. Without exception, every paper listed one or more of three learnings:

★ I learned the importance of being kind.
★ I learned why it's not good to be a bully.
★ I learned that there are children in my class

who don't have many of the things I have.

What Do We Mean by Extreme Trauma?

Harvard Collaboration published by Harvard Health Publications, the media and publishing division of Harvard Medical School, states, "Emotional and psychological trauma is the result of stressful events that shatter a person's sense of security, leading to a feeling of helplessness and vulnerability in a dangerous world" (*Emotional and Psychological Trauma*, n.d.). In other words, childhood trauma can result from anything that threatens a child's life, disrupts their sense of safety and security, or creates an unstable and unsafe environment—for example, sexual abuse, physical or verbal abuse, domestic violence, neglect, separation from a parent, and serious illness.

Situations that leave individuals feeling overwhelmed and alone can be traumatic even if they do not involve physical harm. Crucially, it is not the objective facts that determine whether an event is traumatic but the person's *subjective emotional experience* of the event.

Dr. Perry's speech to the Oklahoma State Education Department in February 2020 includes many examples of students living in urban poverty who witness violent death among friends and family members on a regular basis. Newspaper reports out of Chicago and other urban areas are replete with stories of people living in close proximity to gunfire, injury, and deaths. Educators cannot solve the problems of urban violence, but they can make a difference in the lives of the students who must endure it. As many students living in poverty have expressed, "School is the one safe haven I have."

Addressing the Challenge of Traumatized Students in the Classroom

All educators must learn to recognize the symptoms of trauma. Can you list five symptoms of trauma, in addition to "bad behavior"? Here is a list of some of the most telling symptoms:

- ◆ Student body language (e.g., not making eye contact)
- ◆ Sad facial features
- ◆ Lack of talking or social connection with other students
- ◆ Expressing issues through written "cries for help" in journals or other assignments
- ◆ Failing grades
- ◆ Not turning in assignments
- ◆ Sitting alone during lunch
- ◆ Dressing unusually or in soiled or protective clothing (hoodies, outerwear)
- ◆ Evidence of family dysfunction during a "home visit"
- ◆ Frequent absences or tardiness

Do not retraumatize students by punishing the trauma-induced behaviors they cannot control. Examples of such behaviors include the following:

- ◆ Refusal to speak in class
- ◆ Head down on desk or other signs of depression/exhaustion
- ◆ Lateness to school due to parental factors
- ◆ Constant interruptions or disruptions in the classroom
- ◆ Constantly being, or trying to be, humorous or argumentative

---

 Strategy 219: Develop Trauma-Specific Interventions

- ★ Utilize active listening skills with the student, in private, to encourage the student to discuss his feelings: "Billy, you look very sad. What's going on?" Or, "How can I help?"
- ★ For a moderate issue, meet with the student after class or after school. Talk with a school nurse, psychologist, or social worker for help, advice, or information about the student.
- ★ For serious issues, walk the child to the psychologist's or social worker's office.

Self-Assess Your Level of Sensitivity to Trauma

When it comes to trauma sensitivity, there is essentially one question you need to ask yourself: "What don't I know about this student that might help me reach her?" What exhibits as "bad behavior" may be a symptom of trauma.

Keeping your mind open to this possibility may help you identify the true source of the behavior issue and, ultimately, address it.

Trauma may date back to earlier in a child's life, or it could be related to a very recent or immediate situation. The student may be experiencing trauma on a regular basis out-of-school, or perhaps situational trauma—for example, recently learning of the death of a favored friend or relative or being the subject of peer abuse during school.

A college junior told a story that perfectly illustrates the difference between a teacher who is trauma-sensitive and one who isn't: "When I was in high school, my favorite uncle, with whom I was very close, had died two nights before. In my first class on the day I returned to school, the teacher came over to me, expressed her condolences and said, 'If you need to leave the room, just go ahead, and let me know if there is anything I can do to help ease your grief.' In my next class, the teacher would not give me an inch. She knew of my uncle's passing but did not acknowledge it. 'Get your head off the desk,' she yelled at me. 'Pay attention!'"

This student did not ordinarily experience trauma. Therefore, the sudden death of a relative to whom she felt close might be called "situational trauma." We cannot always know if "situational trauma" may be the cause of a student's atypical behavior, but shouldn't we allow for it?

✓ **Strategies 220–227: Strategies to Accommodate Students Who May Be Experiencing Severe Trauma**

★ *Learn each child's history.* How many things can you list about a child's history that are most important for a teacher to learn?

- ❏ Family's economic status (approximate)
- ❏ Who the student's caregivers are
- ❏ Number of siblings
- ❏ Medical history
- ❏ Previous teachers' narratives
- ❏ What worked previously when this child had difficulties, either academic or behavioral
- ❏ Interests
- ❏ Special talents

What other aspects of a child's history might be helpful for a teacher to know?

★ *Build relationships with parents.*

❑ Home visits with parents or guardians are extremely useful if conducted as a meeting to help the student grow and develop. A recommended format for a home visit can be cooperatively developed by teachers, administrators, and parent representatives.

❑ Ask parents to write a brief note about their child and to include anything they think the teacher should know.

❑ Send a note home, or call, with at least one positive communication each month. Louis Mihalyi, a science teacher, would send home a picture of a child at work in the lab at least once a year, accompanied by a brief note. With email, social media, and other technology readily available, it can be easy for teachers to do this. Most schools and teachers rarely go beyond asking parents for assistance with field trip supervision or fundraising, and these requests are often viewed as "one more thing you want from me." A message that provides positive information about the child, or simply shares information that may be of interest to parents, is more often than not well received, and it serves to demonstrate to parents that the school personnel care about students and their parents or guardians.

❑ You may periodically send open-ended questions that can generate dialogue between parents and children, such as, "Ask your child about the river project we began this week," or "Discuss with your child the actions they should take if they see a student being bullied."

❑ Mr. Mihalyi had it right—as classes become learner-centered, there are more opportunities to invite parents to be authentic audiences for student performances, portfolio reviews, demonstrations of competence, and/or viewing of products resulting from a project. As few as two or three parents can constitute an authentic audience.

❑ Set a low bar for parent participation and let parents feel good when their participation exceeds what you requested. Parents often do not know how much participation is enough. If you communicate clear and simple expectations for parent involvement—for example, attending classroom presentations for an hour twice a year, posing occasional questions at the dinner table, and attending two parent conferences a year—you will often get better results, in one form or another.

❑ A principal in an urban, poverty-stricken neighborhood requires teachers to call home every time there is an absence. He gives staff a script that begins, "I care about Harold and noticed he was absent from school today. I am calling just to find out how he is." While we do not expect many schools to institute this policy, it can reap enormous dividends in terms of positive parent-school relations and problem-solving of family issues.

❑ A guided tour, led by community representatives, through the neighborhood of a teacher's students can be worthwhile. In fact, this should be mandatory for new hires of both professional and non-professional staff. If this is not practical, at least find a way to expose staff to the conditions that some of their students experience as a way of life.

Homework Considerations: When the Home Is Not Conducive to Work

An outstanding veteran teacher tells this story of when she was a young teacher in Colorado:

> I had a 13-year-old student in my math class who was capable of excellent work, but rarely turned in homework assignments that were easily within her ability to complete with little effort. After weeks of cajoling, threatening, and bribing, I decided that enough was enough. As I passed her desk while collecting homework from almost every other student, I stopped and asked, "Do you have your homework today?" She shook her head and looked away. "Look at me," I demanded. "Why don't you have your homework?" She stared blankly at me, so I repeated the demand. I continued to press the issue, my voice probably getting louder each time and the young girl's face getting redder, but without a response. Finally, I became even more serious and demanded one more time, "Why is someone with your ability simply not turning in homework and not offering any reasonable explanation?"

> The young girl exploded, looking right into my eyes for the first time: "You try doing homework or anything else when your step-father rapes you almost every night."

Setting aside the question of whether this teacher should have tried a different, gentler approach with her student, the story shows how problematic it can be to expect students who are experiencing trauma at home to turn in quality homework. Even if you do not grade the homework, if your lesson and tests build on the assumption that students have done their homework, where would that leave this student?

DAN AND DON: Although some schools have adopted a no-homework policy, we are not necessarily recommending that all schools should do so. However, we strongly recommend schools consider that some students have legitimate reasons for being unable to do their homework. Due to the home circumstances of these students, they are often already behind in their work, and the inability to do homework puts them even further behind unless the teacher or school has a way to make opportunities to succeed more equitable.

Strategies 228–235: Strategies for De-escalation and Redirection

★ Use active listening:
  ❏ "You look angry, Samuel. What happened?"
  ❏ "Why don't you take a time-out, Sarah? Take a walk to the girls' room and back or stop by the counselor's room if you like."
  ❏ "Could we talk after school, Jamaal? I'd really like to talk with you and know more about you."
★ Explore evidenced-based approaches.
  ❏ Active listening
  ❏ Journaling
  ❏ Caring behaviors
  ❏ One-on-one teacher-student conferences
★ Understand the cycle of trauma and how to break it. Traumatic incidents lead to student frustration, depression, acting out, withdrawal, drugs or other addictions, poor academic performance, and destructive nonproductive lifestyles. Strategies to break the cycle include intervention, ongoing support, teaching coping skills, or use of an ongoing sponsor or advocate to reinforce support and care.
★ Understand the impact of trauma on brain development and learning.
★ For new students who are English language learners, it is essential to have a school-based resource staff member who speaks the child's language and can communicate with their parents. It is critical that the child and parents know that you like and care about them. All of the learner-centered activities and suggestions in this book can be used to personalize and individualize content, activities, and

expectations for these children. Placing two or more children of the same language or culture in the same classroom is also an extremely important way for these students to encourage and help one another.

★ One of the key questions for all schools, teachers, and students dealing with trauma-related student behaviors or conflicts is, "How do we turn this situation into a learning experience?" There could be a consequence tied to a "Learning and Behavior Contract," or such a contract could be the consequence itself.

★ When students misbehave, there must be consequences, but they should be restorative, not punitive. And there should always be some sort of appeals process. If a student or a teacher believes a consequence is unjust, they have a right to meet with the others involved, and/or the decision-makers if no one else is involved, to discuss the incident for possible repeal or a new consequence. This would be an effective demonstration of due process and citizenship development and a valuable learning experience for students and staff. It is also another way of demonstrating to students that the school cares about them.

Zero-tolerance policies are designed to make the consequences for misbehavior transparent, consistent, and equal (e.g., the athlete, the academic, and the child in poverty are all treated alike). However, such policies often break down because there can always be extenuating circumstances. Equitable, rather than equal, repercussions for every student may have to be considered when making decisions about consequences.

For instance, the first grader who was suspended for having aspirin that his mother put in his backpack. Or the high school senior who was running late for school, but knowing his mother was suicidal and wanting to protect her, grabbed a revolver from the closet on his way out of the house, put it in his backpack, and forgot about it. Should this student receive the same penalty as the student who, with malice, totes a weapon to school?

It is critical for a discipline policy to be applied consistently. However, there can always be unusual circumstances that justify an exception. It only takes one event like the ones just cited for the entire zero-tolerance policy to be legally and morally questioned. It is important that any deviation from a strict discipline policy be perceived as justified while still allowing for those exceptions that are warranted. An appeals process allows for the consistency of a zero-tolerance policy while affording an avenue for exceptions. The appellate group could consist of an administrator, a teacher, a parent, and a student.

✓ Strategy 236: Checklist to Assess Whether Your School Is Trauma-Sensitive

Many excellent books are available on the topic of student trauma, and they are worth exploring for recommendations of what constitutes a trauma-sensitive school. However, many valuable recommendations are simply too costly or require more school restructuring than is reasonable to expect most schools to implement. The authors recommend that, at a minimum, schools implement every item on the following list of ideas for addressing trauma. Our hats are off to any school that goes above and beyond in its efforts to create a trauma-sensitive school. This list is focused on practical application steps that we believe every school can undertake without the excuse, "It's too costly," or "We can't do it."

When you can check off every item on this list, you have earned the right to say that your school is trauma-sensitive.

_____ If a visitor were to walk from one end of your building(s) to the other, would it be clear from posters, displays, and other visual evidence that this is a school that does not tolerate any form of racism, bullying, or discrimination?

_____ When you bring in presenters on trauma, are staff given advance information as a lens through which they can experience the presentation? Do staff know in advance what to expect so they can do some research or at least think about what will be discussed?

_____ For presentations, is follow-through built in? For example, asking a committee to make recommendations based on what the members learn at the presentation.

_____ Does every staff member have an easily accessible list of trauma triggers to look for in students and to use for intervention whenever possible?

_____ Is there a long-range school plan (for at least the next three years) in place for addressing student trauma as a priority? No checkmark if the school has a plan but no one can locate it! (Note: The first year should be detailed; subsequent changes can be outlined with the stated intent to provide more detail at least two months before the end of the prior year.)

_____ If so, does this plan include the following?
  - At least two full training days, every year, to give teaching staff information and practical strategies for understanding and addressing the needs of traumatized students
  - At least one full-day awareness training for all nonteaching staff every year

- A list of agencies with resources available to school staff, parents, and students, with contact information for each
- A detailed, multiyear plan for increasing learner-centered classroom practices, with content, target dates, and evidence to periodically assess success of the plan
- Pilot programs to create models of trauma-sensitive, learner-centered classrooms
- A restorative justice process and other progressive discipline programs to support students exhibiting inappropriate behaviors, and to enable them to learn skills for changing their behaviors
- A list of classroom management techniques
- Stress management practices throughout the day—in every classroom
- Movement techniques that may be used in every classroom to have a calming effect on all students but particularly those experiencing trauma
- Emphasis on a "no-threats" approach to discipline accompanied with well-advertised consequences in a non-threatening approach
- Use of time at every staff meeting to address aspects of trauma sensitivity
- Sample posters, fliers, etc., that can be displayed throughout the school with information on the impact of trauma and strategies for relieving student and staff stress
- Involving students in immersing the school in posters, displays, and other examples of trauma-sensitive information and practices
- Use of daily announcements to immerse students and staff in ideas related to trauma and stress
- A process for orientating and mentoring new employees on the expectations regarding the trauma plan
- A plan to teach students how to be trauma-sensitive advisors for themselves and other students

_____ Does the plan identify the types of training that will be provided for teachers over the next three years, with approximate dates, providers, and lengths of time?

_____ Is there an evaluation process built into the plan and sufficient time to conduct the evaluation near the end of each year?

_____ Is there a committee with the sole responsibility of overseeing all of the above and making sure it happens? Does this

committee meet at least monthly (and additionally as
needed), and does it issue regular, detailed progress
reports to building and central administrators, the board of
education, and recognized teacher and parent groups? Are
these reports available to the public? There should be, at the
very least, one committee for the entire school district; there
can also be committees for each building. An administrator,
or an appropriate staff committee, might consider bundling
all of the foregoing suggestions for a trauma tool kit into a
binder for every staff member.

COMMONSENSE CONCLUSION

Trauma is pervasive, and it can affect students at all levels of education, up to
and including graduate school programs. It can also affect students from wealthy
families, as well as those in poverty. When a school is trauma-sensitive, it is prepared to support all of its students in meaningful, effective ways.

27

Social Justice Is a Critical Element of Good Citizenship

Ms. Ugarte, arguing at a parent meeting that schools don't need to add the goal of good citizenship to the curriculum, insisted, "I pay my taxes. I don't break any laws, and I don't bother anyone! Doesn't that make me a good citizen?"

The shootings of George Floyd, Jacob Blake, and other Black individuals in 2020 may have been a turning point in the struggle for equal rights for people of color that began more than 400 years ago. The immediate fallout of these killings included nationwide protests and statements of support for diversity, equity, and inclusion from many of the country's leading corporations and institutions. Many Americans of all races and ethnicities joined in making equity a major issue in the 2020 presidential election campaign.

As in this entire book, we offer examples of lessons and activities teachers can include in their curriculum that will address these important issues and facilitate student development in critical thinking, understanding the Constitution, and citizenship. Teachers who are understandably concerned about preparing students for standardized tests can be assured that they can do so as a by-product of a well-designed lesson or unit on issues of social justice without requiring additional teacher time for preparation, teaching, or assessment.

DOI: 10.4324/9781003284697-33

Why Teach about Social Justice?

There is little doubt that one of the most important, and often hidden, reasons for a public education system is to help students understand diverse cultural norms. Cultural sensitivity is one of the building blocks for developing individuals, and ultimately a society, that recognizes, appreciates, and practices the qualities of inclusion, justice, and fairness. Unfortunately, many teachers and state curriculum creators want to focus less on fostering cultural understanding and more on "just the facts and major concepts." This perspective is sometimes used to justify a narrower scope of social justice and social-emotional issues in the curriculum.

However, the lack of prioritization on social justice is also a cultural norm, and it needs to be thoroughly addressed if we hope students will develop the citizenship skills and values that are necessary for a healthy democratic society—particularly with Black Lives Matter protests dominating the news since the murder of George Floyd. How many students understand why many Americans believe Black Lives Matter is a valid movement and not a slight to those who want to claim that "all lives matter"?

Adapting Activities and Lessons for Younger Children

The examples in this chapter, as throughout the book, can be used by teachers in the classroom and by parents with their children. Exercises that seem geared toward older children can be modified for success with younger ones. For instance, this question for older children: "Should citizens have access to unlimited health-care services? To any? If any, which?"—might be adapted as follows for younger children: "If people are sick, do you think they should have to pay money to see a doctor, and if so, how much and why?" Younger children can also be asked questions about what it means to be kind and what examples of kindness might look like. What matters is that *all* children are challenged with questions that require them to think critically, hear what their peers have to say, and reach conclusions based on sound reasoning.

 Strategy 237: Examples of Challenging Questions to Start a Discussion on Social Justice

★ Should people who are not Black support the Black Lives Matter movement? Why or why not?

★ Are there reasons people should be concerned about discrimination against groups that they are not part of?

★ Is there a correlation between issues of social justice in our society and bullying in our schools?

★ Is there a conflict between supporting Black Lives Matter and being opposed to defunding police departments, as some are arguing for?

Apart from enabling students to think critically about social justice issues, wouldn't class discussions analyzing current events also appeal to their desire to study relevant topics? And if teachers can link a current event to standards they are required to teach, they will not have to view the time involved in such discussions as "extra" time.

There are four interrelated principles of social justice (Health and Community Services Workforce Council, Queensland, Australia):

◆ **Equity:** The fair distribution, among *all* people, of equal opportunities to obtain resources

◆ **Access:** The opportunity to have equitable access to information, resources, and opportunities for personal and professional growth

◆ **Participation:** Equitable opportunity and expectation to participate in opportunities open to other segments of society

◆ **Rights:** The legal, moral, and ethical right for equity, access, and participation as defined above

Issues in these categories can include but, by far, are not limited to the following:

◆ Should there be a constitutional amendment lowering the voting age to 15?

◆ Should U.S. citizens be able to own handguns? Assault rifles? Machine guns?

◆ Should individuals who have served their prison sentences be allowed to vote? What about people who are currently imprisoned?

◆ Should citizens have access to unlimited health-care services? To any? If any, which?

How Widely Is Social Justice Currently Taught?

While a growing number of teachers are addressing issues of social justice with their students, many do not spend in-depth time helping students explore these issues, develop critical thinking and creative problem-solving skills, and apply their learning to the real world. Some students may focus on social justice through specific courses, such as Participation in Government, the semester-long civics course required of all seniors in New York State. Yet, we argue that social justice can and should be integrated into any course, even those not specifically focused on justice or citizenship. It is unreasonable for students to wait 12 years to explore issues related to social justice, especially since they are more likely to be intrinsically motivated to explore these issues and to develop the skills necessary for effective and active responsible citizenship.

Given that many teachers feel overwhelmed with curriculum and standardized testing demands, one solution is to integrate information and discussions about social justice into the required curriculum. To accomplish this effectively only requires a change in teachers' mindsets. In English classes, for example, it can be as simple as choosing stories and books that can be catalysts for social justice discussions. If Shakespeare is the required literary content, the issues of violence, love, forgiveness, revenge, racism, and family dysfunction are core social justice issues that can easily be used as motivating themes for students to explore through many of the activities discussed in earlier chapters.

Some teachers, and many parents, think children should be shielded from discussions on difficult topics, particularly in the earlier grades. However, if teachers and parents do not appropriately sensitize young students to issues of social justice, citizenship, bullying, bigotry, etc., how can we expect them to become responsible citizens who are free of the kinds of prejudices that infect too many people in our current society?

Many low-income families are aware of abuse, homelessness, crime, and poverty, either through their own experiences or the experiences of those around them. Similarly, many families of color have experienced racism. When families are immersed in these struggles, conversations about them occur naturally within the family and often within the community.

Parents experiencing a more comfortable lifestyle often resist, and sometimes protest, schools' efforts to actively explore social justice issues, believing their children should be shielded from some of the harsher realities of life. What they may not realize is that their children are already exposed to these realities through the media, peer discussions, and experiences outside of the home, often forming opinions that are not based on fact. The question is not whether children, even at younger ages, should be exposed to complex realities. The fact is that they are. The question is whether we want responsible adults to be present while children discuss difficult issues so that there is an opportunity to guide healthy discussion, correct misinformation, and prevent it from spreading.

Sometimes protests related to the use of a particular article or book are the result of parents feeling blindsided when their children report on class discussions around these materials. There are still many people who believe that schools should teach the three Rs, and nothing more. Effective communications about literature you intend to use, and why, can head off possible parental concerns, or at least alert teachers to readings they may need to make optional while providing an alternative for some students.

Not only is dealing with social justice issues in schools necessary for all the reasons cited previously in this chapter, but there is one more compelling reason. Once students complete their schooling, they may find themselves in work or living situations that have much more cultural diversity than what they experienced in their K–12 education and hometown. If we do not prepare students for the realities of the world outside their homes and communities, it will not only be a culture shock when they leave home, but it may also cause them unnecessary difficulty in interacting with people from diverse backgrounds.

Oscar Hammerstein, speaking of how children learn to hate, had it right when he wrote the song, "You've Got to Be Carefully Taught." If we want children to learn kindness, self-respect, and respect for others, then we must "teach" them about these concepts.

✅ Strategies 238–246: Practical Strategies for Teaching Social Justice in the Schools

★ Miguel, a former member of Ms. Larson's fourth-grade class, has left the United States and returned to Mexico with his mother, who was deported due to an immigration issue. Miguel left a note for Ms. Larson to read to his classmates stating how much he enjoyed them and appreciated their help in teaching him English, how sad he was to leave, and his feelings about what he labeled as the "unfair U.S. immigration laws."

After Ms. Larsen reads the letter to her class, the students have many questions and even express interest in changing the immigration laws of which Miguel wrote. Ms. Larson decides to "seize the moment," and take advantage of her students' interest and motivation to learn more about immigration. She posts all the students' questions and tells the class that together they will learn about immigration and get answers to their questions over the next several weeks. They brainstorm all the possible issues related to immigration, including such topics as law, travel, reasons for immigrating, penalties, fairness, gangs, language, religion, income, and many more. The class lists more questions about these issues.

Ms. Larson, then asks the class what resources will help them get answers to these questions, and she lists the possibilities. She suggests many resources that the students were not aware of. She puts students into groups of three composed of individuals whom she believes can work cooperatively and asks them to decide on the three questions they feel are most important to get answers to. Their task is to use the internet, over the next two weeks, to research their questions, document their sources, write a report, develop a proposal for a change on immigration policy, and make a presentation to the class.

During the week, Ms. Larson shows the class a movie on current immigration that provides some perspectives on some of their questions. She also invites a local immigrant parent and a border patrol officer to respond to student questions with answers that the students can use in their reports and presentations. Ms. Larson is careful to screen the people she invites, either by speaking with them personally or getting references from someone whose judgment she trusts. The class also shares their work with Miguel through letters and makes final proposals to their elected representatives on policy changes they believe are important. Ms. Larson also makes sure that she documents which state standards the students are progressing in and which teacher-created standards exceed state requirements for parent or administrator review.

You may not have Miguel in your class; however, you could try this same activity and focus it on Miguel's story or any other.

★ Aleeta Summers is debriefing her tenth-grade urban high school English class on a cultural exchange experience the class had at a local middle-class suburban high school. After brainstorming questions and observations, the students agree that the most important questions to explore are: "Does our country have separate and equal schools? And, if not, why not?" They also agree that each student must answer the questions by writing an in-depth, eight-page research paper or completing a project approved by Ms. Summers.

Over the next several weeks, the students read Jonathan Kozol's *Savage Inequalities*; conduct interviews with the local superintendent, school board president, and local state legislator; view several documentary films on the topic; and read and discuss several articles related to their questions. The students spend two class periods per week in writing groups, sharing and revising their papers based on peer and teacher feedback. Following the completion of their research papers, projects, and a class discussion of their responses, Ms. Summers challenges the class to form groups of three and develop proposals for improving their school. After a week of writing and revising, the class presents its proposals to the principal, superintendent, local board members, and a state legislator.

★ During the first week of the school year, give each student a copy of a periodical from the previous year and direct them to skim it for examples of social justice issues. Then ask them to share the issues they found, either from the periodical or their own knowledge or experience, and list them on newsprint. Have students identify their top three issues of importance, followed by their top choice. Then ask them to list three important questions about their top issue. Have them meet in triads and help each other consider other essential questions for their topics. By the end of the third quarter, each student will be required to complete research on their approved question and submit either a paper or a project approved by you.

★ After brainstorming social justice issues and prioritizing them with the entire class, bring in monthly speakers with expertise to respond to student questions. Students can be required to write a paper reflecting on the relevance and/or meaning the issue has for them personally or for others and whether there is a role for students to become activists in addressing any of the issues discussed. Have triads conduct the guest speaker interviews, working from questions they have developed and prioritized in advance.

★ One teaching strategy to deal with "boring" guest speakers is to create student/teacher role plays focusing on several examples of the social justice issue being studied and then have the expert/ guest speaker respond to each role play. Another strategy is to instruct the guest, in advance, not to prepare a talk but rather to expect a question/answer format. Then, guide students toward developing their own questions based on background information provided by the teacher. Better, yet, have a student or students moderate the Q and A session.

★ Have students brainstorm possible social justice issues and select a different issue for the entire class to focus on each month. Require each student to keep a scrapbook of newspaper, periodical, or internet articles; interviews they conduct with experts; movies or documentaries they view; and reflections on each. Require at least two reflections per week for each month's issue. Then change the social justice issue for the next month with the same requirements. At the end of each month, have students meet in rotating triad groups to share what they think were their most interesting reflections. Use questions to guide students.

★ Each month, spend one week on a different social justice issue with students, using readings, documentaries, speakers, writing assignments, discussions, and interpersonal activities to help students explore the issue.

★ Following any discussion, have students reflect on the issue(s). This is because once we know what an issue looks like, we cannot unsee it. Take bullying, for example. Once you've learned to recognize bullying, you will notice it all the time, whereas previously you might have thought it normal behavior. It is the same for racism and other social justice issues. Possible reflection questions that can be posed for verbal or written responses from individuals, pairs, or groups include the following: What have you learned? What do you know now that you did not know when we began this discussion? How do you feel about what we have studied? What is one song, book, movie, or quote that will remind you of what we have discussed?

Image by Afzal Khan. With permission

★ English teachers who have flexibility with their content can focus on social justice issues through novels and nonfiction using books such as Kozol's *The Shame of the Nation*; Picoult's *Small, Great Things*; Stevenson's *Just Mercy*; Lee's *To Kill a Mockingbird*; and many others. Speakers, field trips, documentaries, poetry, student presentations, and oral proposals to legislators can be meaningful activities to help students gain awareness and grow as civic actors while also increasing skills in reading, writing, researching, listening, discussing, critical thinking, and appreciating good literature.

Learner-Centered Pedagogy Based on Constructivist Theory Is Social Justice in Action

In this chapter, we have discussed engaging students with social justice content. However, the very use of learner-centered strategies and constructivist theory is a demonstration of applied social justice. In a learner-centered classroom, the teacher meets all learners where they are, empowers them to make choices that coincide with their interests and needs, and helps them reconcile their prior knowledge with new information to the degree to which they are able. This is in contrast to the traditional assembly-line style of education in which students are treated as standardized commodities. In effect, learner-centered constructivist pedagogy creates social justice for each student.

COMMONSENSE CONCLUSION

If students are not educated about social justice issues before they graduate, they will lack the skills to be responsible community members, to vote intelligently, or to feel comfortable in any environment that is different from the local setting in which they were raised.

28

Addressing Controversial Issues with Civil Discourse through Effective Use of Student-Centered Practices

"That's a really stupid thing to say," Mr. Veidt responded to a comment on his Facebook page. "You are such an idiot," he continued without offering any direct response to the comments he disputed, nor any evidence to support his point of view.

It is our experience that few teachers address issues such as racism, sexism, gender identification, and other potentially controversial topics. This reluctance may be attributable to concerns over finding time in an already overcrowded curriculum. It could also be due to lack of training and fear of having to deal with parental protests if they appear to be promulgating a position contrary to the beliefs of some parents or community members. When teachers do attempt to address critical social issues or current events, it is an excellent opportunity to teach children to address points with which they disagree with rationale instead of name-calling. This is particularly important because of the modeling of name-calling they are provided daily by celebrities, politicians, and other children.

It is important to notice that some states are now mandating, and others are encouraging, teachers to address potentially controversial topics. Also, bullying is a significant and growing problem in most schools, and it is difficult to address the causes of bullying without discussing the issues of inclusion and equality. This is also why it is important to address the need to support arguments with rationale instead of name-calling since name-calling is a calling card of bullies.

DOI: 10.4324/9781003284697-34

In New York State, for example, the New York State Education Department has issued NYSED CR-S (Culturally Responsive-Sustaining Education), a framework requiring schools to adhere to four principles:

Create a warm and welcoming environment
High expectations and rigorous instruction
An inclusive curriculum
Ongoing professional learning

On the education department's website, it is clearly stated,

> The Culturally Responsive-Sustaining (CR-S) framework is intended to help education stakeholders create student-centered learning environments that affirm cultural identities; foster positive academic outcomes; develop students' abilities to connect across lines of difference; elevate historically marginalized voices; empower students as agents of social change; and contribute to individual student engagement, learning, growth, and achievement through the cultivation of critical thinking. The framework was designed to support education stakeholders in developing and implementing policies that educate all students effectively and equitably, as well as provide appropriate supports and services to promote positive student outcomes.

In California, in October 2021, Gov. Gavin Newsom signed legislation making California the first state to require all students to complete a semester-long course in ethnic studies to earn a high school diploma.

If teachers are inclined, or asked, to address issues of inclusion, social justice, and similar potentially controversial issues, what kinds of activities and approaches can they utilize to address such topics while simultaneously teaching to standards so that they can be a part of the existing curriculum rather than add-ons to increase the workload of already overworked educators?

Using Critical Thinking to Address Issues of Racism, Bullying, and Bigotry

If students are to engage intelligently in discussions of social justice issues such as discussions about racism, bullying, bigotry, and the like, they must learn to think critically and to understand certain universally accepted values such as honesty, integrity, and respect for other points of view. This will not happen unless we create an environment that allows students to reflect deeply on challenging issues and reach their own conclusions (as opposed to merely taking in facts). We need to design activities that encourage students to express their thoughts verbally or in writing so that their parents or teachers can react and facilitate a dialogue.

 Strategy 247: An Example of Challenging Students to Do Their Own Research

For example, instead of telling students about the Dred Scott decision, challenge them to research the case and give them questions to address during their research.

There are topics we should explore with students in the hope that they will shape their attitudes—topics such as respect for people of different races, religions, ethnicities, genders, and beliefs. But even with topics where we might agree there is a right and wrong attitude to hold, we will not change a child's mind by telling them how to think. We must challenge students to explore all relevant facts by asking questions, and we must resist the temptation to provide our personal answers, which is actually an effective student-centered method of addressing any curriculum.

The Risk of Controversy

It is not always possible to avoid parent protests, as evidenced by objections that have at times surfaced against *Huckleberry Finn*, *The Catcher in the Rye*, and *To Kill a Mockingbird*, among others, but the approach we are recommending can limit the risk.

As teachers, our aspiration should always be for students to learn to support their opinions with reasonable rationale. This can be a criterion for praising students as well as assigning grades: "I don't have to agree with what you say or write," students can be informed, "however, I will want to see the basis for your opinion."

If a student presses a teacher for an opinion, a response could be, "I will share my opinion when we are ready to leave this topic, and I will provide my rationale, but for now, I want you to form your own opinion, based on facts and research, and uninfluenced by mine." Then near the end of the lesson, the teacher can offer her personal opinion and rationale and invite student questions and discussion. Of course, if the teacher wants to avoid ever stating an opinion on a particular topic, it reduces further the risk of protests.

Begin with a Process of Conducting a Civil Dialogue

If one of the most important objectives of the nation's schools is to prepare students to become engaged, responsible citizens who can think critically and solve problems creatively, then all educators have a major responsibility to work toward this objective.

Public political discussions in recent years give evidence of the critical need to teach our children how to disagree with respect for those expressing contrary opinions precisely because politicians and celebrities are not always good role models for intelligent discourse. Social media is filled with exchanges such as the following:

"Boy, are you stupid!"
"Get your head out of your butt!"
"Shut the hell up! We don't want to know your dumb opinions!"

Exchanges like these are becoming commonplace and demonstrate the need for us to teach children to address issues, not personalities, and to engage in civilized debates if our objective is truly to influence another's opinion. Calling someone a jerk, even if true, is not likely to get that person to rethink their position.

However, it is not as simple as expecting students to engage in an intelligent, research-based discussion with supportive rationale provided for every point argued, particularly if they are passionate about the topic under discussion.

Teach Students a Process for Engaging in Civil Discourse

It is suggested that as early in the school year as possible teachers should teach students a process for engaging in a class discussion and then should repeat this process throughout the year whenever there is a class discussion on any topic but particularly when the topic is potentially controversial. The following is an outline of a process for conducting a class discussion on any potentially controversial topic.

The process should include these two ground rules in addition to a few others that will be recommended:

Do respond to points with which you disagree with the rationale.
Do not respond with name-calling or insults.

Strategy 248: Example of a Process for Conducting a Civil Class Discussion

Before engaging students in the exploration of an issue, ask them to name a few issues that could create disagreement among them or among any group of citizens. Then pose this question to them: "What are appropriate behaviors to expect of people who are engaging maturely in a discussion of a controversial issue?" Students will be able to generate some useful behaviors that you should list on the board, newsprint, or with technology as a reminder to the class during discussions.

Then inform students you will expect to see these behaviors exhibited at all times but particularly during class discussions when it is easy to become passionate about a topic and forget the appropriate behaviors. Include in the list that follows any behaviors suggested by students a moment ago that have merit.

1. Seek to understand the other person's point of view before seeking to have yours understood. Emphasize to students that you cannot persuade someone toward your opinion if you don't understand the reasons for their opinion.
2. Utilize good listening skills such as paraphrasing what you think you heard the other person expressing, before responding; and waiting a few seconds after you think the other person has completed speaking before you begin to speak. (See amplification on listening skills below.)
3. Distinguish fact from opinion. Ask students in pairs or small groups to list three facts and three opinions and then discuss what the criteria are for each.
4. Stress the importance of relying on more than one source before you choose to believe what is presented as a fact or opinion
5. Distinguish what makes an argument relevant from one that is irrelevant. You can google "irrelevant arguments" and get a list of 15 such as the following:

   The fact that a celebrity advocates a certain perfume is irrelevant unless he/she has credentials as a cosmetics' expert, that a criminal says something does not mean it is irrelevant just because of who is speaking.

You can design activities around each of the foregoing. Spend time discussing these aforementioned criteria so that students understand why they are important; then apply these criteria to all discussions. (You can also do this at home with your children.) Also, have a signal a student or the teacher can use if they believe any of these criteria are being violated. One teacher encourages students to say, "Oops," in which case, the discussion stops while the class discusses whether students agree that a criterion has been violated.

Emphasize the Importance of Listening Skills

Inform your students that while all of the aforementioned criteria are important like skills, researchers have concluded that one of the most important skills for an individual to possess is listening skills. Our use of good listening skills can affect us throughout our lives. It may be worth taking an entire class period to focus on the behaviors of a good listener, as described herein:

Ask students to generate a few suggestions through "pair-share," or as a large group, behaviors that would demonstrate "good listening." Explain to them that some of the behaviors they have shared are similar to what the experts call "active listening." List and briefly describe the major aspects of "active listening":

- ◆ Eye contact
- ◆ Reflect content
  Reflect feelings
- ◆ Ask clarifying questions

Role-play the process of reflecting feelings with another student, with one of you making a statement and the other saying, "When you say that, it makes me feel…"

Demonstrate this again, but then ask a clarifying question, such as, "Are you more frustrated or just angry?" Discuss with students why this is a valuable listening process.

Reinforce student learning of listening skills with a role play involving a student or another adult. Post a list of each of the listening skills (noted earlier) and conduct a class discussion on a controversial issue, such as student suspensions for minor behaviors. During the role play, "stop-action" whenever you demonstrate one of the active listening behaviors and ask students which behavior they observed. You could also demonstrate some inappropriate listening behaviors and ask students what they thought of how it helped or hindered the conversation.

DAN: During a class discussion involving race, one of my Black students stated: "I don't care! I just hate white people." Rather than chastising the student, I responded with something like, "Wow, Jonathan, you have got a lot of anger going on there. What's caused you to hate white people?" This led to a productive discussion in which Jonathan described some past discrimination he and his family experienced and also clarified that he did not hate all white people.

Additional Tips

◆ Remain nonjudgmental by seeking to understand before being understood

◆ Model the listening behaviors you are expecting of students

◆ Admit that they are learning, too, and that you may have to think about an issue more to develop a position on it or do additional reading. Note: Modeling these behaviors and admitting what you do not know is good practice for teachers in school and parents at home, whether or not it is part of conducting a group discussion

◆ Teach students to discern fact from opinion

◆ Encourage students to use multiple sources to evaluate opinions

◆ Create opportunities for creative problem-solving

As a culminating activity to a lesson on how to conduct an intelligent, fact-based discussion, create a class list of all the possible activities, depending on your teaching mode of operation, that you have used to help students understand the issue. Ask the class to individually list the top three activities that you have used to engage them with the topic, and then have them individually rank order their lists from first choice to third choice.

Then put them in groups of three to share, practice "listening empathetically," and decide on the group's top three suggestions in rank order. Follow this, depending on your reading of the class, by having them meet in groups of six and following the same process of narrowing the list to three items in rank order. Have each group present its decisions to the class as you post their decisions on the board or newsprint visibly to the entire class.

Have each group select a group representative to present their recommendations to the entire class and encourage all class members to ask clarifying questions for understanding.

Ask for a hand vote on which suggestion the class should do; post the vote numbers as they are announced. Depending on your mode of operation, it is possible to have each group work on their own project suggestion or tell students that they will all work on one at a time depending on your time availability.

This step is extremely important; it gives students the opportunity to develop their skills in real-world problem-solving, thinking critically, researching, planning, writing, creating presentations, and interacting with people in power.

Set Ground Rules for Class Discussions

 Strategy 249: Examples

STEP ONE:

While setting ground rules, consider those that can be used for all class discussions. They will help students develop the habits of a good listener:

◆ The five-second rule: No student may speak until at least five seconds have passed since the previous person spoke.

◆ A person responding to what someone has said must first paraphrase what he thinks he heard and receive affirmation from the previous speaker.

◆ If it becomes necessary, place a liberal time limit on the amount of time any one person can speak.

◆ No one can speak more than once as part of the same discussion until others have at least had the opportunity to speak.

◆ Finally, perhaps in English class, ask students to react to this Mark Twain quote: *"If we were supposed to talk more than we listen, we would have two mouths and one ear."*

DON: All the members of our immediate family can be pretty verbal. During family discussions, the youngest of our three children, who was five at the time, often had great difficulty participating until we established the five-second rule. This was empowering to her. As I or any of the other family members got passionate during a debate and rushed in to make our point, Raina would quickly point out, "You didn't wait five seconds," and then before one of us could overcome our amused surprise, she would begin talking, and we would have to respect her right to do so.

STEP TWO:

Avoid getting so caught up in the content of the discussion that you fail to place equal value on the importance of teaching students how to discuss. Periodically, halt the discussion and ask students to evaluate themselves on how well they adhered to the behaviors agreed upon and posted for all to see. Sometimes you can simply ask the class as a whole to assess the discussion. Other times you can give students an opportunity to discuss their evaluation in pairs or small groups before asking them to share their conclusions with the entire class. Each time they are asked to think about their own assessment or discuss it with others, they are being challenged to think critically about the behaviors that are critical to a meaningful discussion.

☑ **Strategies 250–254: Activities to Address Issues of Discrimination**

◆ In an NPR interview, two first-grade teachers from Woodlawn, California, described telling their classes the story of Ruby Bridges, who at age six was the first African American to desegregate an all-white elementary school in Louisiana. An easy strategy for any teacher is to share Ruby's story with the class and then put students in pairs or small groups and ask them to produce three questions about Ruby Bridges. After compiling a class list, the teacher can then rotate the questions so that each pair or group is responding to another's questions. Obviously, this process creates opportunities for the teacher to share information and correct misinformation.

◆ For an activity to focus students on significant issues of discrimination, students could be asked to conduct research to discover two facts that either support or refute any of the following:
   ❏ George Floyd, Breonna Taylor, Daniel Prude, and other people of color were unjustly killed by police officers.
   ❏ The average U.S. person of color has an annual income that is as much as 30% lower than that of the average white U.S. citizen.
   ❏ In some occupations, women are paid less than men for doing the same kind of work.
   ❏ The infant mortality rate for children of color is much higher than that for white infants.
   ❏ Medical services and practices, such as providing pain relief, are not always available or offered to people of color.
   ❏ New York schools are classified as having the most racial segregation in the nation.
   ❏ People of color receive harsher sentences for equivalent crimes by white individuals.
   ❏ Many suburban areas throughout the United States refuse to allow the building of affordable housing for lower-income individuals.

❏ Many Civil War monuments and flags honoring Confederate soldiers (whom the Constitution would label as traitors) are still displayed throughout the United States.

◆ Or, for students capable of handling a significant challenge to their analytical capacity, an ambitious teacher might try this: Distribute a newspaper article about the events that took place in Charlottesville, Virginia, during the presidential term of Donald Trump. Have students list and rank order three reasons why they agree, disagree, or are uncertain of their support for Donald Trump's statement that "[t]here were good people on both sides." Follow this up by having students meet in triads and share their positions and reasons while practicing "active listening" skills. End by asking the entire class by a show of hands if anyone changed their positions at all after hearing others' opinions. Then ask for volunteers to share their position changes and main reasons. End by asking students, "What can be done to make sure that future protests are nonviolent?" and have them return to their triads to develop and share proposals, which could be refined and presented by students to their local city council.

Strategy 255: Examples & Questions for Activities focused on discrimination

The following questions contain examples of the kinds of discrimination faced by Black people on a daily basis. These are concepts teachers of all age groups should explore with students, at their appropriate level of understanding, to help reduce racism, bigotry, and discrimination toward any group. A variety of learner-centered activities could be designed around these questions. The questions could be assigned to students individually, in pairs, or in small groups to research and discuss. The results of their research could then be shared through individual essays or class presentations. A journal entry documenting the students' research process could also be required.

◆ Is the disproportionate number of Black individuals who are shot by police without cause or strip-searched for minor traffic violations a problem that affects only Black people, or should others be concerned? Why?

◆ What is meant by the lyric, "He's not heavy. He's my brother!"? (Playing the song by The Hollies, Neil Diamond, or another artist could enhance a discussion.)

- Who is affected by racism, discrimination, bigotry, and prejudice in the United States? How are they affected?
- In addition to Black individuals, what other groups did the Ku Klux Klan discriminate against? What is the evidence?
- What kinds of discrimination most often confront Latinx groups?
- How were Africans treated in 1619?
- How many Catholics have received a major party's nomination to run for president? How many have been elected? Why did it take so long?
- How did enslavement affect those who were enslaved? Economically? Socially? Psychologically? Educationally? Politically?
- What did our Constitution say about the equality of the enslaved population in 1789?
- What occupations were rarely open to women prior to the 1970s? What brought about a change to allow for women to become employed in traditionally male occupations?
- What was the Dred Scott Supreme Court decision? Is it important? Why or why not?
- What was Reconstruction? What happened to former slaves during this period?
- Do we have separate and equal schools today? Why?
- Do current American citizens benefit or suffer when immigrants are granted citizenship? Explain.
- What was the *Brown v. Board of Education* decision? What happened, and did not happen, as a result of it?
- What is "redlining?" How does it affect people of color and those who are impoverished?
- What should our government do to solve the problems of racism, bigotry, discrimination, and poverty?
- What can you do as an individual to help solve the problems of racism, bigotry, and poverty? What specific action will you take? Why will you do this?
- What can you do, as an individual, to help solve the problem of bullying among your peers? What specific action will you take? Why will you do this?
- What do we mean by the term "mass incarceration"? What has been the impact on minority populations?
- What are the origins of policing in this country?
- Have indigenous people had struggles unique to their heritage, and if so, what have they involved? What agreements has the U.S. government made with indigenous people? Have these agreements been honored?

Strategies 256, 257: Two Fun, but Important, Activities for Addressing Controversial Issues

Here are two activities passed along from Raamitha Pillay, an instructor in the School of Engineering at the State University of New York in Canton:

The 9/6 Activity

Each pair of students will need an index card with the number 6 written on it so that it looks like a six from one direction, and it looks like a nine from the opposite direction. Students group in pairs facing each other across a desk, chair, small table, or counter. Place the index card on the table or chair in between the pair so one student sees the number 6 and the other student will see the number 9. Students are asked to persuade the other person that the number is as they see it. Students should stay on their side of the table, not move the index card, and follow classroom rules of communication. Students could spend two minutes in their persuasion discussion.

Ask your students what they observed and experienced in the 9/6 activity. Guide them toward seeing that what was important was that they each see the other's point of view, not whether either could persuade the other.

Now discuss the topic that will probably elicit contrary points of view from your students. Afterward, or throughout, bring them back to the 9/6 activity and point out that it is less important to persuade or be persuaded than to listen and try to understand another point of view.

The Mood Meter

The "Mood Meter" was designed by the Yale Center for Emotional Intelligence and is available for a few dollars, with volume discounts if you google "Mood Meter." The self-assessment meter can be useful if you distribute it to children, and throughout a discussion, do a spot-check assessment by asking students to reflect on whether and/or how their mood has changed but only if they are willing to share. Here's an example: "Jack, are you comfortable sharing with us where you are on the meter right now? Jalil? Barry?" For the students, it is worthwhile for them to learn to take time to reflect on how they are feeling. For teachers, this can enable them to monitor students' feelings throughout a discussion in order to guide their approach.

Or, you could take a quick assessment of the class at a particular time during the discussion of a controversial issue by displaying the "Mood Meter" and asking for a show of hands on the following questions: "How many of you are feeling like this feeling on the Mood Meter?" "How about this feeling?"

The Mood Meter can be used in a variety of ways, including the use of pair-shares or small group discussions so that students can discuss their moods with each other and nurture their empathy skills. The Mood Meter could also be a conversation starter for a parent to use with a child.

 Strategy 258: Examples for Younger Children

For younger children, simpler, yet meaningful, questions could be assigned, again for discussion in pairs or small groups:

◆ What does it mean to love your neighbor?
◆ What should you do if you see someone picking on another child?
◆ Are people whose skin color is different from yours, better, worse, or the same as everyone else?
◆ Are men or women smarter than the other?
◆ Who make better doctors, men or women? Why? Give examples.

The foregoing questions, and others that teachers or parents can create, can be used to challenge young people to research examples of bias toward any group or individual. These questions can also be a catalyst for discussions around bullying, which is a significant problem in schools.

When you do ask students to share, discuss, and report to the entire class, some are sure to ask how they will be graded. If you are asked, we suggest announcing, "As long as you put forth maximum effort, you will receive a high grade on this assignment. I will assess your effort based on how hard you seem to be working within your pair/group and whether you have reasonable research and rationale behind your conclusions, even if I don't necessarily agree with you."

 Strategy 259: An Activity for a Discussion on Sexism

Begin by having students break into four groups (however, resist the temptation to divide them by gender since not every student may identify as male or female). Give each group a large sheet of newsprint and have them assign people to the roles of recorder, facilitator, presenter, and gopher.

Have two of the groups draw a line down the center of their paper with one-half labeled "Advantages of Being a Female" and the other half "Disadvantages of Being a Female." The other groups will divide their newsprint into columns labeled for advantages and disadvantages of being a male.

Give the groups 15 minutes to brainstorm, prioritize, and agree on their top three advantages and disadvantages, with supporting rationale for each. Have each group present its work and answer questions from other groups and yourself as the teacher.

Note: If you have an exceptionally large class, you can create more groups, but trying to limit group size to four is more likely to result in the active engagement of students.

Following the discussion, explore the following questions:

"What examples of sexism exist in this school or community?"
"What can we do about it?"

After brainstorming viable solutions, assign each student to create a proposal in writing for addressing sexism. Have volunteers share their essays with the entire class. Challenge individuals to act upon their proposals.

Here is another activity: Ask students whether this quotation from Billie Jean King reflects their thinking about sexism and lesbian, gay, bi-sexual, transgender, and queer (LGBTQ) issues. If so, how; if not, why not?

"It's just really important that we start celebrating our differences. Let's start tolerating first, but then we need to celebrate our differences."

You might also show the movie *Battle of the Sexes* in conjunction with this quote. It should capture student interest and lend itself to good discussion questions.

 Strategy 260: Create a Lens for Viewing a Video or Reading a Passage

Whenever you do show a film, make questions available to students BEFORE the showing. It is always a good idea to let students know, in advance, the questions you will pose following a reading or viewing. This gives students a lens for their reading or viewing and helps them focus on what the teacher wants them to notice

Another activity: Have your students (or children at home) research Elizabeth Blackwell and provide them with specific questions to address.

For example, how did Blackwell become the first female admitted to a medical school in the United States? Children may be surprised to discover that the higher-ups at Geneva Medical School did not want to accept Blackwell but feared being accused of bias if they did not. So, they handed it down to the students to vote. The students thought it was a hoax, so they voted to admit her, not believing it would happen until the day they showed up for classes.

Challenge students to address the question suggested in the previous paragraph, as well as these or other questions:

◆ After a few months, how was Blackwell received by the administrators of the college? By the students? By outsiders?
◆ How did her admission open the door for other females to enter the field of medicine?

Suggest that students use the internet but caution them against relying heavily on any one source. Suggest, as a resource, but do not insist on it, *The Doctors Blackwell:*

How Two Pioneering Sisters Brought Medicine to Women and Women to Medicine

by Janice P. Nimura.

 Strategies 261, 262: Activities to Address LGBTQ Discrimination

LGBTQ individuals have historically experienced discrimination due to religious intolerance, cultural mores, ignorance, and fear. However, these groups have also seen a huge increase in acceptance, tolerance, and respect from the broader U.S. population, as evidenced by positive media depictions and a slew of legislative victories affirming LGBTQ rights. Despite this evolution, the LGBTQ population continues to experience violence, prejudice, and discrimination. Schools must address these issues. Ask students to discuss whether the phrase "[a]ll (people) are created equal" should apply to those who are LGBTQ? And why or why not? List their ideas on the board and direct them to respond to the question in writing, giving at least three priority reasons to support their positions. Have them share in triads and ask questions of each other. Another question that can be posed is, "Should the sexual orientation of someone else concern me?"

An Activity to Address Religious Discrimination

Once again, fear and ignorance perpetuated by government leaders, parents, peer groups, and some religious leaders have led to increased prejudice and violence against Jews and Muslims. Lack of self-esteem, conspiracy theories, and refusal to read and comprehend the facts are most often the characteristics of the aggressors. Schools can play a critical role in eliminating these behaviors and creating more religious tolerance and respect through engaging learner-centered experiences. Show videos like the 1943 Academy Award-winning *Gentleman's Agreement*, the 1967 film *Guess Who's Coming to Dinner*, or any of the scores of more recent films that focus on issues of diversity and discrimination, such as *Schindler's List* and *12 Years a Slave*. But do not simply show the film—utilize it as a catalyst for discussion. With time at a premium for most teachers, showing brief excerpts of films depicting moral dilemmas to generate dialogue among students can be effective.

In pairs or groups, ask students to brainstorm and rank order reasons for having "freedom of religion" in our Constitution's First Amendment. Then have each small group share their top reason with the class and respond to questions.

DON: An advantage of activities and discussions about topics raised in this chapter (and, in fact, about any class discussion or activity) is what the teacher or parent can learn by being attentive to student comments, questions, and body language. As Dan and I collaborated on this book, we spoke with people from diverse backgrounds and submitted drafts with requests for candid feedback. I am 79 years old and have always considered myself to be a forward-looking thinker on matters of human relations. Yet, I have been amazed at how much my views have changed as a result of what I continue to learn.

Simply reading feedback that certain words or phrases I have used all my life are offensive to certain people has been an eye-opener.

Strategies 263–271: Address Bias with Learner-Centered Activities

Additional activities to try include the following:

◆ Challenge students with questions and activities that will simultaneously require them to think critically and to learn about perceived injustices of the past so they are not repeated in the future. Consider activities such as these:

❑ Have students brainstorm, write essays, and suggest solutions to the following question: "What do you think causes people to discriminate against others, particularly minority groups that have faced discrimination in the past?"

❑ Give students a list of races, nationalities, and religions, and ask them, in pairs or small groups, to conduct research and report (in writing or verbally) on the kinds of discrimination each group has faced. Give students options but try to ensure that each pair or group researches a different group. One method to accomplish this is to allow students to choose a group to study but consider assigning each student to a group they are unfamiliar with.

❑ Use the categories of scientists, mathematicians, historical figures, authors, artists, musicians, athletes, entertainers, and inventors, and do research as a teacher to find names of Black, Latinx, Muslim, Native American, Asian, LGBTQ, and females who made significant contributions in each category. Assign groups of students to research the contributors, and report on their research in a creative way.

❑ Ask students how they think their school should deal with a complaint of bullying or other kinds of discrimination in the school.

❑ Have students "pair-share" on the following question: "Is there a connection between bullying and bigotry, and, if so, what is it?" Follow it up by having a representative from a local antidiscrimination group speak to the class about the question.

◆ Integrate issues of racism, discrimination, and social justice into the mandated and elective curricula.

◆ Create a voluntary professional development group to read and discuss books on racism, discrimination, and other examples of injustice.

◆ Conduct cultural exchange student visits between city school students and suburban or rural school students. Discuss the reality of separate and unequal schools with both groups of students and have students present their findings and proposals to school administrators, parents, and community groups.

◆ Intervene assertively when racial slurs or discriminatory acts are heard or observed. The way you react, or fail to react, is a model for what you can expect from your students. Work with other teachers and the administration to turn these acts into learning experiences for the entire school. Organize a class workshop for all students using roleplays (being careful of roles chosen so stereotypes are not perpetuated) and audience pair-share discussions.

Teachers and students who have grown up in an environment with little cultural diversity often feel awkward discussing issues of racism or other forms of bigotry. However, as New York State, California, and a growing number of other states are demonstrating, addressing issues such as these are becoming mandatory or at least recommended, so it is important to have strategies for this purpose.

 Strategy 272: Initiating a Discussion on Discrimination

To start a discussion on discrimination, a parent or teacher could give the following quiz to youngsters:

Which of these events occurred in the United States before 1970?

◆ World-famed Black entertainer Sammy Davis Jr. was not allowed to stay in the same Las Vegas hotel where he was paid to perform.
◆ A television network received hate mail because as Perry Como and Lena Horne concluded a duet, the tips of their extended fingers accidentally touched as they took their bows.
◆ Singer Billie Holiday was not allowed to use a segregated bathroom in the restaurant where she was entertaining.
◆ Jackie Robinson had to have dinner brought to him in the team bus because Black people were not allowed in restaurants in the southern town where the team was playing.

Strategies 273–277: Examples in Different Disciplines of Linking Activities to Standards

In addition to the many suggested activities in this chapter, here are some that directly link issues of social justice and discrimination to federal and most local and state standards:

◆ In English classes, include in any activity written journal reflections by students on what they think they are learning from the activity, oral reports to the class, and research or readings that provide information the students may need to reference.
◆ In social studies, integrate current events to complement required content.
◆ In math, after citing statistics giving evidence of the harsher impact of COVID-19 on minority populations, consider posing this

question: "If the number of minority-owned businesses in America decreased by 30% in one month, say, March, but increased 30% in April, would the total of minority-owned businesses be back to the level that existed before March?" In other words, ask students if a drop of 30% followed by a gain of 30% brings things back to where they were.

◆ In science, have students investigate whether there are valid comparisons between the impact on minority populations of COVID-19 and either the Tuskegee Study or the Slave Experiment.

◆ Given the previous examples, why not integrate pandemic issues into art, music, physical education, and technology. With a bit of creativity, current events such as the pandemic can be used as relevant student issues to meet required standards.

In Support of Cooperative Learning Activities

Researchers Roger T. Johnson and David W. Johnson of the Cooperative Learning Institute and the University of Minnesota report that putting people of different backgrounds together does not, by itself, help to break down stereotypes and prejudices. They cite research supporting the contention that people who are different from each other will actually have their stereotypes reinforced if they are in a traditionally taught classroom. For example, if people are in a class with someone who uses a wheelchair, but they do not have active engagement with this person, the stereotyped opinions will not change. It is only when people are eyeball-to-eyeball and knee-to-knee, Johnson and Johnson state figuratively and emphatically, that perceptions will change.

COMMONSENSE CONCLUSION

Effective student-centered teaching requires the teacher to trust that if students are challenged with probing questions that require them to think critically, the students will reach conclusions that can enable them to be contributing members of a just society.

29

Lessons from COVID-19

Online Instruction and Utilizing Technology Can Support, Not Replace, Good Teaching

Yvonne enjoys social studies because Mr. Blaine shows lots of movies. Afterward, he asks the students whether they enjoyed the movie and gives them a quiz with some short-answer questions and one or two essay questions. Yvonne googles the movie so she can learn enough to get a good grade on the test. This allows her to play video games while the movie is showing. She doesn't have to be too clever about hiding her tablet from Mr. Blaine because he's usually busy doing a crossword puzzle or reading the newspaper while the movie is playing.

No book on education reform would be complete without discussing the impact of technology on educational practices. With the proliferation of online schooling, many teachers are scrambling for ideas to make online teaching more effective.

A Transformational Perspective

Linda Darling-Hammond, a current international education icon and leader for progressive, research-based education reform, has stated that the pandemic may have a thin silver lining in that it has provided educators, policymakers, and researchers the opportunity to reevaluate our current "factory-assembly-line," test-driven process of education and create a new vision, goals, and action plans for developing a more learner-centered form of education. When the pandemic is behind us, will educators simply revert to

DOI: 10.4324/9781003284697-35

what has been comfortable and familiar, though in most cases dysfunctional, or will we seize the opportunity to create something better for students?

What We Have Learned from COVID-19

After reviewing numerous studies related to online learning during the tragic circumstances brought about by COVID-19, we share our three main conclusions:

1. Technology is a valuable tool when utilized in support of in-person instruction. However, there is no substitute for in-person learning. In addition to students missing out on the socialization aspects of education, the learning of *all* students suffers in varying degrees when learning is online. Higher-performing students, whose learning styles align with traditional teaching styles, suffer the least decline in achievement after moving to online learning. Students with strong in-home support also suffer minimally, because they are generally among the higher-performing students who have reasonably good study habits and have someone at home to ensure they participate in online communications with the teacher and follow through on assignments. Students with less adult home supervision, those who live in poverty, those who are suffering trauma, and those who are already behind on their work usually fall furthest behind when learning is online.

   Also, even higher-performing students can suffer a great deal when learning is restricted to online. Many of these students have unique creative talents and/or learning styles that cannot be noticed and accommodated through online teaching.

   The fact that the COVID-19 experience has provided evidence of the limitations of online instruction is important because there have been rumors that some politicians believe there can be enormous savings by conducting all or most schooling online.
2. The ability of many teachers to use technology effectively in support of classroom learning has been significantly advanced due to the necessity to teach online in many school districts.
3. While many uninformed people have previously viewed teaching as a 9–3 job with plenty of vacations and summers off, at least some have gained a greater respect for the profession during the COVID-19 crisis. Many parents have had to assume the role of at-home

teacher, an experience that may have increased their understanding and respect for the work of full-time teachers. In addition, the media spotlight on how teachers across the country have been responding to and coping with the challenges of the pandemic may also have amplified the public's support and appreciation.

There have always been two ways educators have approached the use of technology: either as a substitute for quality teaching or as a support for sound pedagogical practices. The COVID-19 experience has demonstrated the fallacy of the former and the value of the latter.

Effective Use of Technology

As long ago as 1993, one author entered an urban classroom of second- and third-grade students and observed two-thirds of the young students seated at tables of four working on math manipulatives. Another six students sat at computers obtained through a major state grant. They were using software that reinforced what they had learned from their teacher while working on the manipulatives. The students had to demonstrate a required level of proficiency before the teacher would send them to the computers. This was an example of using technology in support of, rather than as a replacement for, effective teaching.

The COVID-19 pandemic triggered the cancellation of months of in-school lessons, resulting in many schools providing online instruction to students confined to their homes. Given the issue of student and staff safety and protection from the virus, this was the best option possible under the circumstances. Some schools were more able than others to ensure that every student had access to the necessary technology. As often is the case, students from financially strapped families were least likely to keep up with their classmates. This was only mainly due to more limited access to technology and less access to tech-knowledge family support. Of course, families in poverty include concerned parents who would work with their children; however, on average, the parents tend to be less educated and/or have less time to devote to reinforcing their children's study habits due to other commitments such as employment and childcare.

What is concerning is that politicians may think what they have learned from this COVID-19 experience is that technology can replace the classroom teacher. Think of all the money that could be saved if schools were conducted online as some college courses are. Look at the cost savings if school buildings were not needed. Recently in an article headlined "Cuomo Suggests Online

School Could Replace Classroom Instruction," the New York State governor was quoted as saying, "The old model of everybody goes and sits in a classroom and the teacher is in front of that classroom and teaches that class and you do that all across the city, all across the state, all these buildings, all these physical classrooms. 'Why? With all the technology you have?'" (*Real-Time Hudson News*, May 20, 2020)

This kind of thinking does exist; it is part of a thought process we will label as an attempt to teacher-proof education. What those outside of the classroom sometimes fail to realize is that ALL students benefit from the hands-on teaching of an expert with training and experience. The students who suffer the most when their class size is too large, or when technology replaces—rather than supports—the classroom teacher, are those in poverty, those suffering with trauma, those with learning disabilities, as well as those higher-performing students and students whose learning styles do not precisely fit the mold of the average student. In other words, almost everyone.

American Federation of Teachers president Randi Weingarten told MSNBC host Joshua Johnson on November 16, 2020, "Remote learning disproportionately affects low-income students," while in the same interview also stated, "We've learned that kids don't learn as effectively with on-line teaching."

Reducing the role of the classroom teacher using technology is one of many ways governments and educational leaders try to teacher-proof schools. It is critical to recognize that you can no more take teachers out of teaching than you can take medical professionals out of health care. Whether discussing health care or education, there is only so much that can be done through testing and technology. Would you want to go to a doctor who simply reads charts and laboratory reports and then states on a computer what to prescribe without using any of the judgment her training and experience prepared her to rely on?

The risk that technology and other government mandates will become vehicles for attempting to replace—rather than augment and support—the expertise of classroom teachers is present; however, a simple-to-describe-if-not-easy-to-guarantee solution exists: as educators, we must constantly remind the public, and ourselves, that the goal is what is best for our children's education, not what is easiest or least expensive.

In an earlier chapter, there is a description of 76 students participating in an activity in a cafeteria being asked to go to the front of the room to cast a ballot for their choice of a topic to be explored in a lesson. As a tech-savvy teacher observed one student after another walk to the front of the room and cast a ballot, she suggested, "I could bring in chrome tablets and distribute them to every table, and then the process would be quicker and more efficient."

Sounds logical, right? Maybe. It was pointed out that this was part of a lengthy process wherein students would be seated for a long time, and this was a chance for movement.

So, what is the answer? Should technology have been employed to save time, or should the slower method that would generate movement and, perhaps, better functioning of students' brains have been the better strategy? The answer is, "It depends." The criteria for the decision should include how long the total seat-time for students would be, whether there are other times during the lesson when students would be moving about, how much time could be allotted for the lesson, and any other relevant factors. Again, the criteria for the decision as to whether to utilize technology goes beyond whether it is available and would be more efficient. The question must always be, "What would be best for the students?"

 Strategy 278: A Learner-Centered Online Teaching Idea

In a classroom, it is of course easier to group students than when they are isolated at different locations working at their computers. But you can still ask two, three, or four students to work on a task using technology to communicate with each other.

As stated earlier in this chapter, there are many resources available to teachers who seek to utilize technology effectively, so we are not going to add pages to lists that are available through Google or consultation with a tech-savvy colleague. We will recommend one resource designed recently by Alicia Peletz and two colleagues. Alicia was a teacher before moving into her current position as a staff developer with Applied Coaching for Projects (ACP). ACP has published an e-book filled with ideas for utilizing technology when limited to virtual teaching/learning. It is short, and it has many worthwhile ideas. See https://www.appliedcoaching.org/collaboration-e-book.

For example, the question of what, if anything, have we learned from online teaching and learning processes that can be integrated into our regular teaching is a worthwhile question for serious exploration.

To accommodate the conflicting preferences of parents for online or in-person learning, many schools opted for a mixed approach of two or three days a week of each. Due to the number of parents who refused to let their children attend school in person, class sizes were significantly smaller than originally planned, and many teachers who had always taught traditionally from the front of the room consequently found themselves meeting in person with small groups of students while they would have other small groups researching, interviewing, surveying, interning, or experimenting with topics of interest.

Did these teachers discover that this was a more effective learning process than meeting with all 30 students and trying to teach all of them the same thing at the same time? One would hope so. Darling-Hammond's recommendations are critical. As educators, we must also learn from our experiences and "seize the moments" for our growth and that of our students whenever possible (Darling-Hammond, 2019).

COMMONSENSE CONCLUSION

Technology is a terrific asset to a classroom teacher if it is used in support of best instructional practices rather than as a replacement for them.

30

Change How Student Progress Is Reported

Jeremy's mother looked at his report card and said to her spouse, "This is meaningless. I mean, it's nice that he got an 88 in science, even though we joke that he can't tell a rock formation from a glacier. Maybe this week they were focused on other aspects of science that he enjoys. And his English grade is still in the low 70s, even though he spent six weeks in summer school supposedly studying English."

"That concerns me, too," her husband responded. "I spoke with his summer school teacher and asked why he spent so little time with Jeremy on punctuation and so much time on reading comprehension, even though his regular English teacher said his weakest area was spelling and grammar. He told me he wasn't aware of that because Jeremy's record only showed that he had a 72 in English last year."

✔️ Strategy 279: A Reporting Process for Effective Communications

We strongly recommend that schools change how they communicate student progress with parents and other teachers. Our suggestions are based on the following experiences and examples:

★ Too often, teachers have limited ability to access relevant information about students they are required to teach or remediate. In many districts, summer school teachers have little or no access to information about the students in their courses.

★ Report card grades generally reflect a combination of a student's skill levels and other factors—behavior, attitude, and homework

DOI: 10.4324/9781003284697-36

assignments. However, what does an "85%" really tell you about a student's strengths and weaknesses? In English, for instance, one student can excel in spelling, grammar, and punctuation but struggle with reading comprehension and writing, while another student can be the reverse. Yet, in all likelihood, their report cards will simply record that both students earned a "C."

★ Without detailed specifics on a student's skills, her past number or letter grades will be useless to her current teacher's ability to diagnose her needs.

Suggestions for Improving Communications about Expectations for Quality Work

1. In each discipline, identify the few skills and content knowledge areas that are essential for a student to master in order to succeed in the next grade level.
2. Design a performance assessment and rubric for determining whether a student has mastered the desired skill level.
3. Utilize technology so that a parent, teacher, or administrator could simply press a button to view a student's assessments and demonstrated performance levels.

In the following, we break down each step in further detail.

1. Identifying Skills
   Clearly articulate in writing both the curricular expectations and the expectations of your school's administration or teaching staff.
2. Design a Performance Assessment
   To show how a performance assessment might be designed, let us use an example based on a sixth-grade Common Core Standard.

Learning Objective
Students solve real-world and mathematical problems involving area, surface area, and volume.

Performance Task
A cereal company uses cereal boxes that are rectangular. The boxes are made from cardboard and have the dimensions shown.

- ◆ 12 inches high
- ◆ 8 inches wide
- ◆ 2 inches deep

The managers of the company want a new size for their cereal boxes. The new boxes must be rectangular. You will create and propose your own design for the company.

Requirements for the new boxes:

- ◆ The new boxes must use less cardboard than the original boxes.
- ◆ The new boxes must hold the same or greater volume of cereal as the original boxes.

Rubric			
Dimensions	**Criteria for a Score of 3**	**Criteria for a Score of 2**	**Criteria for a Score of 1**
Understands the concept of volume and how to calculate volume	• The company cereal box's volume is correctly calculated. • The student-created cereal box's volume is correctly calculated.	Only one of the box's volumes is correctly calculated.	Both of the box's volumes are incorrectly calculated, but the correct formula is applied.
Understands the concept of area and how to calculate area	The areas of both company and student boxes are correctly calculated.	Only one of the box's areas is correctly calculated.	Both of the box's areas are incorrectly calculated, but the correct formula is applied.
Understands how to apply knowledge of volume to solve a real-world problem	The student-created box has the same or greater volume than the company box.	The student-created box has less volume than the company box.	The student is somewhat unclear on how to calculate volume.

Rubric			
Dimensions	**Criteria for a Score of 3**	**Criteria for a Score of 2**	**Criteria for a Score of 1**
Understands how to apply knowledge of area to solve a real-world problem	The student-created box uses less cardboard than the company box.	The student-created box uses the same amount of cardboard as the company box.	The student-created box uses more cardboard than the company box.

Chart by Pat Flynn with permission.

This rubric makes it easy to understand what sixth-grade teachers expect students to understand about volume.

3. Utilize Technology

Now imagine if the above rubric were readily available to teachers, administrators, and parents via an online portal. A fifth-grade teacher would understand exactly what her students would be expected to know the following year, and a seventh-grade teacher would know what capabilities to expect of her incoming students. If a parent received this rubric and saw that their child had scored a "2" on this task, wouldn't that be far more helpful than simply receiving a report card with an 87% for math?

A district could look at an entire pre-K-to-12 curriculum to ensure the expectations for a certain skill were properly aligned with the appropriate grade levels, meaning the current grade as well as the grade before and the subsequent one.

Three Cautions as You Consider New Approaches

1. The first time a school attempts to assess skill and content mastery through performance assessments, start with just a few items in one discipline. The question to address is, "What are the two or three skills or pieces of content information that a student needs to master in order to have a chance to be successful at the next grade level?" It will be a slow process, initially, to design and implement the assessments, with some time for trial and error. However, once this is accomplished in one discipline at one or two grade levels, you will

have an exemplar that will enable others to develop performance assessments in far less time in every other discipline.

2. Teachers sometimes rebel against separating discipline and homework from skill assessments on a report card. Some teachers use the report card grade to control homework and student classroom behavior. It is legitimate for teachers to ask, "If I can't lower a grade due to a student's behavior, how can I control it?" We acknowledge that there must be consequences for students who ignore homework or cause behavioral problems in class. However, we suggest that the district find alternative means of addressing these concerns so that teachers do not feel the need to use the report card grade as a weapon. A baseball manager cannot reduce a player's batting average as a penalty for disrespectful behavior, but there are other options, such as benching the player, issuing a fine, or requiring counseling. Teachers too must have options for addressing behavior problems without impacting how knowledge and skill levels get communicated.

3. While transitioning into performance assessments, continue using the same report cards. Just add the results of performance assessments on a limited number of highly important skills and content knowledge areas. It may take five years or longer, but eventually, parents, teachers, and students will let you know that they do not need the traditional reporting process any longer. They will find that the performance assessment reports provide a more thorough assessment of a student's abilities and progress. Personalized comments from the teacher, as well as student self-assessment comments, are also valuable bonuses for students and parents.

Additional Considerations for Rating Students

In a research-based, humanistic system, teachers who are relying on performance assessments might rate each student as follows:

"Exceeds/meets/developing XYZ skill, as demonstrated by..."

This framing removes the focus on alphanumeric grades, which risk masking student progress. And the use of "developing" rather than "failing" helps to remove the stigma of failure.

We believe student performance rubrics would be more meaningful if they were individualized for each student but only if not in comparison to other students. Each student is unique and progresses at a different rate. We already know that most students who begin a course with a stronger or weaker background in the requirements are not likely to significantly alter their position relative to their peers. When asked how she believes we should support children being raised in poverty, American Federation of Teachers president Randi Weingarten said, "Wrap services around each student with an individual plan" (2020).

COMMONSENSE CONCLUSION

Communications between teachers and parents about student progress must be specific to students' knowledge, skills, and abilities.

Section Seven

Is Meaningful School Reform Possible?

Agents of Change, Please Step Forward
There Can Be Major School Reform at Minimal Cost

Why do many school reform initiatives
introduced with great fanfare fail?
Often because they are too expensive,
or because they disturb the structure of
daily school operations.

Who are the change agents who can
create learner-centered schools
and classrooms? They can be
administrators, classroom
teachers, parents, community members,
or anyone willing to lead and articulate
what they believe in.

31

Agents of Change, Please Step Forward

Fifth-grade teacher Marty Chan was feeling down as he poured a cup of coffee in the faculty lounge. Speaking to his colleague Arnie Sakall, he lamented, "Every good idea I have gets shot down by Mr. Ferrari. Either it's not something we've ever done, or some committee would have to approve it, or he doesn't know if parents would object." Mr. Sakall tried to soothe him: "Do what you can in your classroom that doesn't require anyone's approval. Mr. Ferrari is retiring soon, and his replacement may be looking for a veteran teacher like you to champion innovative ideas."

Effective, meaningful change can happen, and the most effective change starts from the bottom up. If the people at the top will not lead, they should at least follow and support responsible, creative proposals designed to make teaching and learning more meaningful. By "top" we refer to anyone in a position to influence the direction of schools, who is not actually working in a classroom or school.

◆ Each year a growing number of teachers are learning, practicing, and implementing learner-centered practices and lessons. The authors can identify teachers who have been on the learner-centered journey long enough to say they have completely transformed their classrooms into learner-centered environments.

Administrative positions are being gradually filled by teachers who have been in classrooms where learner-centered strategies were used. They know what is involved, and they know the kinds of support their teachers need to help other teachers and administrators create more learner-centered schools.

DOI: 10.4324/9781003284697-38

◆ University education departments have been the slowest to react, but each year, more of them are preparing and requiring their college students to understand and apply constructivist theory of how people learn.

Teachers and administrators need to be the agents of change if we truly are to restructure our schools to be more adept at meeting the educational and social-emotional needs of *all* students. With all due respect for the intentions of many of our politicians and state and federal education department officials, most have been out of the classroom too long to understand the revolution in teaching strategies that is taking place—a revolution that can transform the way we educate students and significantly increase the skills and knowledge they need to be effective citizens.

COMMONSENSE CONCLUSION

The change agents to transform education must come from among the educators who are in the trenches daily. Local teachers and administrators understand the challenges of educating *all* students. Whether they resist or lead their schools in the research-informed directions cited in this book will determine the length of the journey to improved and equitable opportunities for *all* students.

32

There Can Be Major School Reform at Minimal Cost

Image by Afzal Khan. With permission

Much of what is proposed in this book requires a change in mindset, not a change in school-district budgets. It requires teachers to think differently about how they design lessons and how they assess student learning. Administrators need to see themselves as facilitators of learning. The good leaders already do.

As long ago as 1989, one author was asked by a school superintendent to work with three elementary school staffs in his district to design a plan for totally restructuring each school's approach to educating children. The purpose was for an application for a multimillion-dollar grant. The experience was essentially the same in each building.

DOI: 10.4324/9781003284697-39

This author, as facilitator, led each staff in brainstorming and visioning, and he instructed them to design the best restructuring plan that was in their creative power to conceive. "Ignore cost," the teachers were told. "If it can be defended as being best for children, put it in your plan."

Each of the three staffs took two full days to create their vision of the ideal school, and when their work was completed, their ideas were spread on newsprint around the four walls of the large conference rooms where they had been meeting.

"Take a long, slow look at what you've designed," the author instructed each group separately. "Do you notice anything surprising?" More than 80% of what each staff had separately designed would NOT COST any money. These ideas were created 31 years ago and addressed groupings of students and teachers, interdisciplinary approaches to learning, parent conferences, grading, and reporting grades, as well as many other changes teachers wanted to explore. And what happened as a result? On the one hand, it can be discouraging that the progressive ideas proposed by those teachers 31 years ago are still being implemented. On the other hand, these school districts' work shows that education is beginning to head in the direction that education researchers have been recommending, even if the pace is slower than ideal. The challenge is obvious: Let us pick up the pace of education reform that progressive educators know reflects best practices.

Since the Carnegie Report on education reform (1983), there have been numerous articles written about the lack of progress of reform initiatives. But the doubters are looking in all the wrong places. In Section Two, we state that the classroom is where it is at. The educational lexicon now contains so many terms that were either nonexistent 30 years ago or at best were familiar only to those few researchers and other educators who stayed current with the literature. It is now becoming more common for teachers to have some familiarity with portfolio assessment, journaling, cooperative learning, technology in service to instruction, rubrics, project-based learning, and performance-based authentic assessment. This knowledge demonstrates some basic growth for the education field, but what is consistently lacking is the substance of direct, consistent application of these learner-centered practices to the classroom by the large majority of school districts.

It will take a major effort, and substantial funding, to equalize educational opportunities for *all* students and to combat the hazards of high-stakes standardized testing, racism, and other forms of bigotry. But prioritizing the design of learner-centered classrooms is a start—one that is at the lower end of the spending spectrum. And, critically, it is the vehicle that will allow our nation to step up efforts to provide a quality education for every student in America.

If you agree with the premises of this book, you do not need to become a crusader, but you can become an agent of change. As a teacher, make your classroom a model of learner-centered practices. As an administrator, support and encourage your staff to move in this direction—in other words, be a role model and leader. As a parent, community member, business leader, or school-related employee, voice your support for learner-centered practices and models integrating the affective domain, which is such a critical part of the educational process.

COMMONSENSE CONCLUSION

Ronald Reagan said, "*Don't let* what you *can't do* stop you from *doing* what you *can do*." Teachers and administrators, as agents of change, you can vastly improve our schools if you concentrate first on the classroom and then the entire school. The professional educators, the ones actually in the schools, have the power. They just need to realize it!

Image by Afzal Khan. With permission

I alone cannot change the world,
but I can cast a stone across the
waters to create many ripples.

Mother Teresa

Epilogue

Opportunities for Students Are Inequitable

Drive from a school in a wealthy community to a school in a lower-income part of town in any county. Move through the hallways and look in classrooms. What is the comparison between the resources available to staff and students in each? What about staff-to-student ratios? Technology? The number of certified teachers on staff in proportion to uncertified? And most importantly, what kind of skills, experiences, and emotional and physical health do students bring to school with them that need to be taken into account in setting and assessing standards? With inequitable school resources, do students have equal opportunities to succeed?

Are all school districts providing sufficient funding to offer every student equitable access to the quality of teaching and resources necessary for guaranteeing a quality education? No child should suffer because of the inability of their school to provide a meaningful level of resources or support.

Providing equitable opportunities to *all* students does not mean that every school has to offer exactly the same resources. It does mean there must be a federally distributed list of resources that every school needs to provide to offer equality of opportunities. If individual states and school districts want to go above and beyond, they should not be limited, but they should be held to a standard of resource provision that levels the learning field for *all* students. Unlike suggestions throughout this book, it will require significant funding increases to meet the constitutional requirement of equal opportunities for *all* students.

> Educational Equity means that each child receives what he or she needs to develop to his or her academic and social potential.
>
> National Equity Project
> (https://www.nationalequityproject.org/
> education-equity-definition)

Note: A proposed lesson plan for university education professors to use in conjunction with this book is available at www.learningcentered.org or by request at institutelce@gmail.com.

Chapters on the following topics are similarly available on the website of the Institute for Learning Centered Education or upon request:

- ◆ Initiatives to Improve Student Outcomes
- ◆ There Is a Place for Charter Schools
- ◆ Research-Based Professional Development Can Lead the Way
- ◆ Higher Education Should Lead Education Reform
- ◆ Policymakers: Listen More, Mandate Less

Appendix A

Resources for Advocacies and Journaling

1. **Writing Prompts for Middle School: 101 Things to Write about for Middle School to Supercharge Their Writing Skills—Writing Prompts for Students (Kids Journal Writing) (Volume 2)**
   By Subha Malik, Aug 31, 2017
2. **Teaching Students to Love Journaling**
   By Twila Godinez, June 25, 2012
3. **Journal Keeping: How to Use Reflective Writing for Learning, Teaching, Professional Insight and Positive Change**
   By Dannelle D. Stevens and Joanne E. Cooper, Apr 21, 2009
4. **Advisory in Urban High Schools: A Study of Expanded Teacher Roles (Palgrave Studies in Urban Education)**
   By K. Phillippo, Jul 31, 2013
5. **The Advisory Guide: Designing and Implementing Effective Advisory Programs in Secondary Schools**
   By Rachel A. Poliner and Carol Miller Lieber, Mar 1, 2004
6. **Creating Connections: Middle School Advisory That Works**
   By Erin Tobul and Ellen D'Amore, Oct 1, 2017
7. **Life Lessons for Young Adolescents: An Advisory Guide for Teachers**
   By Fred Schrumpf and Sharon Freiburg, Dec 1, 1993
8. **Changing the View: Student-Led Parent Conferences (Teacher to Teacher)**
   By Terri Austin, Nov 10, 1994
9. **Student-Led Conferencing Using Showcase Portfolios**
   By Barbara P. Benson and Susan P. Barnett, Dec 22, 1998
10. **Becoming the Teacher Students Love**
    By Christopher Harper and Natalie Bruno, Jan 20, 2014
11. **The Future of Education Depends on Social-Emotional Learning**
    By Giancarlo Brotto, Jun 4, 2018
12. **Social-Emotional Learning (SEL) and Education Equity**
    By Joan Cole Duffell, Dec 19, 2019

Appendix B

Resources for Teaching Good Citizenship

You do not need experience teaching citizenship to design effective lessons on the topic. A perusal of the following list should help:

1. **Flourish: A Visionary New Understanding of Happiness and Well-being**
    By Martin E. P. Seligman, Feb 7, 2012
2. **Values Clarification: A Handbook of Practical Strategies for Teachers and Students**
    By Sidney B. Simon and Howard Kirschenbaum, 1972
3. **Moral Reasoning: A Teaching Handbook for Adapting Kohlberg to the Classroom**
    By Ronald E. Galbraith and Thomas E. Jones, Jun 1, 1976
4. **Maslow's Hierarchy of Needs: Understand the True Foundations of Human Motivation**
    By 50Minutes.com, Aug 17, 2015
5. **Teaching Character and Virtue in Schools (Citizenship, Character and Values Education)**
    By James Arthur and Kristján Kristjánsson, Dec 23, 2017
6. **On Education, Formation, Citizenship, and the Lost Purpose of Learning (Reading Augustine)**
    By Joseph Clair and Miles Hollingworth, Nov 30, 2017
7. **Digital Citizenship in Schools: Nine Elements All Students Should Know**
    By Mike Ribble, Oct 21, 2015
8. **Global Citizenship Education**
    By William Gaudelli, Apr 18, 2016

Appendix C

Resources for Teaching Social Justice

(Titles Contain URLs)

1. **What Does It Mean to Teach for Social Justice—SUNY Oswego** (https://www.oswego.edu/~prusso1/Russos_what_does_it_mean_to_teach_for_s.htm)
   Pat Russo, Jun 2004
2. **Teaching for Social Justice by Herbert Kohl—Rethinking Schools** (http://www.rethinkingschools.org/articles/teaching-for-social-justice)
   Herbert Kohl, n.d.
3. **How to Teach Social Justice in the Classroom** (https://resilienteducator.com/classroom-resources/teaching-social-justice/)
   Caitrin Blake, May 13, 2015
4. **Teaching for Social Justice** (https://www.youtube.com/watch?v=neg9FLI1czE)
   Ashley Swanson, Nov 19, 2013
5. **Social Justice Lesson Plans** (www.nasponline.org/social-justice-lesson-plans)
   NEA Human and Civil Rights Awards Program, n.d.
6. **Why Teaching About Social Justice Matters | Teaching Tolerance** (https://www.learningforjustice.org/magazine/why-teaching-about-social-justice-matters)
   Christina Torres, Mar 5, 2015
7. **Publications—Rethinking Schools** (http://rethinkingschools.aidcvt.com/publication/index.shtml)
   Rethinking Schools, n.d.

Bibliography

Aracelli-Primo, M. (2004). *Examining concept maps as an assessment tool.* Standford, CA: Stanford University School of Education.

Aronson, E., Blaney, N., Stephan, C., Sikes, J. & Snapp, M. (1978). *The jigsaw classroom.* Newbury Park, CA: Sage Publications.

Au, W. (2018). *Rethinking multi-cultural education.* Milwaukee, WI: Rethinking Schools.

Barbian, E. & Gonzalez, G. (2017). *Re-thinking bi-lingual education.* Milwaukee, WI: Rethinking Schools.

Bargh, J. & Schul Y. (1980). On the cognitive benefits of teaching. *Journal of Educational Psychology, 72,* 593–604.

Benware, C.A. & Deci, E.L. (1984). Quality of learning with active and passive set. *American Educational Research Journal, 21,* 755–765.

Blunt educator [@Blunteducator]. (2020, October 8). Some teachers taught the curriculum today. Other teachers taught students today. And there is a big difference. [Tweet: iCollege] Twitter. https://twitter.com/icollegeint/status/777435605043122176.

Boyd to receive the 2020 Distinguished Faculty Award from SUNY Canton (2020, May 7). North Country Now. Potsdam, NY Retrieved October 8, 2020, from https://www.northcountrynow.com/honors-recognition/boyd-receive-2020-distinguished-faculty-award-suny-canton-0279847.

Brooks, J. & Brooks, M. (1983). *The case for constructivist classrooms.* Alexandria, VA: ASCD.

Cohen, E.G., & Lotan, R.A. (1995). Producing equal status interaction in the heterogeneous classroom. *American Educational Research Journal, 32,* 99–120.

Danielson, C. (1996). *Enhancing professional practice: A framework for teaching.* Alexandria, VA: ASCD.

DiAngelo, R. (2018). *White fragility.* Boston, MA: Beacon Press.

Deming, W. E. (1982). *Out of the crisis.* Cambridge, MA: The MIT Press.

Dewey, J. (1938). *Experience and education.* New York, NY: Macmillan.

Emotional and psychological trauma. (n.d.). Help guide. Retrieved June 8, 2020, from https://www.helpguide.org/articles/ptsd-trauma/coping-with-emotional-and-psychological-trauma.htm.

Engaging students in learning. (n.d.). Center for Teaching Learning. University of Washington, Washington Center for Teaching and Learning. Retrieved September 20, 2020, from https://teaching.washington.edu/topics/engaging-students-in-learning/.

Fact sheet: Social justice and health. (n.d.). Health and Community Services Workforce Council, Queensland, Australia. Retrieved April 23, 2021, from https://www.checkup.org.au/icms_docs/182820_15_FACTSHEET_Social_Justice_and_Health.pdf.

Felder, R.M. & Solomon, B. A. (n.d.) Learning styles and strategies. Retrieved March 27, 2009, from https://www.engr.ncsu.edu/wp-content/uploads/drive/1QP6kBI1iQmpQbTXL-08HSl0PwJ5BYnZW/1988-LS-plus-note.pdf.

Flynn, P., Mesibov, D., Vermette, P.J., & Smith, R.M. (2004a). *Applying standards-based constructivism: A two-step guide for motivating elementary students.* Larchmnt, NY: Eye on Education.

Flynn, P., Mesibov, D., Vermette, P.J., & Smith, R.M. (2004b). *Captivating classes with constructivism: Preparing educators for the Common Core standards.* Oregon, WI: Rainmaker Education.

Gardner, H. (1983). *Frames of mind: The theory of multiple intelligences.* Cambridge, MA: Harvard University Press.

Goodlad, J. (1984). *A place called school.* Alexandria, VA: ASCD.

Howe, L. & Howe, M. (1975). *Personalizing education.* England, UK: Hart Publishing Co.

Hunter, M. (1994). *Enhancing teaching.* New York, NY: Macmillan.

Jackson, P. (1987). *The practice of teaching.* New York, NY: Teachers College Press.

Johnson, D. & Johnson, R. (1987). *Learning together and alone.* Hoboken, NJ: Prentice Hall.

Johnson, R. (2018). *Children of the dream.* New York, NY: Basic Books.

Kohn, A. (1999). *The schools children deserve.* San Franciso, CA: Houghton Mifflin.

Lessinger, L. (1963). Test building and test banks through the use of the taxonomy of educational objectives. San Franciso, CA: *California Journal of Educational Research, 15*(5), 195–201.

Lipton, L., & Wellman, B. (1998), *Patterns and practices in the learning-focused classroom.*, Bloomingdale, MI: Pathways Publishing.

Lyiscott, James. (2019). *Black appetite, white food.* London, UK: Routledge.

Marzano, R.J. (1992). *A different kind of classroom.* Alexandria, VA: ASCD.

Moving beyond the classroom: The growing role of teacher leaders. (2018). *Education Week.* Retrieved June 20, 2020, from https://www.edweek.org/teaching-learning/moving-beyond-the-classroom-the-growing-role-of-teacher-leaders.

National Research Council. (2000). *How people learn: Brain, mind, experience, and school.* Washington, DC: National Academy Press.

Newman, F. (1997). *Authentic achievement: Restructuring schools for intellectual quality*. Hoboken, NJ: Jossey Bass.

Novak, J. (1991). Clarify with concept maps: A tool for teachers and students alike. *The Science Teacher, 58*(7), 44–49.

Novak, J. & Gowin, D. B., (1984) *Learning how to learn*. Cambridge, MA: Cambridge University Press.

Ogle, D. S. (1986). K-W-L group instructional strategy. In A.S. Palinscar, D. S. Ogle, B.E. Jones, & E.G. Carr (Eds.), *Teaching reading as thinking* (Teleconference Resource Guide), pp. 11–17). Alexandria, VA: ASCD.

Perkins, D. (1999). The many faces of constructivism. *Educational Leadership, 57*(3), 6–11.

Pernell, B. & Theoharis, J. (2017). How New York became the capital of Jim Crow north. *The Washington Post*. Retrieved November 12, 2020, from https://www.washingtonpost.com/news/made-by-history/wp/2017/08/23/how-new-york-city-became-the-capital-of-the-jim-crow-north/.

Perry, B. D., (2018, May 22), Childhood trauma. [presentation]. *ACEs 2018 Conference on Confronting Childhood Trauma*. Oklahoma State University, Tulsa, OK.

Piaget, J. (1973). *To understand is to invent*. New York, NY: Grossman.

Pink, Daniel (2009) *Drive: The surprising truth about what motivates us*. New York, NY: Riverhead Books.

Popham, J. (2004). A game without winners. *Educational Leadership, 62*(3), 46–50.

Put down that notebook! New studies find taking notes is bad for your memory. (2018, September 14). *Panopto*. Retrieved June 20, 2020 from https://www.panopto.com/blog/put-down-that-notebook-new-studies-find-taking-notes-is-bad-for-your-memory/.

Ravitch, Diane. (2013) *Reign of error*. New York, NY: Vintage Books.

Ravitch, Diane. (2008). *The death & life of the great American school system*. New York, NY: Basic Books.

Ravitch, Diane. (2020). *Slaying Goliath*. New York, NY: Vintage Books

Richardson, V. (Ed.). (1997). *Constructivist teacher education: Building a world of new understanding*. London, UK: Falmer Press.

Rogers, Carl. (1969). *Freedom to learn*. New York, NY: Pearson.

Rothstein, Richard. (2004). *Class and schools*. New York, NY: Teachers College Press.

Rothstein, Richard. (2017). *The color of law*. New York, NY: Liveright.

Rothstein, Richard (2008). *Grading education*. New York, NY: Teachers College Press.

Schlick Noe, K. & Johnson, J. (1999). *Getting started with literature circles*. Norwood, MA: Christopher-Gordon Publishers.

Schon, Donald A. (1983). *The reflective practitioner: How professionals think in action*. New York, NY: Basic Books.

Schwartz, D. & Bransford, J. (1998). A time for telling. *Cognitive and Instruction*, 16(4), 475–522.

Shuell, T. (2003, October 5). *Learning theories* [presentation]. Northeastern Educational Research Association, Ellenville, NY.

Simon, S.B. & Kirschenbaum, H. (1971). *Values clarification*. New York, NY: Dodd-Mead.

Six benefits of critical thinking and why they matter. (n.d.). Wabisabi Learning. Retrieved August 8, 2020, from https://wabisabilearning.com/blogs/critical-thinking/critical-thinking-benefits.

Sylvester, R. (1971). Benjamin Bloom and his taxonomy. *Instructor*, February 1971.

The benefits of a trauma-informed school community. (2018, November 14). *Sage Thrive*. Retrieved September 5, 2020, from https://www.sagethrivetoday.com/the-benefits-of-a-trauma-informed-school-community/.

Thorndike, E., (2011). *The law of effect*. New York, NY: Macmillan.

Tomlinson, C.A. (1999). *The differentiated classroom: Responding to the needs of all learners*. Alexandria, VA: ASCD.

Tovani, C. (2000). *I read it, but I don't get it*. Portsmith, NH: Stenhouse Publishers.

Twelve solid strategies for teaching critical thinking skills. (n.d.). Wabisabi Learning. February 6, 2018, Retrieved August 8, 2020, from https://wabisabilearning.com/blogs/critical-thinking/teaching-critical-thinking-skills.

Vermette, P.J. (1994, March). Four fatal flaws: Avoiding the common mistakes of novice users of cooperative learning. *The High School Journal*, 255–260.

Vermette, P.J., Foote, C.J., Battaglia, C., Mesibov, D., Bird, C., & Harris-Ewing, S. (2000). Understanding constructivism(s): A primer for parents and school board members. *Education*, 122(1), 87–93.

Vermette, P.J., & Foote, C.J. (2001). Constructivist philosophy and cooperative learning practice. *American Secondary Education*, 30(1), 26–37.

Vermette, P.J. & Konkoski-Bates, B. (2004, May 18). *Working the room: Helping middle level teachers make good decisions during students' learning efforts* [presentation]. Great Lakes Association for Cooperation in Education, Toronto, Canada.

What is a performance task? (n.d.). Defined Learning. Retrieved October 24, 2020, from https://blog.definedlearning.com/blog/what-is-a-performance-task.

White, E. B. (1945). *Stuart Little*. New York, NY: Harper Row.

Why teachers should create vision boards with their students. (n.d.). Study All Knight. Retrieved October 12, 2020, from https://www.studyallknight.com/why-teachers-should-create-vision-boards-with-their-students.

Wiggins, G. & McTighe, J. (2005). *Understanding by design*. Alexandria, VA: ASCD.

Wise, Tim. (2004). *White like me*. New York, NY: Soft Skull Press.

Wlodkowski, R. J. (1986). *Motivation and teaching: A practical guide*. Washington, DC: NEA.

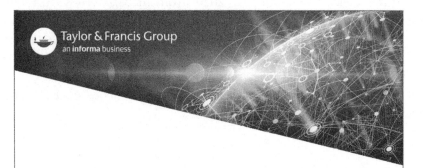